Reformational Missiology

Reformational Missiology

An Evangelical Lutheran Perspective for Global Mission

MIKE RODEWALD
and SAMUEL DERESSA

Foreword by Robert Kolb

WIPF & STOCK • Eugene, Oregon

REFORMATIONAL MISSIOLOGY
An Evangelical Lutheran Perspective for Global Mission

Wipf & Stock
An Imprint of Wipf and Stock Publishers
199 W. 8th Ave., Suite 3
Eugene, OR 97401

www.wipfandstock.com

PAPERBACK ISBN: 979-8-3852-6216-8
HARDCOVER ISBN: 979-8-3852-6217-5
EBOOK ISBN: 979-8-3852-6218-2

VERSION NUMBER 03/11/26

Cover design and figures throughout were created for this publication by Caleb Rodewald.

Dedicated to Abigail Yonas by Samuel Deressa
and
Cindy Rodewald by Mike Rodewald

Feelings come and feelings go,
And feelings are deceiving;
My warrant is the Word of God—
Naught else is worth believing

—A poem attributed to Martin Luther

Contents

Illustrations

Foreword

WHAT DOES WITTENBERG HAVE to do with Addis Ababa? What does Augsburg have to do with Chennai? Many scholars with little historical-contextual sensitivity have said, "Very little." In fact, as Samuel Deressa and Mike Rodewald demonstrate in this volume, Luther's perception of the challenges of daily life and God's speaking to these challenges from the pages of Scripture aid Christians in their witness in twenty-first-century societies and cultures around the world. His Small Catechism continues to bring instruction from the word of God for life lived in faith to speakers of nearly two hundred languages on six continents. His insights into the rhythm of life and the biblical presentation of God and his human creatures help believers today across the spectrum of Christian churches in finding the comfort and power of the promise of new life in and through Jesus Christ.

Deressa and Rodewald are uniquely equipped for this task. Deressa absorbed Luther's insights in his native Ethiopia and has ministered in the United States for over a decade; Rodewald absorbed Luther's insights in his native United States and then ministered for some years in Africa before beginning his working supporting translation of Scripture in the majority world. These veterans of cross-cultural witness have experienced the challenges of bringing God's word to the nations. They have put Luther's understanding of God's mission for his people into practice. Their common and contrasting experiences have opened their minds to the dynamic that still bursts out of the writings, the insights, of Martin Luther, into whose way of thinking they were introduced in their contrasting cultural birthplaces. What they have produced in this volume engages modern missiological scholarship and presents insights gained from Luther's way of thinking. They effectively interpret those insights for those are expressing their faith in Jesus Christ with others who share their culture and those who have traveled into new cultural settings.

My experiences have shown me firsthand how deeply Luther's words and spirit have penetrated people around the world. On July 9, 2006, some seven thousand people gathered in Tranquebar on the east coast of India to take part in the celebration of the three hundredth anniversary of the landing of Bartholomäus Ziegenbalg and Heinrich Plütschau. These German Lutheran missionaries had been sent out under the aegis of the Danish Lutheran king, Frederik IV. Their work led to the creation of a powerful Lutheran church, in part due to Ziegenbalg's sensitivity to the task of bringing the gospel of Jesus Christ to people outside the European cultural zone. He learned Tamil and initiated the work of translating the gospel into that language. He even poured lead into molds of Tamil letters so that the Holy Scripture, a catechetical paraphrase of Luther's Small Catechism, and other Christian literature could be printed in Tamil. He conducted ethnological studies of Hindu culture. He got himself jailed by Danish colonial authorities for his defense of a falsely accused Tamil woman. He and Plütschau stood at the beginning of a long line of Lutheran missionaries from Europe and North America, some sent by Anglican mission agencies in the eighteenth century, who worked together with the people of principalities across the subcontinent to proclaim Christ as Lord and Savior. The spirit of the people of Tranquebar that day reminded me of the US citizens in Perry County, Missouri, or in villages across Wisconsin, Minnesota, and the Dakotas, who celebrate their Lutheran roots in the manner of Brazilians in Rio Grande do Sul, Australians in South Australia, or South Africans in KwaZulu-Natal. Luther continues to provide spiritual sustenance to the descendants of European immigrants and the people they met and live among in many cultural settings.

Luther lives—in the case of the use of his Small Catechism, for instance, within and outside Lutheran churches—because he found in the Bible, according to Heinrich Bornkamm, "a mirror of daily life" as he experienced it.[1] His seeing the similarities between, for example, Sarah and Abraham and couples in his own day—and noting the contrasts as well—enlivened the biblical text for his own hearers. That sensitivity to the historical differences and to the commonalities of human life, with its

1. Bornkamm, *Luther and the Old Testament*, 11–44.

problems and opportunities, with its dead ends and its open invitations, echoes through the ages with a timbre that strikes a chord in our ears today.

Some modern scholars have accused Luther of having no sense of mission. Volker Stolle's collection of "Luther Texts on Mission" lays that old canard to rest. Although the Wittenberg reformer's ruler did not offer the support for overseas mission that imperialist monarchs in Spain, Portugal, France, and England offered, he had a sense of the church in other parts of the world and the need for Christian witness, both at home and abroad. He conceived of God as a talker, a God of conversation and community, who had been speaking from Gen 1 through the rest of Scripture, finally promising the fulfillment of his reign in Rev 22. This presentation of God flowed naturally into an emphasis on the witness of the children of God. In 1523 Luther wrote, "If it is true that [all Christians] have God's Word and are anointed by him, then it is their duty to confess, to teach, and to spread the word. . . . It is certain that a Christian not only has the right and power to teach God's Word but has the duty to do so on pain of losing his soul and of God's disfavor."[2] Luther anticipated what modern linguists call "performative speech." He taught that the Holy Spirit actually executes the re-creation of sinners through his word of promise in oral, written, and sacramental forms. Luther's strong doctrine of creation helped him appreciate the full range of God's providence and his imaginative use of selected elements of his created order to convey salvation and rebirth to his people.

Luther's devotion to Jesus Christ as eternal Lord and the Savior of the nations highlighted the comfort and power conveyed in the wisdom and power of the foolishness and impotence of the cross, while emphasizing that Christ was raised to restore our righteousness (Rom 4:25). Luther's high appreciation of the presence of the Holy Spirit in his own life and in the life of his church led him to rejoice in the Holy Spirit's use of people like him to deliver his saving promise of new life in Christ and guiding his faithful reaction to the promise in a life of new obedience. This is a message that speaks to people in crisis in every culture.

Rodewald and Deressa show how this "carrying across," the "translating" of the witness to our Creator and his reign that we have from ancient Hebrew and Hellenistic cultures functions not only in the post-Enlightenment of the "West" but also in animistic societies. These societies are in some ways closer to Luther's childhood surroundings than

2. Quoted from Luther, *That a Christian Assembly*, 309–10, cited in Stolle, *Church Comes*, 21.

we are. Luther's capture of the essence of the biblical message addresses universal concerns effectively. It is our task to translate his insights, carrying them over the thresholds of cultural uniqueness to meet our contemporaries where they are.

The authors give readers insights into the faithful exercise of this commission. Both at home and wherever else the Holy Spirit might lead us, we are called to carry the forgiveness of sins, life, and salvation to others. Rodewald and Deressa perceptively guide readers through the question of whose the mission is. They emphasize that God is totally responsible for bringing the saving gospel of Christ to others and bringing them to faith in Christ. At the same time, they recognize that God has made us, his people, responsible for giving witness to his love delivered in Christ's sacrifice and resurrection. This paradox reflects Luther's conviction that we must be listening to both halves of God's message for us. God presents to us his saving action in the atonement rendered by Christ and in the conversion of sinners into children of God accomplished by the Holy Spirit. He also tells us what he expects us to be doing. He does not explain how the gift of his promise of new life that is his total responsibility fits together with his demand that we be fully responsible for the tasks he assigns us. Luther believed simply that he makes that happen.

This volume guides readers into the practical aspects of cross-cultural witnessing, examining the building of the bridges between cultures as believers of their own cultures meet those outside the faith, whether they live halfway around the globe or next door. For Christians live in the culture of the church as it has developed out of two thousand years of church history in their own national and social cultures. Many other cultures often shape their dominant religious practice in some form of animism, whether in the US American manager who relies on magic stones for guidance or in the farmer of the traditional religion in a majority world village who hopes his juju will keep the rains coming this season. Luther had grown up with a form of Christianity that still reflected the ritualistic practices of the traditional Germanic religions that had been given Christian labels in the conversion efforts three quarters of a millennium earlier. He still speaks to people whose feel for the sacred reflects this animinstic, ritualistic worldview. Luther's feel for the dilemmas of daily life in his own time reflects the culture of sixteenth-century Germany.

At the same time the Wittenberg professor caught the essence of the crises that God's design for human life inevitably produces with its cracking and crushing of our spirits when we fail to be the human creatures he wants us to be. Thus, his way of thinking translates easily into the "post-modern" West. Luther's sermons addressed his hearers' sense of shame on occasion, their sense of guilt more often, but above all, he addressed their fears. Indeed, he explained that they rightly feared God's wrath, but he also addressed their fears of hunger, flooding, loneliness, and failure. He cultivated a sense of the presence of the crucified and risen deliverer of evil perpetrators and broken victims of his age. He gives us a model for speaking of both God's expectations and his comfort and consolation to the secure and the broken of our own time wherever and whenever we can. Furthermore, his medieval sensitivities knew that it takes a village to make life possible, and so he constructed a model for Christian living that brought temporal support as well as eternal hope to others.

In this volume readers encounter the voices of two experienced cross-cultural communicators who have taken a five-hundred-year-old script and translated it into the language that addresses Christ's church and the cultures in which it is called to give witness today. These readers will enjoy the conversation.

Preface

We, the authors of this book, come from distinct cultural contexts, yet our paths converged—perhaps by chance, or perhaps by divine design, depending on one's worldview. This collaboration began with an unplanned encounter: when the driver assigned to pick up Samuel Deressa at the airport encountered difficulties, Mike Rodewald stepped in. The occasion was a conference where Samuel was scheduled to speak, and what followed was a spirited conversation that revealed our shared wonder at God's story of salvation, the enduring power of his word throughout history, and our own roles within his mission. That initial exchange grew into a partnership and, ultimately, this book—a contribution to global mission, for there is no greater purpose than making Christ known as Savior across every cultural context.

In this work, we present a distinctly Lutheran Christian perspective on mission, rooted in the conviction that God's mission (*missio Dei*) is fundamentally his own work, carried out through the dynamic power of his word. This word takes multiple forms: it is present read through Scripture, signed or proclaimed audibly in preaching and witness, embodied sacramentally in the waters of baptism, and made present in the Lord's Supper. Each of these means serves as a vehicle of divine grace, through which God creates, sustains, and extends his kingdom.

Central to our understanding is the recognition that mission is not primarily a human endeavor but rather God's own redemptive activity in the world. The Holy Spirit works through the word—both written and incarnate—to awaken and nurture saving faith in those who hear and receive it (Rom 10:17). This theological framework, derived from the Reformation's *sola scriptura* and *sola fide* principles, insists that mission originates in God's initiative, not human strategy. The church as God's people, therefore, does not *possess* mission but *participates* in what God is already accomplishing.

This divine activity is not a recent development but has been evident throughout salvation history—from the covenantal promises to Israel, the prophetic calls to repentance, the incarnation of Christ, and the apostolic proclamation to the nations. The same Word that spoke creation into being (Gen 1), that became flesh in Jesus (John 1:14), and that was preached by the apostles continues to accomplish God's purposes today (Isa 55:10–11). This continuity assures us that mission remains God's work, even as he calls his people to be instruments of his grace.

The gospel, as the good news of Jesus Christ—his life, death, resurrection, and reign for the salvation of sinners—is inherently complete and sufficient. It requires no human embellishment, for it is *God's* power for salvation (Rom 1:16). Yet the divine commission to proclaim this gospel (Matt 28:18–20, Acts 1:8) involves human messengers, and with this participation comes both privilege and peril. The very act of communication—shaped by language, culture, and human frailty—introduces complexities that can obscure, rather than clarify, the gospel's transformative message.

This book grapples with the tension between the gospel's objective efficacy and the subjective challenges of its transmission. Historically, well-intentioned missionary efforts have sometimes entangled the gospel with cultural assumptions, political power, or theological accretions, erecting unintended barriers to its reception. Colonial-era missions, for example, often conflated Western civilization with Christianity, while contemporary evangelism can reduce the gospel to a privatized transaction, divorced from its cosmic redemption narrative. Such distortions raise a critical missiological question: *If we proclaim the gospel and no one hears—that is, if the message is misunderstood, ignored, or rejected due to human interference—has the gospel truly been proclaimed?*

To address this, we turn first to Scripture's own witness. The biblical pattern of mission demonstrates that the gospel transcends human limitations (e.g., Jonah's reluctant preaching to Nineveh; the Spirit's work despite Paul's "weakness," 1 Cor 2:1–5). Yet Scripture also warns against hindering the gospel through hypocrisy (Rom 2:21–24) or cultural insensitivity (Acts 15:1–29). Lutheran theology, with its emphasis on *Christus praesens* (Christ present in the word), assures us that the gospel's power lies not in the messenger but in the Spirit's work through the word.

As the Augsburg Confession declares, "The Church is the assembly of saints in which the gospel is purely taught and the sacraments are rightly administered."[1] This frames the church's mission not as a quest for pragmatic success but as a vocation of *faithfulness* to the means of grace.

However, confessional fidelity does not negate the need for critical reflection on *how* we proclaim. Drawing on Lutheran missiology, we examine methods that prioritize both theological integrity and contextual sensitivity. For instance, the distinction between *law* and *gospel* guards against moralistic distortions, while the principle of *adiaphora* (matters not essential to faith) allows for cultural adaptability in forms of worship and witness. We also engage contemporary debates: How does the gospel speak into pluralistic or post-Christian contexts? What does it mean to proclaim Christ in settings where the term *gospel* itself has been co-opted or corrupted?

Ultimately, this book argues that the church's mission is neither a human project nor a passive reliance on divine sovereignty but a dynamic partnership—what Luther called *Deus operans in nobis* (God working in us). The gospel *has* been proclaimed when it is spoken in truth, even if rejected, for the word does not return empty (Isa 55:11). Yet we are summoned to "become all things to all people" (1 Cor 9:22)—not by compromising the message but by removing unnecessary stumbling blocks so that Christ alone may be heard.

We hope this book will deepen readers' missiological understanding, equipping them to reflect critically on purpose, history, and methodology as they participate in God's mission. May it inspire both personal growth and renewed commitment to the task of making Christ known in every corner of the world.

1. Augsburg Confession 7.1–2 (*BC*, 43). Hereafter, AC. Citations of the Lutheran confessions are cited by part, article, and marginal number, as applicable. All citations of the *Book of Concord* throughout refer to the Kolb and Wengert edition.

List of Abbreviations

AC	Augsburg Confession
Ap	Apology of the Augsburg Confession
BC	*Book of Concord*
CMS	Church Mission Society
EECMY	Ethiopian Evangelical Church Mekane Yesus
ELCA	Evangelical Lutheran Church in America
IMB	International Mission Board (Southern Baptist Convention)
LC	Large Catechism
LCMS	Lutheran Church—Missouri Synod
LMS	London Missionary Society
LOP	Lausanne Occasional Paper
LWF	Lutheran World Federation
LW	Luther's Works, American Edition
RTS	Religious Tract Society
SA	Smalcald Articles
SC	Small Catechism
WA	Luther's Works, Weimar Edition (critical German edition)

Introduction

The mission of the Christian is not a human invention but a divine mandate, rooted in the very nature of God as the one who sends and redeems. This book seeks to explore this reality through the lens of Lutheran Christian theology, demonstrating how its distinctive emphases—justification by grace, the theology of the cross, and the centrality of word and sacrament—shape a robust and dynamic approach to mission in today's world. This book is structured to move from theological foundations to historical developments, then to contemporary challenges, and finally to practical engagement, ensuring that mission is understood not merely as a set of strategies but as an outworking of God's own redemptive work in history.

Theology and mission are inseparable within the Christian tradition, yet the distinct contributions of Lutheran theology to global mission have often been overshadowed by broader Protestant or evangelical frameworks. This book seeks to articulate Lutheran theology for mission—rooted in the Reformation's theological insights—while engaging the complex realities of the twenty-first-century church.

Yet one may ask, *What is mission?* As David Bosch states, "Mission means being involved in the redemption of the universe and the glorification of God. Evangelism is the core, heart, or center of mission, it consists of the proclamation of salvation in Christ to nonbelievers, in announcing forgiveness of sins, in calling people to repentance and faith in Christ, in inviting them to become living members of Christ's earthly community and to begin a life in the power of the Holy Spirit."[1]

1. Bosch, "Evangelism," 98.

The term *mission* has a rich and complex history, with its origins dating back to the sixteenth century. Initially, the term was primarily associated with the doctrinal understanding of the Trinity, specifically the sending of the Son by the Father and the sending of the Holy Spirit by both the Father and the Son. This conceptualization of mission highlighted the divine sending and purpose within the Godhead. It did not explicitly extend to human involvement in spreading the Christian faith until the Jesuits, under the leadership of Ignatius of Loyola, expanded the usage of the term to encompass the spreading of the Christian faith, including among pagan populations and even non-Catholic Protestants.[2] They viewed the spreading of the Christian faith as a central part of their mission.

Yet, for centuries, different denominations—including evangelical, Catholic, and Lutheran churches—have held varying, and sometimes conflicting, interpretations of what constituted authentic missionary work. While some groups prioritized conversion efforts among non-Christian populations, others focused on internal renewal or doctrinal purity. It was only through sustained ecumenical dialogue in the twentieth century that these disparate perspectives began to converge.[3]

There are two confusions that remain unsolved among many churches. First, there are some who have argued that mission or the *missio Dei* is simply everything that God sends the church to do in the world.[4] As Stephen Neill rightly contends, however, when mission becomes everything that churches do in relation to the world, it ends by meaning nothing at all.[5] Second, churches have always been struggling with the question of how to properly balance evangelism and social ministry. Many church bodies have lost the evangelistic aspect of mission by defining mission in terms of humanization, development, and liberation. Luther's holistic understanding of mission can shed light on such confusion. This book offers a clearer and more theologically grounded perspective on these persistent confusions by critically engaging through a biblically grounded evangelical Lutheran Christian approach for mission. While some continue to equate *missio Dei* with any activity the church undertakes in the world—risking, as Stephen Neill warns, the dilution of mission into an indistinct concept—this work provides a more precise

2. Bosch, "Evangelism," 98.

3. See Sunquist, *Understanding Christian Mission*, 8–9.

4. See Stott, *Christian Mission*, 24.

5. Neill, *Creative Tension*, 81.

definition, distinguishing between the church's general witness and its specific missionary mandate.

The first section, "Foundations for Mission," establishes the theological parameters for all subsequent discussion. Beginning with the *missio Dei* as the fundamental reality of God's self-revealing and redemptive action in the world, we examine how Lutheran theology understands mission as primarily God's work and nature before it becomes the church's task. This divine action takes concrete form in the proclamation of Christ crucified, through which God creates and sustains faith. The second chapter explores the ecclesiological implications of this understanding, arguing that the church as God's people exists not for itself but as an instrument of God's reconciling work. Here we engage critically with Protestant missiologies, demonstrating how Lutheran theology avoids the extremes of ecclesiastical triumphalism on one hand and mere humanistic activism on the other. The final chapter in this section traces the development of missional theology in recent decades, showing where Lutheran Christian insights have been overlooked and how they might insert and enrich the broader conversation and even serve as corrective where warranted.

"Historical and Theological Development," the second section, provides the necessary historical context for understanding Lutheran Christian contributions to mission theology and practice. While Martin Luther's direct engagement with cross-cultural mission was limited by his historical context, his theological breakthroughs established principles that would later bear fruit in Protestant missionary movements. We examine how Luther's doctrine of the word, his understanding of vocation, and his distinction between the two kingdoms provided the theological infrastructure for subsequent missionary expansion. The historical survey then traces how these Lutheran emphases were preserved, modified, or neglected in the great Protestant missionary movements of the eighteenth through twentieth centuries, with particular attention to how Lutheran mission societies and churches developed their own distinctive approaches to evangelism and church planting.

The third section, "Contextual and Cultural Challenges in Mission," brings theological and historical reflection to bear on the complex realities of contemporary mission practice. The chapters in this section address the perennial challenge of communicating the gospel across cultural boundaries without either compromising its content or rendering it unintelligible to new audiences. Special attention is given to the encounter with animist worldviews, where the gospel's claim of Christ's victory over spiritual powers must be carefully articulated in relation to existing cosmological understandings. These chapters combine theological reflection with anthropological insights, demonstrating how Lutheran theology's emphasis on Christ's finished work provides both critical distance from and meaningful engagement with diverse cultural contexts. The discussion of translatability emphasizes that the gospel is not a cultural artifact but living truth that speaks anew in every language and setting.

The final section, "Collaboration and Practical Engagement," moves from analysis to implementation, exploring how Lutheran theological commitments shape concrete mission strategies. In a world where traditional missionary methods are increasingly questioned and where global Christianity's center of gravity has shifted to the Global South, we argue for mission partnerships that respect both theological identity and cultural particularity. The concluding chapter's metaphor—"If opportunity doesn't knock, build a door"—captures the proactive, creative approach to mission that flows from Lutheran theology's confidence in God's prior action. Here we provide case studies and practical models for mission engagement that honor Lutheran distinctives while responding flexibly to contemporary challenges.

This volume is offered to scholars, missionaries, pastors, and students who seek to understand how the theological riches of the Lutheran Christian tradition can inform and transform mission practice in our time. By rooting mission in God's own being and action, by learning from both the strengths and weaknesses of historical models, by engaging honestly with cultural challenges, and by envisioning new forms of collaborative witness, this work aims to foster a more theologically grounded and practically effective missiology for the twenty-first-century global church.

HOW TO READ THIS BOOK

The book is structured to guide readers through a progressive engagement with Lutheran missiological thought—from its theological foundations to its practical applications in today's world. Each chapter may be read alone, but to maximize the book's value, readers are encouraged to approach it with attention to its intentional organization, interdisciplinary dialogue, and practical implications. The book's four-part structure moves from theological foundations (section 1) to historical developments (section 2), then to contextual challenges (section 3), and finally to practical engagement (section 4). Readers new to precepts within Lutheran Christian missiology should begin with section 1 to grasp the core theological commitments that shape everything that follows. Those with a strong background in Lutheran theology may choose to enter at later sections but should note how each part builds upon the previous. The final section on collaboration and mission strategy (section 4) is a good read in light of the earlier discussions, as it applies Lutheran theological insights to contemporary mission practice.

This book is unapologetically rooted in Lutheran theology and missiology—particularly its emphasis on *missio Dei*, justification by grace, and the theology of the cross. It may be used for missiological awareness and training for the mission sojourner at any stage in their mission journey, particularly of value for those serving within cross-cultural mission. But precepts of mission do not exist in isolation. Readers are encouraged to compare and contrast our evangelical Lutheran Christian perspective with other Protestant, Catholic, and Orthodox mission theologies. Each chapter raises questions about how Lutheran theology and missiological precepts complement, challenge, or diverge from broader missiological trends. Those from non-Lutheran faith traditions will find that the book does not merely advocate for Lutheran exclusivity but demonstrates how its theological emphases can enrich global mission discourse.

Throughout the book, a key question remains: *How does Lutheran theology, with its distinctive emphases, shape a faithful and effective approach to global mission today?* Readers should evaluate whether the book's argument holds—does the resulting missiology offer something unique and necessary for the contemporary church? Does it avoid both cultural imperialism and theological compromise? By reading with these considerations in mind, we hope that the reader will find a valuable resource for the church's ongoing mission in the world.

Section One

Foundations for Mission

1

The *Missio Dei*—God's Mission

Foundation for Mission

THE QUESTION IS ASKED for the Christian sojourner in mission: Why? Answers and motivations arise through cultural and denominational perspectives.[1] Some serving in missions may be motivated by soteriological purpose—to save people from damnation. Or some are motivated by compassion and the desire to help those in need; others, by ethnocentric purpose—driven to bring the ways and benefits of a sending culture to those in another culture. Some serve with ecclesiastical motive, wishing to expand their versions of church or denomination. Others seek to bring about the kingdom of God by causing all to be reached, a salvation-historical reason towards the world transformed through Jesus' return.[2] And some just seem motivated toward personal fulfillment, seeking their own mission activity to make a difference.

These efforts are not without result. Many have heard and come to faith through the gospel proclaimed by those driven with such motivation. That is a comfort. But such motivations are subsidiary to the primary motivation and scriptural foundation for mission defined under the missiological term *missio Dei* (Latin for "God's mission/sending"). Significantly, the *missio Dei* serves as corrective to those who view missions as the activity of churches, mission societies, or even individual missionaries.

1. See such as Hickman, "14 Reasons" or IMB, *Foundations.*
2. Bosch, *Transforming Mission*, 389.

DEFINING GOD'S MISSION

The *missio Dei* as defined missiological concept was first presented by theologian Karl Barth[3] during a 1952 conference of the International Missionary Council in Willingen, Germany, and elucidated in the years following by others, including early Lutheran missiologist Georg Vicedom.[4] The term itself can be traced through church history to such as Augustine, but its wider understanding and use followed the conference. The *missio Dei*, and its synonym *God's mission*, acknowledges mission as derived from God's nature—the sending and calling activity in mission initiated by God himself. It includes God's people—the universal church—integral to mission. Encapsulated, the *missio Dei* articulates mission in the Trinitarian sense—God sending his Son (John 10:15; 17:18, 21),[5] Father and Son sending the Holy Spirit (John 14:26, 15:26, Luke 24:49),[6] and Father, Son, and Holy Spirit sending God's people, the church,[7] into the world (John 17:18–23, 20:21).[8] In God's mission, God is the initiator of mission, and mission into the world is the action of our Triune God through his people. This foundation for Christian mission not only motivates God's people into mission but also serves to guide proclamation methodologies for those serving in mission.

But the precept of God at work through his word was present before it was gathered and defined under a single term. Martin Luther boldly

3. Bosch, *Transforming Mission*, 389.

4. See Vicedom, *Mission of God*.

5. "Just as the Father knows me and I know the Father" (John 10:15); "As you sent me into the world" (John 17:18); and "Just as you, Father, are in me, and I in you" (John 17:21).

6. "But the Helper, the Holy Spirit, whom the Father will send in my name" (John 14:26); "But when the Helper comes, whom I will send to you from the Father, the Spirit of truth, who proceeds from the Father" (John 15:26); "And behold, I am sending the promise of my Father upon you. But stay in the city until you are clothed with power from on high" (Luke 24:49).

7. The meaning of the term *church* is understood to be derived from the Greek *ekklesia* in the New Testament, which expresses *ekklesia* both as the people of God / body of Christ in the general sense and as believers contained within assemblies of various shades and degrees of faithfulness organized within multiple contexts. "For where two or three are gathered in my name, there I am among them" (Matt 18:20).

8. "As you sent me into the world, so I have sent them into the world. . . . That they may all be one, just as you Father, are in me, and I in you, that they also may be in us, so that the world may believe that you have sent me. . . . So that the world may know that you sent me and loved them even as you loved me" (John 17:18–23); "As the Father has sent me, even so I am sending you" (John 20:21).

proclaimed in his writing, "God has always been accustomed to collect a church for Himself even among the heathen,"[9] and, "Therefore God gathered a church in the world not only from the one family of patriarchs but from all nations to which the Word made its way."[10] Mission, as God at work in the world through his word, is exhibited in both of Luther's statements.

Additionally, for those Christians who acknowledge the historical evangelical Lutheran confessions formed in the sixteenth century as an accurate exposition of Scripture, the concept, if not term, is expressed within. The power of the gospel is not in what we do, rather it is by the Holy Spirit in those who hear (see Rom 1:16, 15:18–19). "To obtain such faith God instituted the office of preaching, giving the gospel and the sacraments. Through these, as through means, he gives the Holy Spirit who produces faith, *where and when he wills, in those who hear the gospel*."[11] And, though the gospel is not a human message (Gal 1:11–12), neither is it a magical one: "No one has ever written or suggested that people benefit from the mere act of hearing lessons they do not understand, or that they benefit from ceremonies not because they teach or admonish but simply *ex opere operato*, that is, by the mere act of doing or observing."[12] Additionally, "we may know that the Word and sacrament are efficacious even when they are administered by wicked people."[13]

We see the precept, if not the term, clearly expressed in Lutheran Christian foundation. Our Trinitarian God is at work through his people where the gospel is proclaimed, heard, and faith given through the Holy Spirit. God sends and uses us but is not reliant upon human worthiness or the holiness of those gathered into visible groups self-identifying as believers for the word at work to be efficacious. Within the *missio Dei*, our purpose as those God calls is not to attain a prescribed level of perceived spiritual maturity in order to be titled as *missionary*. God calls us to be faithful to his purpose wherever he calls us and uses us as his people through whatever circumstances and relationships we find ourselves in so that others might hear the good news too.

9. Luther, *Genesis, Chapter 45–50*, 135.
10. Luther, *Genesis, Chapters 31–37*, 227.
11. AC 5.1–3 (*BC*, 40); emphasis mine.
12. Ap 24.5 (*BC*, 258).
13. Ap 7/8.19 (*BC*, 177).

THE CHURCH INTEGRAL WITHIN GOD'S MISSION

Not every reader may supply the same meaning for *church* as applied within the *missio Dei*. This is not surprising. According to Merriam-Webster, church as a noun may mean "a building," "officialdom of a religious body," "the whole body of Christians," a "denomination," a "congregation," "divine worship," "the clerical profession," and "of or relating to the established church."[14] In addition, the meaning may be modified by specific context.[15]

But within the *missio Dei*, *church* applies synonymously to the larger understanding of church expressed through the Greek word *ekklesia* (literally "called out ones") as appears within Eph 3:10.[16] In this larger application, *ekklesia* expresses the church as the people of God, the body of Christ, and/or all believers who find themselves within the more or less organized visible iterations of institutional or local churches within the world's many contexts.[17]

We acknowledge that institutional or local expressions of the "visible church" may contain both believers and those that pretend to be believers. Together they may even accomplish activity for missions. God works through his word even where proclaimed through someone without faith. But that is a comfort, not a goal. God is not sending those without faith into mission. Rather he calls us into belief as his people and sends us as his church. Georg Vicedom succinctly captures the notion of God's people serving in God's mission: "The Church is not called on to decide whether she will carry on the mission or not. She can only decide for herself whether she wants to be Church."[18]

14. *Merriam-Webster*, s.v. "church," https://www.merriam-webster.com/dictionary/church.

15. There are a number of descriptive iterations of *church* provided through authors, denominations, and/or mission agencies: invisible church, visible church, established church, global church, local church, institutionalized church, emerging church, universal church—to list some examples. In addition, local government requirements and designations may result in different expressions of *church*—state church, underground church, free church, house church, ethnic church, etc. The meaning of *church* in each is not static.

16. "So that through the [*ekklesia*] [that is, "church," "called out ones"] the manifold wisdom of God might now be made known to the rulers and authorities in the heavenly places" (Eph 3:10).

17. This larger understanding of *ekklesia* is historically and often yet symbolized today in some faith traditions by capitalizing *church* as *Church* to denote the people of God and/or universal body of believers and in this way differentiate from a local structure or institution (see quotes et al. for examples).

18. Vicedom, *Mission of God*, 6.

THE ROLE OF GOD'S PEOPLE UNPACKED

God's message of salvation is universal, meant for all nations (Matt 28:19). Mission is our Trinitarian God at work through his people. God calls and sends us as the church integral to others receiving and hearing the message (Rom 10:14–17) through the proclamation of the word and administering the word at work through the sacraments commanded through Scripture—baptism (Matt 28:19) and the Lord's Supper (Luke 22:19). Thus is God's mission into the world.

Mission is not primarily a human effort but the work of the Triune God—Father, Son, and Holy Spirit—accomplished through his people. The church does not act on its own authority but is sent by God to proclaim the gospel so that others may hear, believe, and be saved. The apostle Paul emphasizes this when he asks, "How then will they call on him in whom they have not believed? And how are they to believe in him of whom they have never heard? And how are they to hear without someone preaching?" (Rom 10:14). Faith comes through hearing the word of Christ (Rom 10:17), and the church is the means by which God delivers this message to the world.

But perhaps the reader has felt a bit of paradox in the reading. This is not without foundation. Just as Christianity acknowledges the paradox of God as three persons in one, so the *missio Dei* presents the paradox of God's people as integral and necessary to the task of gospel proclamation yet not significant or crucial—a missiological concept not possible to fully explain, but accepted. Acknowledging this paradox helps define our role in mission as God's people. The gospel is all it needs to be. Our role in his mission is not to help God do something he cannot accomplish without us. Rather it is to reduce barriers to the gospel—language, culture, form, personal, et al.—so that the limitations of our sinful human natures do not distort the message we carry nor stand in the way of others hearing the good news of the power of God unto salvation for all through Jesus. God uses his people—the church—through method that lowers barriers to the Holy Spirit, producing faith *where and when he wills* in those who hear the gospel.[19]

This mission is fulfilled in two essential ways: the preaching of the gospel and the administration of the sacraments. The proclamation of the word brings the message of salvation to those who have not yet heard, as

19. See section 3, which poses and probes the missiological question, "If we proclaim the gospel and no one hears, has the gospel been proclaimed?"

Jesus commanded when he said, "Go into all the world and proclaim the gospel to the whole creation" (Mark 16:15). Alongside this preaching, the sacraments—baptism and the Lord's Supper—serve as visible signs of God's grace. Baptism marks the entrance into the covenant community, as Jesus instructed (Matt 28:19), while the Lord's Supper sustains believers in faith, as he said, "Do this in remembrance of me" (Luke 22:19). These sacraments are not mere rituals but means through which God strengthens his people and unites them to Christ.

MISSIONS OR THE *MISSIO DEI*?

It is a comfort that it is not necessary to apply a correct understanding to the *missio Dei* for mission to occur within God's mission. After all, mission is God at work, and as noted previously, many have heard the gospel through those with subsidiary motivations, some such even fueling major Western missionary movements. Yet the *missio Dei* serves as corrective. It sets us toward serving in mission as participation in what God is doing in the world rather than a focus on what we are doing for the gospel.

But switching places with God through subsidiary motivation is not the only contemporary misapplication by those in missions. South African missiologist David Bosch noted the gradual erosion of the understanding of God's mission in statements as, "God's own mission is larger than the mission of the church."[20] In such, the church's role in gospel proclamation is reduced—God's mission becomes the work of the Holy Spirit outside of God's people. It is an unnecessary conclusion. We, the church as God's people, have been called integral into the proclamation process. The danger and consequential result of such redefinition[21] moves mission away from a gospel proclamation role integral to mission toward again assisting God, this time to help reconcile creation through such as unity, peace, justice, or mercy initiatives. These efforts are not without value, but where they redefine or replace the nucleus of the *missio Dei*, they indicate subsidiary intent and point away from God's primary purpose

20. Lutheran World Federation, *Together in God's Mission*, 8, quoted in Bosch, *Transforming Mission*, 391.

21. "We understand the mission of God as relational. We call on LWF to continue and intensify its responsibility to convene, coordinate and enable mission cooperation and mutual accompaniment between different member churches, including their related agencies engaged in holistic mission" (Lutheran World Federation, "Resolution"). Also see Rice et al., "Reconciliation as the Mission of God."

in, with, and through his people. Bosch notes the slippery slope. Those who ignore the integral role of the church as God's people and chosen instrument for gospel proclamation ultimately arrive at such statements as, "'Missio Dei' means that God articulates himself without any need of assisting him through our missionary efforts in this respect."[22] In such circumstance, we note the danger—church and mission become what is decided by those defining it.

CONCLUSION

Why are we in mission? We are called by the gospel, enlightened with God's gifts, sanctified, and continued in true faith through the power of the Holy Spirit just as God calls and gathers others throughout the world in the same way. God is not dependent upon human motivation within the *missio Dei*. The failings of our sinful human nature tend to erect barriers to his purpose. But the scriptural model of mission accepts this paradox—our omniscient and perfect Triune God at work producing faith in us and sending us, integral, limited, and imperfect, within his mission.

Our understanding of the *missio Dei* informs our missiology, methods and paradigms for mission. We study the word of God through Scripture so that we grow in faith and knowledge of God's action and grace in history, today and into the future. This serves as our anchor for our study of the world. We study the world so that we may more fully know ourselves and see the barriers we erect as sinful human beings to God and his action within the *missio Dei*. This helps to determine methods and strategies for taking the gospel into the world so that we do not proclaim a message not heard. We don't need to make a difference in God's mission. The difference has already been made through Jesus. We neither control mission nor accomplish mission. God was at work through his people long before our time here on earth. Others will come after us. Our Triune God does not need our specific efforts for his mission to unfold. But he chooses each of us that others may know Jesus too by the power of the Holy Spirit, and this is the time we have been given to serve in his mission. We are called to be in mission. There is no greater purpose. The kingdom of God arrives wherever the word of God makes its way—within the *missio Dei*.

22. Aring, *Kirche als Ereignis*, 88; quoted in Bosch, *Transforming Mission*, 392.

2

Unraveling the Interplay Between the Church and the Mission of God

A Lutheran Christian Perspective

Even though a vast array of research has been published on Martin Luther's theology, there seems not adequate research on the missiology of Martin Luther. Luther's understanding and contribution to mission theology are often disregarded. Yet, as rightly noted by David Bosch, "in fact, [Luther] provided the church's missionary enterprise with clear and important guidelines and principles."[1] This chapter will focus on church and mission from a Lutheran perspective.

This chapter delves into Martin Luther's conception of the church and its mission. Historically rooted in the teachings of Martin Luther, Lutheranism emphasizes the church as a sacramental and communal gathering of believers, united by faith in Christ and the proclamation of the gospel. Yet, the mission of God extends beyond the mere existence of the church, encompassing a broader vision of God's redemptive work in the world. For Luther, the church's mission in our world is ultimately the work of the Triune God—*missio Dei*. That means, as Ingermar Öberg rightly emphasized, "when the church seeks to fulfill the Great Commission, one should always remember that, ultimately, the Father, the Son, and the Holy Spirit, through the word and sacraments and through human means, builds, expands, and sustains the church or God's reign in

1. Bosch, *Transforming Mission*, 244.

time."[2] The mission implies a call to actively participate in the ongoing creative work of the Triune God, be it through evangelism, social justice, or holistic ministry.

However, the continuous identification and articulation of the church's role within God's mission remain subjects of robust debate and theological reflection. Challenges arise due to contextual shifts, differing interpretations of Scripture, cultural influences, and evolving ecclesiological frameworks. This chapter explores Luther's conception of the church and its mission, and the believer's vocation within this mission, underlined by engagement with the word and the sacraments. It delves into the importance of sacraments in Luther's theology as potent tools for maintaining faith, especially baptism and Holy Communion. This leads us to examine Luther's perspective on the intrinsic link between sacraments and mission and how this ushers believers into a priesthood that actively serves others and reflects God's love.

LUTHER ON CHURCH AND MISSION

In 1537, Luther wrote in the Smalcald Articles, "God be praised, a seven-year-old child knows what the church is: holy believers and 'the little sheep who hear the voice of their shepherd.'"[3] Believers hear the voice of God when the gospel is preached. He wrote in 1523 that "the sure mark by which the Christian congregation can be recognized is that the pure gospel is preached there."[4] Elsewhere, in his Large Catechism, he wrote, "I believe that there is on earth a holy little flock and community of pure saints under one head, Christ. It is called together by the Holy Spirit in one faith, mind, and understanding. It possesses a variety of gifts, and yet is united in love without sects or schisms."[5] For Luther, holiness of the church was not to be found in external rituals or practices but in the transformation of individuals through the word of God and the sacraments.

As also articulated in the Augsburg Confession, the church is defined as "the assembly of believers among whom the gospel is purely preached and the holy sacraments are administered according to the

2. Öberg, *Luther and World Mission*, 81–82.
3. SA 3.12.2 (*BC*, 324–25).
4. Luther, *That a Christian Assembly*, 305.
5. LC 3.51 (*BC*, 437–38).

Gospel."[6] The Reformers' conception of the church, including Luther, is one in which the church operates as an instrument for the dissemination of the word of God, while simultaneously acknowledging the sacraments as physical, tangible representations of God's grace.

Therefore, the church's mission, according to Luther, is fundamentally rooted in the proclamation of God's word and the administration of sacraments. In other words, mission is an intrinsic part of the church's mandate—founded and animated by the dynamic of God's word coupled with sacraments' administration. In his commentary to Ps 19:1, when discussing the place of the word of God in believers' life, Luther wrote, "Wherever one finds the gospel . . . there is His church, and in that place there are certainly living saints. There men praise Him, and He rules over them, even though they are but young people and children. Inevitably, however, there will be old people too."[7] It is this unique understanding of the church's mission and components—that is, the word and sacraments—that sets the course for subsequent developments in Protestant ecclesiology.

For Luther, the gospel held the power to re-create individuals, ushering them from a state of sin into a restored relationship with God as righteous children. This re-creative word of the gospel was not limited to specific forms of communication but extended to various mediums such as oral, written word, and sacramental.[8] Luther saw the written Scriptures as a crucial vehicle for the gospel message to reach and resonate with individuals. Through the Bible, believers could encounter the living word of God, experience conviction, repentance, and ultimately find salvation in Christ Jesus. He argued, "All these instruments out to be placed before our eyes, and we are to grasp only the Word, which God gives through His means."[9]

6. AC 7.1 (*BC*, 42).

7. Luther, *Psalms 117*, 13. Luther also states, "The true mark by which the Christian congregation can be recognized is that the pure Gospel is preached there. For just as the banner of an army is the sure sign by which one can know what kind of lord and army have taken the field, so, too, the Gospel is the sure sign by which one knows where Christ and his army are encamped" (Luther, *That a Christian Assembly*, 305).

8. For more detail, see Kolb and Arand, *Genius of Luther's Theology*, 175–203.

9. Luther, *Über die Taufe*, 150; my translation. See also pp. 20–26.

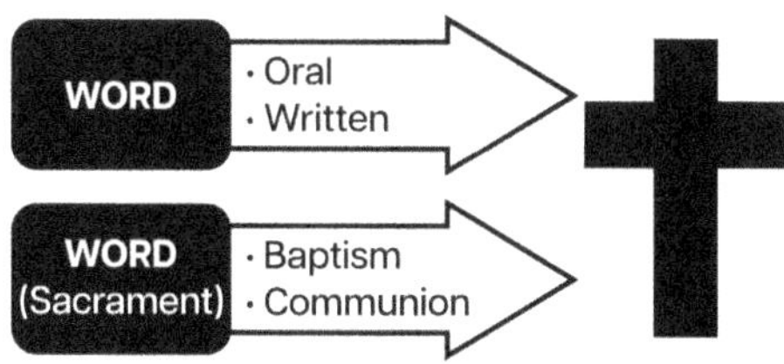

Figure 1: Word (Sacrament)

Luther's teachings emphasized not only the written and oral forms through which the word of God is conveyed but also reserved a significant place for the sacramental forms. Luther's understanding of the sacraments, particularly baptism and the Lord's Supper, underscored their capacity to convey God's grace and bring about spiritual renewal. In baptism, he saw the manifestation of God's saving work, where believers are cleansed of their sins and initiated into the body of Christ. He stated in the Small Catechism that baptism "brings about forgiveness of sins, redeems from death and the devil, and gives eternal salvation to all who believe it, as the words and promise of God declare."[10] Similarly, Luther viewed the sacrament of the Lord's Supper as an essential expression of the re-creative word of the gospel. In partaking of the bread and wine, believers commune with Christ and encounter his presence in a unique and transformative manner. The sacrament serves as a means of receiving his grace and a source of spiritual nourishment for the journey of faith. Through the sacraments, Luther believed that the re-creative word of the gospel was not merely proclaimed but experienced in a tangible and sacramental way.

He explained in his Small Catechism,

> The words "given for you" and "shed for the forgiveness of sins" show us that forgiveness of sins, life, and salvation are given to us in the sacraments through those words, because where there is forgiveness of sin, there is also life and salvation. How can bodily eating and drinking do such a great thing? Eating and drinking certainly do not do it, but rather the words that are recorded: "given for you" and "shed for you for the forgiveness of sins." These words, when accompanied by the physical eating and drinking, are the essential thing in the sacrament, and

10. SC 4, Q&A 2 (*BC*, 359).

> whoever believes these very words has what they declare and state, namely, forgiveness of sins.[11]

Discussion about the relationship between church and mission from a Lutheran perspective requires understanding the two dimensions of the church as an institution. As stated in the Apology of the Augsburg Confession, the church "is not only an association of outward rites and ties but is primarily an association of faith."[12] On the one hand, Christians live in relationship and interaction with God (*coram Deo*)[13] through the word and sacraments. Luther argues that a church is where the word of God takes center stage, gathering saints—a community of believers—and transforming their lives. The church's primary role emerges as nurturing and equipping believers for proclaiming the word. On the other hand, Christians interact and relate with society and the world at large (*coram mundo*), fulfilling its mission of being "salt" and "light" in the world. It involves social responsibility, acts of service, love, and freedom. From Luther's perspective, all believers are ultimately called to join God's mission—a mission in which God works in and through them.

A close reading of Luther leads to the understanding that the church should at all times keep the right balance between the two dimensions of the church. That means the church cannot solely focus on its relationship with God (*coram Deo*) to the exclusion of its mission to the world and societal responsibilities (*coram mundo*). Balance is key as these two dimensions intersect and influence one another—a spiritual relationship with God should naturally spill over into societal impact, and our societal engagement should be deeply rooted in and guided by our faith in God.

11. SC 6, Q&A 3, 4 (*BC* 362–63).

12. Ap 7/8.14 (*BC*, 174).

13. *Coram Deo*, a Latin phrase that means "before the face of God," refers to a Christian's relationship and interaction with God—that is, one's life lived in the presence of, under the authority of, and to the honor and glory of God.

Figure 2: Relationship/Responsibility

For Luther, where there is the word of God, there is an assembly of saints—the church. God gathers his people through the word. It is the proclamation of the gospel that makes the church. The gospel mediates the Holy Spirit, who "calls, gathers, enlightens, and sanctifies the whole Christian church on earth and preserves it in union with Jesus Christ in the one true faith."[14] In other words, the church is a creation of the word (*creatura verbi*) and not of human origin. Luther describes the church as the "mother" that "begets and bears every Christian through the Word of God, which the Holy Spirit reveals and proclaims, through which he illuminates and inflames hearts so that they grasp and accept it, cling to it, and preserve in it" so that they all become part of a community of new birth.[15] God calls and equips all Christians, *communio sanctorum*, or the priesthood of all believers, to be involved in missions through the proclamation of the good news.

For Luther, individual believers are "called through the gospel" because faith comes from hearing and hearing through the word of Christ (Rom 10:17). Luther postulated that every instance of genuine faith is an act of God's grace and intervention in the individual's life. The proclamation of God's word, therefore, was pivotal to evoke faith in individuals. Yet it is through the church that the gospel continues to be proclaimed. As Bernhard Lohse rightly states, for Luther, "God's redeeming and justifying activity occurs in and through the church."[16] When explaining how this happens, Luther states, "The Spirit first leads us into his holy

14. Gritsch and Jenson, *Lutheranism*, 124.

15. LC 2.42 (*BC*, 436). See also Peterson, "Church," 51.

16. Lohse, *Martin Luther's Theology*, 281.

community, placing us in the church's lap, where he preaches to us and brings us to Christ."[17]

As David Bosch rightly points out, Luther based his entire "paradigm" for missions on Rom 1:16: "I am not ashamed of the gospel, because it is the power of God for the salvation of everyone who believes."[18] Luther believed in the power of God's unfailing word and that "the gates of hell would not prevail against it" (Matt 16:18). The word of God is not limited to time and space but is rather "driven farther through the preacher to and from in the world, driven out and persecuted; nevertheless, it is always being made more widely known to those who have never heard it before."[19]

Yet, it is important to understand the two dimensions of God's way of calling (gathering) the believing community. As Klaus Detlev Schulz states, "One aspect of the church is that she is the community of saints which have been gathered through the mission of the triune God; whereas, the other dimension is her active participation in God's mission of bringing the saving Word to others."[20] In other words, according to Luther, the church is formed through the preaching of the good news of Jesus Christ and calling sinners to repentance. Then the primary role or mission of the church becomes to continually nurture, form, and equip believers to proclaim the word to their neighbors. In his commentary on Luke 24:46–47, Luther argues that all Christians are called to "preach among all peoples and direct everyone to repent."[21] In his commentary on Isa 60:11, Luther also states, "Your gates will always stand open, they will never be shut, day or night." And he continues, "This is what it means to have open gates, that *the church is always at its task of calling sinners to repentance*, of preaching, training, teaching, comforting, and absolving. *Men enter this church every day, just as they enter Wittenberg today and are brought into the body through the Word.*"[22]

17. LC 2.37 (*BC*, 435–36).

18. Bosch, *Transforming Mission*, 240.

19. Stolle, *Church Comes*, 24–25.

20. Schulz, "Missional Significance," 134.

21. Stolle, *Church Comes*, 27.

22. Luther, *Lectures on Isaiah*, 319; emphasis mine.

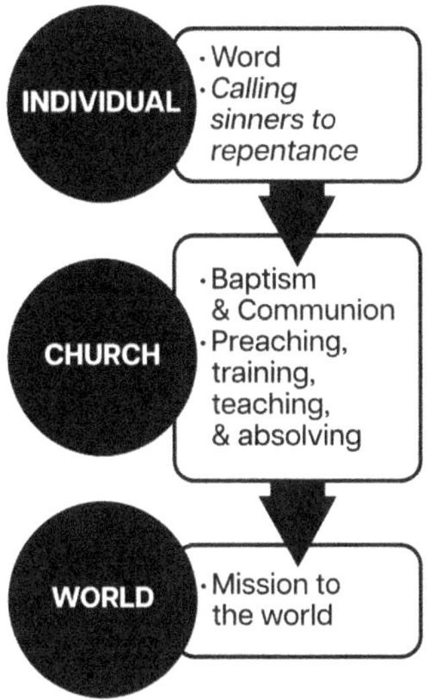

Figure 3: Individual-Church-World

Therefore, all Christians are called to be involved in God's mission because God works in and through the called believers. As Luther indicated in *The Bondage of the Will*, the Triune God "does not work in us without us, because he has created and preserved us that he might work in us and we might cooperate with him, whether outside his kingdom through his general omnipotence or inside his Kingdom by the special virtue of his Spirit."[23] This means God works in us (or continues to form and empower us) as we engage or "cooperate" in his work.

SACRAMENTS AND MISSION

Furthermore, sacraments in Luther's theology played a crucial role in sustaining faith. Luther believed that the sacraments—namely, baptism and Holy Communion—were means of grace, which were to be administered under the church's authority. For Luther, sacraments are not mere symbols but rather both effective signs, carrying God's promise as well as actualizing this promise of God's love and grace.

For Luther, baptism and mission are intrinsically linked. Baptism signifies the creation of the new creature in Christ who is then called and

23. Luther, *Bondage of the Will*, 243.

enabled to participate in the mission where he or she becomes co-workers in the *missio Dei*. Upon baptism, we become part of the community of saints (*communio sanctorum*), a priestly community. Luther states, "As far as it goes, we are all consecrated priests through baptism, as St. Peter says in 1 Peter 2[v. 9], 'You are a royal priesthood and a priestly realm.' The Apocalypse says, 'Thou hast made us to be priests and kings by the blood' (Rev. 5:9–10)."[24]

Luther argued that baptism not only initiates the believer into the Christian community but also ushers them into the priesthood of all believers, a concept that radically redefined the laity's role within the church. However, Luther's conception of the priesthood of all believers encompasses a dual dimension, consisting of an internal (*coram Deo*) and an external (*coram mundo*) aspect. The internal dimension of Luther's concept of the priesthood of all believers (*coram Deo*) focuses on the individual's relationship with God. Following baptism, a Christian enters into a personal relationship with God, characterized by direct access to him without the need for an earthly mediator. Luther grounded this idea in the New Testament assertion that "there is one God and one mediator between God and mankind, the man Christ Jesus" (1 Tim 2:5).[25] Thus, in this relationship, the Christian is justified by faith alone and can directly commune with God, acknowledging Christ as the sole mediator. This conception signifies the uniqueness of each believer's relationship with God, fostered through faith and grace, which is unaffected by any human institution or clergy.

The external dimension (*coram mundo*) highlights the Christian's responsibility toward the world motivated by love and service. Post baptism, as part of the priesthood of all believers, each Christian is called to serve others and demonstrate God's love in all their interactions. According to Luther, this dimension of the priesthood involves a horizontal relationship with fellow believers and neighbors, reflecting God's law of love. Each act of service undertaken by a believer, whether helping a neighbor or discharging their secular duties faithfully, reflects their priestly role and participation in God's mission. Thus, the act of baptism is a missional act, unifying the universal church in fulfilling Christ's commission to "go and make disciples of all nations, baptizing them in the name of the Father and of the Son and of the Holy Spirit" (Matt 28:19).

24. Luther, *To the Christian Nobility*, 127.

25. For more detail, see Arand, "Two-Dimensional Understanding."

Luther argues,

> If he (the Christian) is in a place where there are no Christians he needs no other call than to be a Christian, called and anointed by God from within (upon his/her baptism). Here it is his duty to preach and to teach the Gospel to erring heathen or non-Christians, because of the duty of the brotherly love, even though no man calls him to do so.[26]

Thus, by placing baptism as a pivotal element in the mission narrative, Luther emphasized the church's role in Christian initiation and spiritual growth. His focus on baptism's perpetual relevance underscores the ongoing dynamic between individual faith, ecclesial life, and participation in the wider mission of God. This understanding paves the way for a more nuanced engagement with mission, acknowledging the reciprocal influence of individual faith journeys and the larger Christian community in participating in God's mission.

In his writing titled "A Treatise on the New Testament, That Is, the Holy Mass," Luther also argues that those who take part in Holy Communion must actively participate in the ongoing creative activity of the Triune God through proclaiming the love and grace of God. This is in relation to Paul's clear statement: "Whenever you eat this bread and drink this cup, you proclaim the Lord's death until he comes" (1 Cor 11:26).

According to Martin Luther, communion provides more than mere symbolism or religious ritual. In Luther's own words, "The significance or effect of sacrament is fellowship of all the saints."[27] This interpretation emphasizes communion as an act connecting participants not only with the life, death, and resurrection of Christ but also with the communal body of adherents—past, present, and future. In the rite of Holy Communion, believers share in the fundamental fellowship with Christ and all the saints, becoming compatriots in the divine saga of redemption and salvation. The Eucharist is viewed as an instance of God sharing his existence with us through tangible elements such as bread and wine. Consequently, "we become united with Christ, and are made one body with all the saints."[28] This union is more than spiritual; it plays out in practical expressions of communal life.

26. Luther, *That a Christian Assembly*, 310.
27. Luther, *Blessed Sacrament*, 50.
28. Luther, *Blessed Sacrament*, 51.

Luther further proffers that partaking in the "Blessed Sacrament of the Holy and True Body and Blood of Christ" provides an avenue through which "all the spiritual possessions of Christ and his saints are shared with and become the common property of him who receives this sacrament."[29] This view fosters the understanding of grace as a shared inheritance, made accessible to all believers through the sacrament of communion.

Moreover, Luther advocates for a second dimension of fellowship within the eucharistic ritual—that of fellowship with our contemporary neighbors. His interpretation insists that "we are [also] to be united with our neighbors, we in them and they in us."[30] Therefore, participation in the Eucharist is not an isolated action but rather an act consummating the believers' integration into a wider communion of saints, as well as deepening their connectedness with their contemporary Christian community—leading to active participation in God's mission in the world.

Quoting Luther,

> To receive this sacraments in bread and wine, then, is nothing else than to receive a sure sign of this fellowship and incorporation with Christ and all saints. It is as if a citizen were given a sign, a document, or some other token to assure him [her] that he [she] is a citizen of the city, a member of that particular community.[31]

For Luther, there exists a connection between Eucharist and the mission of the church. When we participate in Holy Communion, we take part in "his life and good works, which are indicated by his flesh."[32] To participate in Holy Communion means to share the perichoretic life of the Triune God (his abundant love and blessing) with the whole of creation—which is manifested through our involvement in the ongoing creative work of God. In taking the blood under the wine, we also take part in "his passion and martyrdom, which are indicated by his blood."[33] We take part in the suffering of Christ, that was meant for our salvation, and in the suffering of the whole creation—and this is how the church's mission is connected to its eucharistic life.

This way, Luther offers a fresh perspective on this complex dynamic, stressing that the Holy Communion is not just a method of remembering

29. Luther, *Blessed Sacrament*, 51.
30. Luther, *Blessed Sacrament*, 51.
31. Luther, *Blessed Sacrament*, 51.
32. Luther, *Blessed Sacrament*, 60.
33. Luther, *Blessed Sacrament*, 60.

Christ's sacrifice but fundamentally a channel through which God actively shares God's self with all of creation. It is a juncture of divine self-giving, to which the faithful respond with an attitude of gratitude and surrender. This responsive gratitude is not merely verbal in nature but requires a holistic commitment of oneself "and all that we have, with constant prayer."[34] Luther insists that our thanksgiving should extend beyond mere verbal expressions, spilling over into the rest of our lives. Our lives, resources, and aspirations should all bear the marks of our grateful response to God's gift.

Implicit within this giving of thanks is the act of self-surrender: "With this, we are to yield ourselves to the will of God, that he may make of us what he will, according to his own pleasure."[35] This makes the Eucharist a ritual of surrender, as believers yield their individual wills and futures to the transformative power of God's will. This surrender is not passive or fatalistic but characterized by trustful submission to the divine will and design. The Eucharist therefore becomes a participatory act of faith symbolizing one's submission to, and engagement with, the divine will—*engagement in God's mission to the whole world.*

Eucharistic fellowship is a fellowship that requires willingness to share others' burdens and suffering. It is through the practice of such sharing that the Christian community is engaged in mission. We encounter God in and through each other's life. By carrying each other's burdens with the love of Christ, we form a communal culture through which each member is formed into the likeness of Christ, and we equip each other for *missio Dei.* As Luther emphasizes, "By the means of this sacrament, all self-seeking love is rooted out and gives place to that which seeks the common good of all; and through the change wrought by love there is one bread, one drink, one body, one community."[36]

For Luther, to experience such transformation, one must

> take to heart the infirmities and needs of others, as if they were [one's] own. Then offer to others [his/her] strength, as if it were their own, just as Christ does for [him/her] in the sacraments. This is what it means to be changed into one another through love. . . . To lose one's own form and take on that which is common to all.[37]

34. Luther, *Treatise on the New Testament*, 98.
35. Luther, *Treatise on the New Testament*, 98.
36. Luther, *Treatise on the New Testament*, 67.
37. Luther, *Treatise on the New Testament*, 61–62.

PRACTICAL IMPLICATION OF LUTHER'S THEOLOGY OF THE CHURCH AND MISSION

Imagine a congregation named Mountain Peak Church which is passionate about worship, devoting most of its time and resources on sermons, prayers, worship songs, and communion. They believe their primary duty is to foster a deep relationship with God. However, this strong spiritual focus has led them to overlook the pressing needs of their community. They have no outreach programs or dedicated efforts to support the surrounding vulnerable individuals, thus missing an opportunity to enact tangible, real-world impacts of their faith.

On the other hand, imagine another congregation named Jubilee Community Church. This congregation is deeply dedicated to community service, running several outreach programs such as food drives, free health clinics, and homeless shelters. They passionately believe in Jesus' teachings of "loving your neighbor as yourself." However, in their urgency to serve the world, they often neglect their personal and corporate spiritual growth. Worship services, prayer times, and the reading of Scriptures are often given lesser attention, resulting in a faith that is more about "doing" than "being."

These two examples show Christian communities where either the *coram Deo* (vertical relationship with God) or *coram mundo* (horizontal relationship with humanity) facet of Christian faith is emphasized to the exclusion of the other. In both cases, there is an imbalance. The Mountain Peak Church needs to consider how their faith calls them to action and service in the world. In contrast, Jubilee Community Church needs to consider how a deeper relationship with God can transform and motivate their work further. A harmonious blend of both dimensions can lead to a more holistic, meaningful, and impactful Christian faith and witness.

When a church, like Mountain Peak Church, focuses solely on their relationship with God (*coram Deo*), certain negative practical implications could arise. The first implication might be a decline in church membership. While the core congregation may feel fulfilled in focusing on prayers and spiritual devotion, new members or those seeking a faith that interacts with the world might feel alienated. As a result, they may decide to leave or not join at all, leading to a steadily decreasing congregation.

Secondly, a lack of societal engagement could result in an imbalance in discipleship and spiritual growth. Discipleship is not only about studying the Bible and communicating with God but also learning from Jesus' lifestyle of serving others. The congregation might have a less varied and rich experience of Christ's teachings, which in turn could stagnate their spiritual growth.

Alternatively, when a church, like Jubilee Community Church, focuses solely on their societal responsibilities (*coram mundo*), there could be significant detrimental effects as well. One potential consequence is that the spiritual growth of church members could be at stake. Without a strong emphasis on a personal relationship with God, spiritual growth might become secondary, leading to a faith that can feel hollow and uncentered. The church members might miss out on the vital, transformative experience of deeply knowing, understanding, and connecting with God on a personal level. Furthermore, the church might not heavily emphasize evangelism. While church members are actively serving their community, they may not be spreading the gospel or inviting people to have a personal relationship with Jesus. This could limit the spread of faith and hinder the growth of the church community.

In both extremes of focus, there is a risk of creating a church either so caught up in the heavenly realms that it does not impact the earthly world, or a church so absorbed in earthly matters that it loses sight of the heavenly anchor of faith. A balanced approach—embodying both *coram Deo* and *coram mundo* aspects—is essential for a vibrant, growing church with spiritual depth and societal impact.

CONCLUSION

For Luther, the church is fundamentally an assembly of believers, bound together by the word of God and sacraments as tangible representations of God's grace. However, this assembly is not merely passive; it is actively engaged in the proclamation of God's word and administration of sacraments. The church, from Luther's perspective, is inherently missional, and every believer, upon baptism, is initiated into this duty of God's mission.

The linking of baptism with mission radically redefines the role of the laity and emphasizes the church's role in spiritual growth and participation in God's mission. Furthermore, Luther's understanding of the Eucharist as an act that fosters fellowship with Christ, the community of saints, and one's contemporary neighbors sets forth a model of a vibrant, engaged, and action-oriented ecclesiology. The Lord's Supper within the eucharistic liturgy is God's giving us once again his body and blood, given and shed for us, with forgiveness and true human life renewed. With this renewed life, we are sent into the world. The sacraments, therefore, not only serve as means of grace but are also intrinsically linked with the mission of the church.

Ultimately, Luther's mission paradigm calls for a community constituted by the word and sacraments, actively engaged in the dissemination of the gospel and service to the world. It encourages believers to be co-workers in the *missio Dei*, to be formed into the likeness of Christ, to carry each other's burdens, to nurture each other's faith, and to constantly be involved in God's work. Based on this understanding, Luther's conception of church and its mission is deeply rooted in engagement with the world—a world crying out for the good news of God's love and grace. In sum, Luther's thoughts provide a robust theological foundation for a dynamic, vibrant, and missional ecclesiology.

Section Two

Historical and Theological Development

3

Luther and Christian Mission

SOME SCHOLARS HAVE ARGUED that Lutherans are indifferent to mission because the Reformers have had a bad missionary legacy. Gustav Warneck (1834–1910), one of the early missiologists, was in fact the first to note that Reformers did not have a legacy of missionary work. He argued that they did not "even [have] the sense of mission, in the sense in which we understand them today" (*Missionsmann in unserm Sinne*).[1] From among the recent church historians, William R. Hogg, in his book *Ecumenical Foundations*, also argues that Luther, "disavowed any obligation for Christians to carry the gospel beyond their fellow-countrymen."[2] Both Warneck and Hogg argued that Martin Luther had never preached about mission and had never encouraged Christians of his day to be involved in evangelism. According to them, Luther and other Reformers had never discussed the idea of foreign missions.[3] Paul Avis refers to this as "the strange silence" of the Protestant Reformers.[4]

It is true that the Lutheran Christian movement started as a confessional movement within Christendom and that its goal was renewal of the church through the word of God. Luther met few unbaptized believers throughout his entire life. Therefore, most of his writings were focused on how to reform or revitalize the Christian church. In fact, he

1. Warneck, *Outline of a History*, 9.
2. Hogg, *Ecumenical Foundations*, 1–2.
3. Warneck, *Outline of a History*, 9; Hogg, *Ecumenical Foundations*, 2.
4. Avis, *Theology of the Reformers*, 168.

and the other Reformers were criticized by one of the Catholic scholars in the sixteenth century, Robert Cardinal Bellarmine, who said, "Heretics are never said to have converted either pagans or Jews to the faith, but only to have perverted Christians."[5]

However, a closer look at Luther's writing, his exegetical writings of the Old and the New Testament, his sermons, and thematic writings reveals that mission and evangelism are at the heart of Luther's theology. Luther understood his scholarly works to be deeply confessional and missional in nature. For Luther, mission as *missio Dei* is both evangelism (the primary mission of the church) and serving our neighbors. In this chapter, I will explore Luther's theology of mission and how his broader understanding of mission helps the Christian church today understand its mission for the world.

MISUNDERSTANDING LUTHER

As stated above, Warneck's conclusion about Luther was that he had no interest in exploring and helping the church understand the need for mission since (a) his main focus was on reforming the church that was set in a "Christendom" context and therefore had no "idea of mission" (*Missionsgedanke*); and, (b) he lacked direct contact with the heathen world and therefore did not see the need for foreign missionary activity (*missionstat*).[6] He argued that the Reformers did not support "a regular sending of messengers of the gospel to non-Christian nations, with a view of Christianizing them."[7] When it comes to the Reformers, including Luther, Warneck argued that it was their "fundamental theological views [that] hindered them from giving their activity, and even their thoughts, a missionary direction."[8] Warneck's successors such as J. Richter, H. W. Schomerus, E. Schick, and Dane L. Bergman also followed his line of thought.[9] They argued that Luther's deficiency in missionary awareness

5. Quoted in Bosch, *Transforming Mission*, 248.

6. Warneck, *Outline of a History*, 9–11. Warneck wrote, "The comprehension of a continuous missionary duty of the Church was limited among the Reformers and their successors by a narrow-minded dogmatism combined with a lack of historical perspective" (Warneck, *Outline of a History*, 159).

7. Warneck, *Outline of a History*, 10.

8. Warneck, *Outline of a History*, 9.

9. For detail, see Öberg, *Luther and World Mission*, 1.

was due to his limited focus on internal issues and a lack of opportunity for the global mission.

Warneck, like many of his contemporaries, understood mission as evangelism—namely, reaching out to people of all nations with the gospel of Jesus Christ for salvation. Already in 1891, Warneck defined the task of mission as evangelization and church planting. He argued, "For by 'mission' we must not understand anything else than this sending, continuing through every age of the church, which carries out the commandment, 'Go and make disciples of all nations.'"[10]

Quoting Warneck,

> Jesus' sending is for the salvation of souls. The salvation of souls is and remains everywhere the essential core work of Christ's messenger. When this core work is misplaced from its central role, a clouding of the sending task has begun. . . . Conversion of a people must begin with individual conversions, and those individual conversions must compose a long phase of the mission period.[11]

Warneck's understanding of mission is shared by many of his contemporaries and is founded on the missionary character of the four Gospels. In Matthew, Jesus commissioned his disciples to "go and make disciples of all nations, baptizing them in the name of the Father and of the Son and of the Holy Spirit" (Matt 28:19). Many refer to this as the "Great Commission," to be called as a witness for the gospel. In Mark, Jesus said to his disciples, "Go into all the world and preach the gospel to all creation" (Mark 16:15). In Luke, Jesus reminded his disciples that their call is to preach "repentance for the forgiveness of sins in his name to all nations, beginning at Jerusalem" (Luke 24:47). In John's Gospel, the risen Jesus said to his disciples, "As the Father has sent me, even so I send you" (John 20:21). God sent his Son to the world (Gal 4:4); and on the day of Pentecost, the Son sent forth his Spirit (Acts 2:1–7). The Spirit then equips and sends the church into the world. Therefore, this idea of "sending and going" shaped the church's understanding of mission for centuries.

Seven decades later (1970s), Stephen Neill, a professor of missions and ecumenical theology at the German University of Hamburg, in his book *A History of Christian Missions*, argued that "in the Protestant world,

10. Warneck, *Outline of a History*, 10.

11. Cited in Hoekendijk, *Kirche und Volk*, 90.

during the period of the Reformation, there was little time for thought of missions."[12] Concerning Luther, he wrote, "It is clear that the idea of the steady progress of the preaching of the Gospel through the world is not foreign to his thought. Yet when everything favorable has been said . . . it all amounts to exceedingly little."[13] Another twentieth-century scholar, Kenneth Scott Latourette, also concluded that Luther lacked an organized missions movement due to a division within Protestant thought.[14]

A few years later, a Lutheran scholar, Carl Braaten, repeated Stephen's argument and stated that "the theology of the Reformers and confessional writings are totally devoid of any missionary consciousness."[15] According to Braaten, the reason for the Reformers' lack of missionary activity or theology of mission, in general, was their opinion that the Great Commission had been fulfilled during the time of the apostles. The opinion of Braaten and other scholars on Luther was based on Luther's interpretation of Ps 82:4, in which Luther cited Mark 16:15 (NIV: "Go into all the world and preach the gospel to all creation") and then added, "Since then, however, no one has had this apostolic command."[16] Quoting Braaten,

> [It is not that] Luther and his fellow reformers denied the universality of the gospel. They simply sensed no present need to express it, because the mission to all the nations has already been accomplished on a worldwide scale in the age of the apostles. The church of today has only to preach the word and administer the sacraments where it is already established.[17]

In the 1980s, J. Herbert Kane added a similar argument, stating that the Reformers, including Luther, "taught that the Great Commission pertained only to the original apostles; that the apostles fulfilled the Great Commission by taking the gospel to the ends of the then known world; that if later generations were without the gospel, it was their own fault."[18] According to Kane, Luther made no noteworthy contribution to theology of mission.

12. Neill, *History of Christian Missions*, 220.
13. Neill, *History of Christian Missions*, 189.
14. Latourette, *Christian World Mission*, 28. See also Latourette, *Great Century*, 42.
15. Braaten, *Flaming Center*, 15.
16. See Luther, *Psalm 82*, 64.
17. Braaten, *Flaming Center*, 15.
18. Kane, *Concise History*, 73.

In the early 2000s, a few other scholars also began to criticize Luther for his lack of mission theology. One of them was Paul Avis, who argued that "when both Luther and Calvin commented on the Great Commission (Matt 28), they remain bafflingly silent on the duty of present-day Christians to carry on the work of the apostles in bringing the gospel to every creature."[19] Hence Avis's reference to "the strange silence" of the Protestant Reformers.[20] So how did Luther not get this idea or concept of mission? How could Luther, who explored the book of Psalms, the Prophets, the Gospels, and Paul's writings, miss the universal purpose of mission or the Great Commission?

Luther did not discuss cross-cultural mission at length. Yet, he articulated mission here and there in his many writings, such as his biblical commentaries, exegetical writings, sermons, and so on. Among these writings, it was Luther's interpretation of Ps 82, where he stated that Jesus' command to proclaim good news to the world "was fulfilled as the Apostles proclaimed the great deeds of God," that created confusion for some scholars.[21] However, there are two important points to note as we explore Luther's view on mission. First, Luther's interpretation of Ps 82 should be read in context: Luther is not arguing that mission to the world has come to an end during the time of the apostles. Rather, he is saying that there is a distinction between the apostles' calling, which he refers to as a "general calling" to all nations, and the "public preaching" or "street corner preaching" of our time, which according to Luther should be done when a preacher has a clear calling from a given community. Preachers or missionaries of our time, as he argued, should be called by a defined community to carry out the task. For Luther, the apostles were different, for they were pioneers in starting the Christian mission movement and therefore had the "general call" to "go to all the land" and preach the gospel.

Second, as rightly noted by many Luther scholars, the Great Commission or global mission is a one-sided nineteenth-century view of mission. Therefore, one should grasp the deeper meaning of God's mission as laid bare by Luther rather than judge him on the standard of a narrow and one-sided view of mission.[22] As David Bosch also emphasized in responding to Luther's critics, "Mission doesn't begin when somebody

19. Avis, *Theology of the Reformers*, 168.

20. Avis, *Theology of the Reformers*, 168.

21. Luther, *Ersten 25 Psalmen*, 546; my translation.

22. See Elert, "Missions."

goes overseas; it is not 'operational theory' (*Betriebstheorie*), nor is it dependent upon the existence of separate 'mission agencies.'"[23] Below, I will discuss how Luther provided the church with an important theological framework that is helpful for the mission works of the church at the present time.

LUTHER ON CHRISTIAN MISSION

Even if Warneck and other scholars had argued that Luther had no sense of mission (mission as evangelism), Luther had referred to the popular Great Commission text of Matt 28 in his commentaries on the Psalms written at Coburg in 1530 as follows: "The days and nights will declare the glory of God and the works of His hands in the languages of all people and in all lands. . . . This was fulfilled as the Apostles proclaimed the great deeds of God in many tongues and it continues to be fulfilled in the whole world, for the gospel which was discriminated into various languages through the apostles continues to resound in those same tongues unto the end of the world."[24] So Luther contends that the mission task, which is bringing the light of Christ to the world, is not over during his time and that it will continue to the end of the age. He states, "The Gospel will be preached in all lands, nations, and languages, not only among the Jews, not only in Jerusalem but in all tongues."[25]

Luther was clear in his statement, "It is necessary *always* [for the church] to proceed to those to whom no preaching has been done, in order that the number of Christians may be greater."[26] In his commentary on Isa 40:9, he also writes that "every Christian is also an evangelist, who should teach another and publish the glory and praise of God."[27] In fact, Luther's mission in sixteenth-century Germany was to teach the true gospel of Jesus Christ. What he did was educate people about the true biblical understanding of Jesus and how one was saved. He emphasized that Christians are saved by grace alone, not by good works.

23. Bosch, *Transforming Mission*, 249.

24. Luther, *Ersten 25 Psalmen*, 546; my translation.

25. Luther, *Psalm 8*, 122.

26. Luther, *Auslegung über etliche Kapitel*, 215; emphasis and translation mine. Also quoted by Braaten, *Apostolic Imperative*, 70.

27. Luther, *Lectures on Isaiah*, 13.

In his comments on Ps 117:1 (NIV: "Praise the LORD, all you nations; extol him, all you peoples"), Luther emphasizes that God's salvation is not limited to either the Jews or the pope's church. He argued that "the Gospel and Baptism must come to the whole world."[28] Referring to Mark 16:15 (NIV: "Go into the world, and preach the gospel to all creation"), he affirms world mission with the following words: "Wherever there are heathens—or a country or a city—there the Gospel will penetrate and will convert some to the kingdom of Christ. . . . For the Gospel and Baptism must come to the whole world, as they have indeed come and every day come again."[29] He argued,

> The Christians should also through the Word harvest much fruit among all the Gentiles and should convert and save many, and thus they shall devour around about them like a fire that is burning in the midst of dry wood and straw. The fire of the Holy Spirit, then, shall devour the Gentiles according to the flesh and prepare a place everywhere for the Gospel and the Kingdom of Christ.[30]

For Luther, Christians are called to direct people to Christ and Christ alone. In his commentary on 1 Peter, he states that all Christians "must preach about Jesus Christ that He died and rose from the dead, and why He died and rose again, in order that people may come to faith through such preaching and be saved through faith." Then he stresses, "This is what it means to preach the genuine Gospel. Preaching of another kind is not the Gospel, no matter who does it."[31]

In his explanation of John 1:7 about John the Baptist, Luther also contends that "just as he [John] was the forerunner of Christ and directed people to him, so the spoken word of Gospel should preach only Christ and point only to him."[32] When explaining the reason why Christians should always take proclamation seriously, he states, "John was sent so that he should be the voice in the wilderness who with his office signifies [the] spoken preaching of the Gospel. Just as the wilderness was unable, on its

28. Luther, *Psalm 117*, 13.

29. Luther, *Psalm 117*, 12–13. In his comments on Ps 117:1, Luther emphasized that "God is not only the God of the Jews but the God of the heathens also, and not only of a small part of heathendom but of all heathens throughout the world" (Luther, *Psalm 117*, 8–9).

30. Luther, *Commentary on Zechariah*, 326.

31. Luther, *First Epistle of Saint Peter*, 10.

32. Luther, *Main Christian Service*, 66–67. John 1:7 (NIV) reads, "He came as a witness to testify concerning that light, so that through him all might believe."

own, to comprehend this light, even though it was present, John had to reveal and to bear witness of it. To this day natural reason on its own is unable to comprehend it, even though it is present in the world. [Therefore,] the spoken word of the Gospel must reveal and proclaim it."[33]

So for Luther, Christians should take their evangelistic role seriously because it is only through the proclamation of the true gospel that people can come to know and believe in God. This is in reaction to some Christians who thought that because Christ is already revealed in nature (*Christus revelatus*) or in other religions (as some pluralistic theologians would argue), there is no need to proclaim the gospel.[34] Luther rejected this notion of a saving natural revelation and emphasized that it is only the Christ who is preached (*Christus preadicatus*) that can offer the light of grace to all people.[35] He argued that Christ must be preached for the gospel to create faith. In his commentary on John 1:12–23 (v. 12 NIV: "Yet to all who did receive him, to those who believed in his name, he gave the right to become children of God—children born not of natural descent, nor of human decision or a husband's will, but born of God"), Luther emphasized that it is only when the gospel is preached and received in faith that people can become the children of God. This is how God liberates people from Satan, sin, and death. This conviction of Luther provides us with a clear understanding about a Lutheran approach to evangelistic mission. Quoting Luther,

> One cannot come to faith or lay hold on the Holy Spirit without hearing the Word first, as St. Paul has said (Rom. 10:14): "How are they to believe in Him of whom they have never heard?" and (Gal. 3:2): "you have received the Holy Spirit through the proclamation of faith." If they are to hear His Word, then preachers must be sent to proclaim God's Word to them; for not all the heathens can come to Jerusalem or make a living among the

33. Luther, *Main Christian Service*, 67.

34. Luther argued, "To this day natural reason on its own is unable to comprehend [the gospel], even though it is present in all the world. The spoken word of God must reveal and proclaim it" (Luther, *Main Christian Service*, 66–67).

35. Particularly in his commentary on John 1:9 (NIV: "the true light that gives light to everyone was coming into the world"), he states that Christ "gives light to everyone," which means that he alone gives the true light of salvation (through the word) and is revealed for all humanity, including Jews and gentiles (Luther, *Main Christian Service*, 70).

> small company of the Jews. He lets them stay where they are and calls upon them, wherever they may be, to praise God.[36]

Luther states that there are two main challenges or obstacles to mission. The first is Satan and his kingdom, which is always opposed to God's ongoing activity in our world. There is always a battle between God's kingdom and Satan's kingdom. Luther states that in the wake of the preaching of the word, Satan and "so many smart people, so many holy and powerful men [who become his instruments]—in fact, the whole world together with the gates of hell would persecute the Word."[37] The second obstacle, according to Luther, is "the ingratitude of people, contempt and weariness with the Word."[38] He states that it is hard for Christians to witness Christ in public because they have the "fear of danger, sometimes the hope of gain and often the advice of friends [which] intervenes." For Luther, this is the reason why the psalmist in Ps 51:15 had to say, "Open my lips, Lord, and my mouth will declare your praise."[39]

Who are these people that need to be evangelized? In the Large Catechism, Luther describes those as "all other people outside Christianity—whether heathens, Turks [Muslims], Jews, or false Christians and hypocrites—[even if they] believe in and worship only the one true God, they still do not know what His mind towards them is and cannot expect any love or blessing from Him."[40] Also in the Large Catechism, in his explanation of the phrase "the kingdom come" in the Lord's Prayer, Luther states,

> We pray that His name may be so praised through God's Holy Word and a Christian life that we have accepted it may abide and daily grow in it, and that it may gain approval and acceptance among other people. *We pray that* [the gospel] *may go forth with power throughout the world.* We pray that many may find entrance into the kingdom of grace, be made partakers of redemption, and be led to it by the Holy Spirit, so that we may all together remain forever in the one kingdom now begun.[41]

36. Luther, *Psalm 117*, 9.
37. Luther, *Psalm 45*, 219–20.
38. Luther, *Psalm 45*, 220.
39. Luther, *Psalm 51*, 393.
40. LC 2.66 (Pless and Vogel, 420).
41. LC 3.52 (Pless and Vogel, 481–82); emphasis mine.

MISSION AS THE TRIUNE GOD'S WORK (*MISSIO DEI*)

As described above, Warneck's and others scholars' critiques of Luther were mainly grounded in their understanding of mission as evangelism or Great Commission. But for Luther, the mission of the church is not confined to evangelism. For him, mission is God's work (*missio Dei*), the Triune God's ongoing creative engagement with the world which cannot be confined or limited to organized mission activities to reach out to the heathen. It also involves greater social responsibility and striving for justice within the scope of the Christian gospel. Many Lutheran scholars have so focused on the vertical accent in Luther's thought (the relationship between God and humanity) that they gave little or no room for Luther's horizontal factors (service to our neighbor). But as Karl Holl pointed out in the early 1920s, a one-sided theocentric approach to mission (the vertical accent) ignores the Reformer's emphasis on the Christian's call by baptism to be Christ to his or her neighbor.[42]

Luther's theology of mission is grounded on the Triune God's purpose to redeem and restore humanity. For Luther, mission is first and foremost God's mission (*missio Dei*). This means, according to Schulz, "God is the subject. Our activity must subordinate itself to God's doing, and any success is due to Him."[43] Luther identifies two purposes (mission) for which the church exists. The first and primary purpose is preaching the gospel, which is the responsibility of all Christians as a sent community—the sending nature of the Triune, missionary God: the Father sending the Son, and the Father and the Son sending the Holy Spirit.[44] The gospel is the word made flesh, for God sent the Son into the world "that the world might be saved through him" (John 3:17). Jesus Christ then taught, equipped, and sent his apostles to baptize all nations. He vested with them the power of the Holy Spirit and commissioned them to be his witnesses. Luther uses the word *Sendung* (sending) and the Latin word *mittere* (to send) when he speaks about bringing the gospel to the nations. Spreading the gospel is the duty of all Christians (the priesthood of all believers). Secondly, Christians are called to love and serve our neighbors. In fact, Luther's missional imagination is filled with neighbors; God puts all Christians in this world for them. It is Luther's

42. Holl, "Luther und die Mission," 234.

43. Schulz, *Mission from the Cross*, 50.

44. "He permits us to live here in order that we may bring others to faith, just as He brought us" (Luther, *First Epistle of Saint Peter*, 11).

emphasis on "faith alone" and "love alone" that ties the two aspects of mission together.[45]

In reference to Christian mission, God has put all Christians in this world so that they can serve all people in love. Mission to our neighbors is not only limited to serving others but also identifying ourselves in them through love.[46] Luther contends, "We conclude, therefore, that a Christian lives not in himself, but in *Christ* and in his *neighbor*. Otherwise he is not a Christian. He lives in Christ through *faith*, in his neighbor through *love*."[47]

At Luther's time, as we often observe among Christians today, the emphasis was given only to *faith*—to human beings' relationship to God. Some even assumed that since we are saved by "faith alone," we are free from works related to our neighbor.[48] Yet, Luther contends, "our faith in Christ does not free us from works but from false opinions concerning works, that is, from the foolish presumption that justification is acquired by works of love."[49] Rather, according to Luther, "everyone who is a neighbor [has] received the command to do us all kinds of good. So we receive our blessings not from them, but from God through them. Creatures are only the hands, channels, and means through which God bestows all blessings."[50]

Faith active in love is experienced in worship. Describing the German word for worship, *Gottesdienst*, Luther emphatically states that "there is no greater service of God (*Dienst gottis*) than Christian love which helps and serves the needy, as Christ himself will judge and testify at the Last Day, Matthew 25 [verses 31–46]."[51] Mission as service to our neighbor flows from our worship life. Our liturgical experience leads to dedicated service to our neighbor: "That is how a Christian acts. He is conscious of nothing else than that the goods which are his are also given

45. Luther, *Concerning the Ministry*, 9.

46. See Simpson, "Being Neighbor."

47. Luther, *Freedom of a Christian*, 371; emphasis mine.

48. Deressa "Church and Development in Ethiopia."

49. Luther, *Freedom of a Christian*, 372–73.

50. LC 1.26 (*BC*, 389).

51. Luther, *Ordinance of a Common Chest*, 172. Luther made similar points in his other writings such as his "short" and then "long" sermons on usury (Luther, *Sermons on Usury*, 306–7).

to his neighbor. He makes no distinction but helps everyone with body and life, goods and honor, as much as he can."[52]

MISSION AND THE THEOLOGY OF THE CROSS

Warneck's mistaken conclusion about Luther probably emerged from his little awareness of Luther's early writings, including the *Heidelberg Disputation* (1518), where Luther explores the theology of the cross as foundational for understanding the basics of theology, which I believe provides us with a framework for articulating a Lutheran Christian approach to theology of mission and mission of the church. This writing of Luther, including a few others such as his *Lectures on Romans* (1515–1516) and the *Disputation Against Scholastic Theology* (1517), were not given emphasis until after World War I, when people began to find or rediscover a prophetic meaning in those writings to speak against Christian idolatry in their contemporary situation.

Luther's theology of the cross (*theologia crucis*) provides us with the framework for understanding the church's mission in the world. Among Luther's writings, the *Heidelberg Disputation* is a good place to start to explore Luther's theology of the cross. In this writing, Luther argues that the starting point for every kind of theology is *either a theology of glory* or *a theology of the cross*. A theology of glory begins from below (human praxis), and the theology of the cross begins from above (the divine). For the theology of glory, the starting point is human experience related to the beauty of creation, an event in history, or something tangible with a positive impact on human life. A theologian of glory always looks for God in the strong, divine power, wisdom, glory, and/or discerned blessing. A theologian of the cross, on the other hand, understands that God reveals himself not in the "brightest and best" but rather through the weak and the foolish. The theologian of the cross identifies him where he has hidden, in the suffering of his Son—Jesus Christ.

The theologian of the cross is described in thesis 19: "That person doesn't deserve to be called a theologian who looks upon invisible things of God as though they were clearly perceptible in those things which have actually happened."[53] In other words, a theologian of glory imagines that he can know God through human wisdom and merits. In thesis 20,

52. Luther, *Sacrament of the Body*, 352–53.

53. Luther, *Heidelberg Disputation*, 52.

Luther described a true theologian as follows: "He deserves to be called a theologian, however, who comprehends the visible and manifest things of God seen through suffering and the cross."[54] Here, Luther clearly argues that God only reveals himself through the suffering of Christ.

Luther also identified two kinds of righteousness (not an integral part of the *Heidelberg Disputation*, but about the same time), two ways of understanding what it means to be human. These two kinds of righteousness which Luther articulated served as a framework for his understanding of what it means to be involved in the ongoing creative activity of God. One is "passive" righteousness, the vertical sphere of our lives indicating God's justification of sinners only because of his grace and mercy. The second one is "active" righteousness, actively participating in mission to the world through caring for God's creation.[55] As theologians of the cross, this theological framework of Luther helps us to understand the vertical bar of the cross symbolizes our fellowship with Christ and our mission for evangelism, and the horizontal bar symbolizes the other aspect of mission—social action—God's ongoing engagement with the world to insure his justice for the poor. Yet our fellowship with Christ and our mission as a sent community to evangelize the unevangelized should always be given priority because God commissioned the church to preach the gospel of Jesus Christ.

Luther's emphasis on the cross of Christ as the foundation for all theology and the church's mission also provides us with a framework for how we understand what it means to be a missional church. How is being a theologian of the cross and mission related? Firstly, mission as the proclamation of the gospel among the nations is made possible by the sacrifice of Jesus Christ on the cross. One becomes a theologian of the cross by hearing the word and proclaiming it. Just as God works through his word, the believer must therefore also proclaim that word: "We are nothing more than his mouth and tongue."[56]

One other implication of Luther's theology of the cross, as pointed out by Paul Althaus, is that it emphasizes mission as servanthood and rejects any motives of triumphalism or imposing forms of Christendom on others.[57] Jesus invited his disciples to take up the cross and follow him,

54. Luther, *Heidelberg Disputation*, 52–53.

55. See Kolb and Arand, *Genius of Luther's Theology*, 12–13, 25–31; see also Kolb, "Two Kinds of Righteousness"; Lumpp, "Luther's 'Two Kinds of Righteousness.'"

56. Preus, "Theology of the Cross," 127.

57. Althaus, *Theology of Martin Luther*, 27–34.

which means that the cross is part of the apostolic vocation. The theology of the cross views the Christian person as one called to serve or suffer. The servant is called to be obedient, even to the point of giving oneself up. As Luther contends, "It is impossible for a person not to be puffed up by his good works. . . . That wisdom which sees the invisible nature of God in works as perceived by man is completely puffed up, blinded, and hardened."[58] Yet the cross "destroys man's self-confidence" so that instead of wanting to do everything by himself, it allows God to use him for his purpose.[59]

Most importantly, a missional church is a church that fully participates in God's sacraments, which then leads to our participation in mission. According to Luther, the "sacrament [of the body of Christ] signifies the complete union and the undivided fellowship of the saints."[60] To take part in Holy Communion is to have fellowship with Christ and all the saints. In the Eucharist, the Triune God shares his God-self with us through bread and wine, and "we receive a sure sign of this fellowship and incorporation with Christ and all saints."[61] As Luther contends, while partaking in this Sacrament, "all the spiritual possessions of Christ and his saints are shared with and become the common property of him who receives this sacrament."[62] Furthermore, according to Luther, in eucharistic fellowship, "we are [also] to be united with our neighbors, we in them and they in us."[63]

CONCLUSION

Luther in his works emphasizes that mission is being part of the ongoing creative activity of the Triune God. For Luther, mission as *missio Dei* is both evangelism (the primary mission of the church) and serving our neighbors. God sent his Son to save the world, and the Son sent his Spirit to drive God's reign forward. And the Spirit equips and sends the church into the world to preach the good news of Jesus Christ and to love and serve their neighbors. The preaching of the "living word" (*viva vox*)

58. Luther, *Heidelberg Disputation*, 53 (thesis 22).
59. Luther, *Heidelberg Disputation*, 55 (thesis 25).
60. Luther, *Blessed Sacrament*, 50.
61. Luther, *Blessed Sacrament*, 51.
62. Luther, *Blessed Sacrament*, 51.
63. Luther, *Blessed Sacrament*, 51.

takes priority because only the gospel can create faith and give eternal life. When the gospel is preached, it mediates the Holy Spirit, who "calls, gathers, enlightens, and sanctifies the whole Christian church on earth and preserves it in union with Jesus Christ in the one true faith."[64]

Luther, through his writing, challenges the church to be missional at all times. Even though in his biblical expositions he perceived Germany and Europe as fields of mission, he had emphasized that the gospel will continue to go forth to all corners of the world and calls people to faith in Christ Jesus (Matt 6:10, 22:9–10). He also emphasizes that mission involves loving and serving our neighbors. For him, evangelism and social service are both integral parts of mission. In other words, Christ calls and sends the church to both preach the good news of Jesus Christ and to love and serve their neighbors.

64. Gritsch and Jenson, *Lutheranism*, 124.

4

Redefining the Church's Mission

The Evolving Missional Conversation and Lutheran Contributions

In his thought-provoking book *Simply Christian*, renowned theologian N. T. Wright poses crucial questions that delve into the essence and purpose of the church. He challenges readers to reflect on what the church truly is, who belongs to it and how, and, perhaps most critically, what the church is for. This last question—"What is the church for?"—stands out as a poignant inquiry that delves into the heart of the church's mission and calling.[1]

In a world where the church is often defined by what it opposes or rejects, Wright's inquiry shifts the focus to a more positive and constructive perspective. Instead of dwelling on what the church stands against, he compels us to consider what the church stands for and why it exists. This shift in perspective invites believers to ponder their purpose and role in the world, emphasizing the proactive mission of the church as agents of God's love and grace.

Wright's insights challenge believers to move beyond a passive understanding of the church as a mere institution or organization. Instead, he calls on the church to embrace its identity as the living body of Christ, actively engaged in the ongoing creative activity of the Triune God in the world. This dynamic view of the church highlights its mission to be a beacon of light, hope, and redemption, reflecting the love and grace of

1. Wright, *Simply Christian*, 201.

God to all. The question is, How can a church be effectively engaged in the ongoing transformative mission of the Triune God?

This chapter explores the missional church conversation in America, a growing movement within the Christian community that emphasizes the church's call to be an active and transformative presence in the world. This movement emphasizes the church's call to participate in God's mission of reconciliation, justice, and love in the world. The missional church conversation in America is a dynamic and evolving movement that challenges traditional models of church and invites Christians to step out of their comfort zones, engaging with the world around them in a way that reflects the love and compassion of Jesus Christ.

In the landscape of missional church conversation, the voice of Lutheran scholars has been notably absent. While various theological traditions have made significant contributions to this conversation, Lutheran scholars have been less prominent in the discussion. Even though the reasons for this may not be entirely clear, it is essential to recognize the richness of Lutheran theology and its potential to contribute significantly to the ongoing dialogue around mission and engagement in the church. In this chapter, I will explore the history and contributions of the missional church conversation and delve into how Lutheran theology can offer unique insights and perspectives to enrich this conversation.

MISSIONAL CHURCH CONVERSATION IN NORTH AMERICA

In the 1960s, a wave of innovators emerged as the forerunners to the missional church conversation, challenging the status quo of Western Christendom. Visionaries such as Elton Trueblood, John Howard Yoder, Howard Snyder, Donald McGavran, Lesslie Newbigin, J. C. Hoekendijk, and Elizabeth O'Connor recognized the changing landscape of Western Christianity.[2] They raised critical questions about the traditional practices and structures of the church, highlighting the need for adaptation in the face of shifting cultural realities. These pioneers foresaw a disconnect between the established church norms and the essence of the gospel,

2. Some of the resources developed at this point in the history include Trueblood, *Incendiary Fellowship*; Snyder, *Problem of Wine Skins*; McGavran, *Understanding Church Growth*; Newbigin, *Household of God*, Hoekendijk, *Church Inside Out*; and O'Connor, *New Community*.

urging for a reevaluation and transformation of the church's mission and purpose in response to the evolving societal context.[3]

One significant turning point in the conversation occurred in the early 1980s when Lesslie Newbigin, an influential theologian, sparked a thought-provoking dialogue with his monograph *The Other Side of 1984: Questions for the Churches*.[4] This publication stimulated a crucial conversation about the intricate relationship between the gospel and culture. Newbigin's concerns centered on the emergence of a post-Christian and even anti-Christian era in Western society, which introduced a new and daunting reality for churches in the Western world.

In *The Other Side of 1984*, Newbigin advocates a crucial shift in perspective by centering the *missio Dei* as the focal point of theological engagement. His broader body of work critically examines the interaction between "the gospel and the late-modern Western culture."[5] Central to his argument is the challenge of articulating Christ's universal lordship without succumbing to the pitfalls of Constantinianism. He asserts,"We are now faced with a new task which may be defined as follows: how to embody in the life and teaching of the Church the claim that Christ is Lord over all life, without falling into the Constantinian impasse?"[6]

In his book *Foolishness to the Greeks*, Newbigin asks the following question: "What would be involved in a missionary encounter between the gospel and these whole way of perceiving, thinking, and living that we call 'modern Western culture'?"[7] As Roxburgh emphasizes, "Newbigin's framing of the missionary situation of the West seemed to offer a fresh and critical window into a new assessment of the church and how its leaders might function."[8] Through these works, Newbigin urged theologians and church leaders to embrace a more creative approach, encouraging them to actively seek ways to engage in God's mission within this challenging cultural landscape. By acknowledging the shifting dynamics

3. For example, Roxburgh identifies eight cultural shifts: globalization, pluralism, rapid technological change, postmodernism, staggering global need, loss of confidence in primary structures, return to romanticism, and the democratization of knowledge (Roxburgh, *Missional Map-Making*, 90–110).

4. Newbigin, *Other Side of 1984*, 34.

5. Newbigin, *Other Side of 1984*, 6. Van Gelder and Zscheile, *Missional Church*, 5.

6. Newbigin, *Other Side of 1984*, 7.

7. Newbigin, *Foolishness to the Greeks*, 1.

8. Roxburgh, "Missional Leadership," 128.

of the era, Newbigin exhorted the church to adapt its methods and strategies to effectively communicate the timeless message of the gospel.[9]

Newbigin's groundbreaking works were a challenge to many churches within Europe and America, where churches were primarily operating within a Christendom context with a church-centered approach to mission. Traditionally, the mission for most Western churches involved sending missionaries to proclaim the gospel in cross-cultural contexts. Newbigin's perspective challenged this conventional understanding and served as a timely reminder of earlier theological works that framed mission as the *missio Dei*. The *missio Dei* emphasizes that God is always at work in the world and invites the church to actively participate in his redemptive purposes. Ed Stetzer writes, "The concept of *missio Dei*, the mission of God, is the recognition that God is a sending God, and the church is sent. . . . From our understanding of the *missio Dei* . . . God's people are to participate in the divine mission to manifest and advance God's kingdom on earth through the means of sharing and showing the gospel of God's kingdom in Jesus Christ."[10]

This understanding brings a shift in focus from viewing mission primarily as a human endeavor to recognizing that it is fundamentally rooted in God's character and action in the world. Whereas the historical perception of mission within many Western churches predominantly emphasized foreign mission projects, these projects were driven by a desire to bring the gospel to distant lands considered to be in need of salvation and enlightenment, both spiritually and culturally. Consequently, mission boards were established to undertake this specific objective on behalf of sending churches. The mission boards and churches shared the understanding that their mission was primarily directed at the "pagan reaches" of the world, where they felt compelled to introduce not only Christianity but also the so-called "Western civilization."

Newbigin's call to reorient our thinking about mission sparked a significant conversation among theologians and church leaders focused on *missio Dei*, a term which David Fitch defines this way: "*Missio Dei* means that God is already at work in our lives and the lives of all around us. . . . [This doctrine] points us squarely into the middle of this world where God is, discerning where God is working, knowing what God has

9. Guder, *Missional Church*, 4.

10. Stetzer, *Planting Missional Churches*, 19.

done in the past continues into the present—not as something that we must do but as something God is always already doing."[11]

This is how the Gospel and Our Culture Network (GOCN) started in the United States.[12] The GOCN contextualized Newbigin's European-based analysis for a North American context. GOCN has played a pivotal role in reshaping the conversation within American churches regarding the intersection of the gospel message, culture, and mission. Firstly, the network delved into understanding the dynamic landscape of American culture, aiming to discern the transformative shifts that shape individuals' lives and identify where God is at work within them. Secondly, GOCN sought to uncover fresh perspectives on how the gospel provides the necessary resources for an assured and compelling witness to Jesus Christ. In other words, they sought to uncover fresh ways to articulate the timeless message of the gospel in culturally meaningful and intelligible ways. Finally, the network embarked on an exploration of a missiological ecclesiology, specifically tailored for the diverse contexts of North America. This exploration sought to understand how churches can become missional communities that effectively embody and proclaim the gospel within their specific cultural, social, and geographical contexts. The network delved into questions of church vocation, structures, leadership, worship practices, and mission strategies, aiming to equip churches to engage meaningfully with the diverse and rapidly changing North American context.[13]

The earlier book by GOCN, *The Missional Church* in 1998, which is a groundbreaking work, introduced the term *missional* and its implications for reimagining the nature and purpose of the church in the complex landscape of the twenty-first century. The term *missional* encapsulated a fresh perspective on the church as a community actively participating in the mission of God in the world. This theological claim is illustrated by the book *The Mission of the Church: Five Views in Conversation*. While the specific theological perspectives vary, each representative of these five views espouses that "the church does not merely send missionaries; rather, the church itself is God's missionary people. Mission becomes the defining character of the church as the reflection of the divine character of God as a missionary God."[14] As Jürgen Moltmann also rightly argued,

11. Fitch and Holsclaw, *Prodigal Christianity*, 28–30.

12. Guder, *Missional Church*, 3–4.

13. Guder, *Missional Church*, 7–8.

14. Ott, *Mission of the Church*, xix.

"It is not the church that has a mission of salvation to fulfill in the world; it is the mission of the Son and the Spirit through the Father that includes the church."[15]

It was in specifically referring to this shift that David Bosch stated,

> Mission was understood as being derived from the very nature of God. It was thus put in the context of the doctrine of the Trinity, not of ecclesiology or soteriology. The classical doctrine on the missio Dei as God the Father sending the Son, and God the Father and the Son sending the Spirit was expanded to include yet another "movement": The Father, Son and the Holy Spirit sending the church into the world. As far as missionary thinking was concerned, this linking with the doctrine of the Trinity constituted an important innovation.[16]

As Darrell Guder states, "The ecclesiastic understanding of mission has been replaced during this century by a profoundly theocentric reconceptualization of Christian mission. We have come to see that is not merely an activity of the church. Rather, mission is the result of God's initiative, rooted in God's purposes to restore and heal creation."[17] This concept provided a departure from the traditional understanding of the church solely as a religious institution focused on its own internal affairs. Academics seized upon this innovative concept, recognizing its potential to awaken the church to its missional calling.[18]

Central to the missional church conversation is the biblical understanding of the church as "sent ones," a concept that forms the bedrock of missional transformation (John 20:21). At the core of this understanding is the mission of Jesus himself, who came "to seek and to save the lost" (Luke 19:10 NIV). This mission is not exclusive to Christ alone but extends to every believer who is called to carry out the same mandate. Just as Jesus was sent by the Father, so too are his followers sent into the world (John 17:18).

The impact of the *Missional Church* book was far-reaching, as its ideas permeated academic circles and ecclesiastical conversations. The book's radical reimagining of the church's nature and purpose in the twenty-first century evoked powerful imaginations, igniting a new wave of theological reflections and practical applications. Numerous subsequent

15. Moltmann, *Church in the Power*, 64.
16. Bosch, *Transforming Mission*, 389–90.
17. Guder, *Missional Church*, 4.
18. Van Gelder and Zscheile, *Missional Church*, 1.

publications have emerged, building upon the *Missional Church* paradigm and exploring its implications for diverse ecclesial contexts.

In the North American context, four key themes have continued to emerge and shape the ongoing conversation around the missional church movement. These themes—including mission as participation in God's kingdom, mission as discipleship-making for participation in God's mission, mission as a "glocal" endeavor encompassing global and local aspects, and mission as an engagement with modern and postmodern culture—have been instrumental in guiding churches toward a transformative understanding of their role in God's redemptive work.

Figure 4: Missional Church Emphasis (image by Samuel Deressa)

The Kingdom-Centered Mission

This understanding focuses on the idea that the mission of the church is to participate in God's kingdom work on earth.[19] It emphasizes the holistic nature of God's redemptive plan and calls for the church to be actively involved in bringing about God's kingdom values of justice, love, and mercy that reflect the values of the kingdom.[20]

One good example is the work by Ralph Winter, who offers a profound insight into the concept of God's kingdom in the grand narrative

19. For detail, see Winter, "Three Mission Eras."

20. Hunsberger, "Called and Sent," 94.

of the Bible. He encapsulates the essence of the biblical narrative with the statement, "The Bible consists of a single drama: the entrance of the Kingdom, the power, and the glory of the living God in this enemy-occupied territory."[21] In this context, Winter highlights the overarching story of the Bible as God's relentless mission to inaugurate his kingdom within a world besieged by sin and darkness. This drama is not merely a series of disjointed events but a cohesive and purposeful movement orchestrated by God to reclaim his creation and reestablish his sovereign rule.[22]

As elucidated by theologians Craig Van Gelder and Dwight Zscheile, the focus on the kingdom of God has been instrumental in guiding scholars and ecclesiastical leaders to a more holistic understanding of the gospel. This dialogical approach to missiology, according to Craig and Dwight, shifted the focus from an exclusive focus on individualized salvation, predominantly aimed at securing eternal life, to a more comprehensive understanding of redemption. It is argued that this approach is necessary not only to uphold the integrity of the gospel message but also to align ecclesiological practices with the overarching purpose of God's mission.

Furthermore, Craig and Dwight argue that this theological approach—focused on the kingdom of God—demands a critical reassessment of the church's self-understanding and its role within the broader framework of divine redemption. The church, they contend, is not an insular institution but an integral participant in God's overarching redemptive narrative. This perspective necessitates a missional ecclesiology that is both expansive and deeply engaged with the world, as the church's mission must align with the comprehensive scope of God's redemptive work.[23]

Discipleship and Mission

This understanding highlights the inseparable connection between discipleship and mission. It stresses the importance of equipping and empowering believers to be active participants in God's mission, emphasizing that discipleship is not just about personal growth but also about engaging in the mission of God to make disciples of all nations. This perspective views every member of the church as a disciple who is called to

21. Winter, "Kingdom Strikes Back," 210.

22. Winter, "Kingdom Strikes Back," 210.

23. Van Gelder and Zscheile, *Missional Church*, 29.

live out their faith in their everyday lives, impacting their communities and the world around them.[24]

As discussed above, the contemporary missional church movement, characterized by a focus on engaging communities outside traditional church settings, has seen an upsurge in churches attempting to be more mission-oriented. However, Mark Breen argues that the success of this movement hinges on a foundational element: discipleship. He argues the missional church movement is destined to fail without a strong foundation in discipleship.[25]

Breen's emphasis on discipleship is grounded in biblical theology. The New Testament illustrates the discipleship model through Jesus' relationship with his followers, where intentional mentoring and teaching were central (Matt 28:19–20, 2 Tim 2:2). Breen underscores that Scripture does not advocate for mission apart from discipleship; rather, mission flows organically from a life committed to learning and living out biblical principles under the guidance of a mature Christian mentor.

Breen identifies several challenges that arise when mission is attempted independently of discipleship. First, there is a risk of superficial engagement, where activities are carried out without deep spiritual roots. Second, without discipleship, there is a lack of accountability and sustainability, leading to burnout and disintegration of mission efforts. The absence of a discipling framework often results in a fragmented community with limited spiritual growth and impact.

Glocal Mission

The *glocal* aspect of mission shifts the focus from a binary understanding of mission (global vs. local) to a more holistic perspective that recognizes the interconnectedness of all mission contexts. It encourages churches to engage both locally and globally, recognizing that God's mission transcends geographical boundaries and requires a multidimensional approach. It also challenges churches to engage with both global issues and local needs, acknowledging that effective mission work requires a

24. For details, see Maddix and Akkerman, *Missional Discipleship*; Willard, *Great Omission*; Bonhoeffer, *Cost of Discipleship*.

25. Breen, "Missional Movement."

balance between addressing global injustices and meeting the needs of their immediate communities.[26]

Missiologists, those who study and facilitate the practice of mission work, argue that one of the most effective ways for local congregations to start global ministry is by reaching out to the immigrants from various parts of the world residing in their neighborhoods. This strategy offers a multitude of benefits that reverberate far beyond geographical and cultural boundaries.[27] Engaging with these immigrant populations presents churches with unique opportunities for ministry.

One exemplary model of the glocal approach to mission work can be found in the insightful contributions of Michael Frost and Alan Hirsch, articulated in their influential book *The Shaping of Things to Come*.[28] Within this work, Frost and Hirsch delve into the paradigms of evangelism through the lenses of the "Bounded-Set" and "Centered-Set" approaches. These frameworks offer distinct methodologies for how churches perceive their mission, both locally and globally. The Bounded-Set approach, representing a traditional view, delineates the church by clearly defined boundaries that separate those who are considered "in" from those who are "out." This model tends to emphasize adherence to doctrinal beliefs, moral codes, and social norms, which can create an exclusionary environment that isolates those who do not conform to these established criteria.[29]

In contrast, the Centered-Set approach revolutionizes the understanding of evangelism by defining the church through the orientation of individuals toward a central figure—Jesus Christ—rather than through rigid boundaries. Membership in this model is not determined by a checklist of qualifications but by the proximity of one's relational and spiritual journey toward Jesus. This perspective encourages inclusivity, offering a space where people from diverse backgrounds and stages of faith can find belonging and community. Frost and Hirsch, while acknowledging their indebtedness to Chris Harding from Youth for Christ in Australia for this conceptualization, manage to express it in a comprehensively transformative manner that challenges conventional church practices.

The implications of the Centered-Set approach for glocal ministry are profound. By emphasizing relational proximity to Jesus over strict

26. Engelsviken et al., *Church Going Glocal*.

27. Wan, *Diaspora Missiology*, 6.

28. Frost and Hirsch, *Shaping of Things to Come*.

29. Frost and Hirsch, *Shaping of Things to Come*, 50.

membership criteria, churches can effectively engage with the multicultural and immigrant populations within their local contexts. This shift fosters an inclusive environment where diverse cultural expressions and spiritual journeys are celebrated rather than judged. The relational nature of this approach prioritizes genuine connections and shared spiritual growth, making it particularly effective in a globalized society where pluralistic values and experiences are prevalent.

The Bounded-Set model, which defines the church by clear boundaries based on adherence to doctrinal beliefs and moral codes, aligns closely with the historic confessional stance of the Lutheran tradition. This model underscores the importance of sound doctrine and the necessity of maintaining doctrinal purity within the church, as articulated in the Lutheran Confessions. The emphasis on clear boundaries is not merely an exercise in exclusion but a means of preserving the integrity of the faith handed down through generations.

In contrast, the Centered-Set approach, which focuses on the orientation of individuals toward Jesus rather than adherence to doctrinal boundaries, can be seen as problematic. While the intention to focus on Jesus is commendable, this model risks undermining the importance of doctrinal clarity and confessional integrity. Orthodoxy in teaching and practice is essential for the true proclamation of the gospel and the administration of the sacraments. The ambiguous criteria for inclusion in a Centered-Set community could lead to a dilution of the distinct theological identity that is central to Lutheran ecclesiology.

Moreover, the Centered-Set approach's inclusivity, while seemingly appealing in a pluralistic and globalized world, may inadvertently lead to relativism where essential theological tenets are compromised for the sake of broader acceptance. The church's mission is to faithfully teach and uphold the truths of Scripture. A shift toward a less defined, more inclusive model risks the erosion of these crucial doctrinal foundations.

Engaging Culture in Mission

This theme delves into the importance of contextualizing the message of the gospel in a rapidly changing and diverse cultural landscape. It calls for a thoughtful and intentional approach to engaging with modern and postmodern culture, recognizing the need to communicate the timeless truths of the gospel in ways that resonate with contemporary society.

A good example of this approach is the work by Ronald Sider, *Churches That Make a Difference*. This book provides a comprehensive overview of churches that embrace a holistic approach to sharing the gospel within their communities.[30] The book emphasizes the telos of offering a complete message of salvation through a combination of evangelism and social action. Sider identifies six key foci that define churches that make a difference:

- Focus on ministries of personal spiritual transformation, recognizing it as a catalyst for social change.
- Focus on social services as a means to open doors for evangelism and spiritual engagement.
- Focus on ministries of reconciliation, demonstrating unity in Christ through actions that promote peace and understanding.
- Focus on community development, reflecting God's love for whole individuals and communities by addressing their holistic needs.
- Focus on justice ministries that embody the liberating message of the gospel by advocating for fairness and equality.
- Focus on reaching skeptics by showcasing tangible impacts and demonstrating the transformative power of the church's presence in society.

However, it garnered criticism from some quarters for its limited engagement with the practical aspects of congregational life. Critics argued that the contributors seemed disconnected from the realities of leading and nurturing missional communities. These critiques called for a deeper understanding of how the concept of the missional church translates into lived experiences and transformative action within congregations.[31]

With *Treasure in Clay Jars*, Barrett and her co-authors sought to bridge this gap by delving into the development of missional leaders within the dynamic context of congregational settings.[32] This book was intentionally crafted to address the gap identified in the previous work and provide practical insights on cultivating missional leadership within congregational contexts. It encompasses a rich exploration of the

30. Sider et al., *Churches That Make a Difference*, 36–44.

31. Kimball, *Emerging Church*.

32. Barrett et al., *Treasure in Clay Jars*.

challenges, opportunities, and transformative practices that shape the development of missional leaders.

Yet, as stated above, the concept of the "missional church" has gained significant traction among scholars as they explore the identity and mission of the church. The emergence of the missional church introduced a paradigm shift, presenting a theocentric reimagining of mission. Under this framework, the Trinity assumes a central role in mission. It recognizes God as a missionary God, beckoning all individuals to enter into communion with him and with each other, while also commissioning his people to participate in his ongoing creative endeavors within the world.[33]

By focusing on *missio Dei*, this movement challenges congregations to move beyond the four walls of the church building and engage with their local communities. It encourages believers to view their everyday lives as opportunities to embody the gospel and bring about positive change in the world. Furthermore, the missional church conversation has been successful in highlighting the importance of contextualization. By recognizing the diversity of cultural, social, and religious contexts in which the church exists, proponents of the missional church paradigm advocate for relevant expressions of faith that resonate with local communities. This contextual approach has the potential to bridge cultural barriers and make Christianity more accessible and meaningful to a wider range of individuals.

TRINITY AND MISSION

Central to missional church conversation is the notion that mission is defined and described from a Trinitarian perspective. The mission of the church is not a human endeavor but a divine mandate entrusted by the Triune God. The biblical foundation of the church's missional role is deeply rooted in the teachings of the Scriptures, where the sending of the church is a reflection of the unified purpose of the Father, Son, and Holy Spirit. As David Bosch announced in his magnum opus in the oft-quoted claim, "Mission is thereby seen as a movement from God to the world; the church is viewed as an instrument for that mission. There is a church because there is mission, not vice versa. To participate in mission is to

33. Bosch, *Transforming Mission*.

participate in the movement of God's love toward people, since God is a fountain of sending love."[34]

In the Gospel of John, Jesus explicitly prays for his disciples, saying, "As you sent me into the world, so I have sent them into the world" (John 17:18). This intimate connection between the sending of Christ by the Father and the sending of his followers underscores the divine origin and authority of the church's mission. Jesus further affirms this commission when he says, "As the Father has sent me, even so I am sending you" (John 20:21), emphasizing the continuity of the divine mission from the Father to the Son to the church.

Why did Jesus come into this world? In the Gospel of John 3:17 (NIV), Jesus reveals the divine purpose behind his coming: "For God did not send his Son into the world to condemn the world, but to save the world through him." The essence of God's sending of his Son is grounded in his redemptive love and the desire to offer salvation to all humanity. The words spoken by Jesus to Nicodemus underscore the core mission of his earthly ministry—to bring salvation and redemption to a fallen world.

Just as he was sent by the Father, Jesus sent out the twelve disciples into the world. In Luke 9:2 we read, "He sent them out to proclaim the kingdom of God." The disciples were empowered by the authority of Jesus to proclaim the kingdom of God and heal the sick, marking the beginning of their journey as ambassadors of the Triune God. In John 20:21, Jesus told his disciples, "Peace be with you. As the Father has sent Me, even so I am sending you." In Matt 28:19–20, known as the Great Commission, Jesus instructs his disciples to go and make disciples of all nations, baptizing them in the name of the Father, and of the Son, and of the Holy Spirit. This triadic formula highlights the unified work of the Triune God in the mission of the church, where believers are called to make disciples in the name of the Father, Son, and Holy Spirit. As Newbigin states, "The Church is sent into the world to continue that which he came to do, in the power of the same Spirit, reconciling people to God."[35]

In Acts 1:8, before his ascension, Jesus promises the empowering presence of the Holy Spirit to his disciples, declaring, "But you will receive power when the Holy Spirit comes on you; and you will be my witnesses in Jerusalem, and in all Judea and Samaria, and to the ends of the earth" (NIV). This verse demonstrates the Triune God's active involvement in

34. Bosch, *Transforming Mission*, 390.

35. Newbigin, *Gospel in a Pluralist Society*, 230.

equipping and guiding the church in its mission to bear witness to the gospel to the ends of the earth.

Therefore, the missional mandate of the church is a sacred calling entrusted by the Triune God, where the Father, Son, and Holy Spirit work together in perfect unity to empower and guide believers in advancing the kingdom of God. As the church, we should embrace our role as "sent ones" by the Triune God, carrying out his mission with faith, obedience, and reliance on the divine guidance of the Father, Son, and Holy Spirit. May we walk in the footsteps of Christ, empowered by the Spirit, and driven by the love of the Father, as we proclaim the good news of salvation to all nations, fulfilling the divine mandate of the Triune God.

This understanding of mission as inherently connected to the Triune God challenges the traditional view of mission as merely a task or program that the church engages in. Instead, it emphasizes that mission is an essential aspect of the very nature of God, who is inherently relational and sends forth his love and redemption into the world. As David Bosch explains, "To say that church is missionary does not mean that mission is church-centered. It is *Missio Dei*. It is Trinitarian."[36] As he contends, "mission [is] understood as being derived from the very nature of God. It [is] thus put in the context of the doctrine of the Trinity, not of ecclesiology or soteriology."[37]

From this Trinitarian perspective, the mission of the church is not just about preaching the gospel or doing good works but about embodying the love, unity, and community of the Triune God in all aspects of our lives. It calls us to see ourselves as co-participants with God in his ongoing work of reconciliation and redemption in the world. This understanding also challenges us to reconsider our understanding of church as merely a place we go to on Sundays or a community of like-minded individuals. Rather, it calls us to see the church as a living organism, constantly being sent out into the world to bear witness to the love and grace of God. As Craig Van Gelder states, "The church is missionary by nature because God has sent it on a mission in the world under the leading of the Holy Spirit. It is to bear witness to God's redemptive reign. Just as God is a missionary God, so the church is to be a missionary church."[38]

In essence, the Trinitarian foundation of missional theology reminds us that mission is not just something we do but is an integral

36. Bosch, *Transforming Mission*, 493.

37. Bosch, *Transforming Mission*, 390.

38. Van Gelder, *Essence of the Church*, 98.

part of who God is. As image-bearers of God, we are called to reflect the Triune nature of God in our relationships, our actions, and our mission in the world. This perspective transforms our understanding of mission from a mere task or program to a way of life—a way of being sent out into the world to bear witness to the love and grace of God in all that we do.

This understanding of the Trinitarian nature of God shapes the very core of missional theology and practice. To truly embody the mission of God in the world, the church must first and foremost reflect the loving, relational nature of the Triune God. Just as the Father, Son, and Holy Spirit exist in perfect unity and harmony, so too should the community of believers strive to live in loving and unified relationships with one another. The early church serves as a model of unity and communal living in the book of Acts (2:42–47, 5:42). The believers were devoted to fellowship, breaking bread together, and sharing their possessions with one another. This sense of community and mutual support is a foundational aspect of the church's mission, emphasizing the importance of love and unity among believers (John 13:34–35, 1 John 3:16–17). This way, the doctrine of the Trinity compels us to think beyond individualistic notions of salvation and mission and to embrace a communal and participatory understanding of God's redemptive work. It challenges us to see ourselves not as isolated individuals on a personal spiritual journey but as members of a community called to participate in the ongoing mission of God in the world.

As members of the church, Christians are created and called to mirror God's image to the world—which implies that the Christian community, in its Trinitarian image, should live in a way that reflects life with the Triune God.[39] This is the very reason why the doctrine of the Trinity is at the heart of the missional church conversation. The essence of missional theology is a particular view of mission as part of God's identity.[40]

LUTHERAN THEOLOGY VS. MISSIONAL CHURCH CONVERSATION

Lutheran approach to missiology, a concept that has often been perceived as conflicting, has been a topic of discussion within theological circles for a long time. This skepticism can be traced back to Gustav Warneck. His

39. Zizioulas and McPartlan, *Communion and Otherness*, 4–5.

40. Guder, *Missional Church*, 5.

criticism of Martin Luther has been passed down through generations, suggesting that Luther did not have a clear theology or understanding of mission. This has led to a common belief that Lutheran theology inherently lacks the necessary resources for robust engagement in mission work.[41]

The core of this criticism revolves around the idea that Lutheran theology tends to focus inward and prioritize doctrinal purity, which can hinder its effectiveness in missionary work. According to Warneck, Luther's teachings do not adequately address the concept of mission, making Lutheranism weak and insufficient in terms of missiology. This viewpoint argues that true, impactful missiological practice requires a theological foundation that actively embraces and participates in the missionary mandate, a quality that some critics believe is missing in Lutheran theology.[42]

Nevertheless, it is important to acknowledge that this criticism has not gone unchallenged. There are individuals within the Lutheran tradition who argue that Luther's writings and broader Lutheran theology possess untapped potential for missiology. They suggest that when viewed from a different perspective, Lutheran theology can offer profound insights and resources for mission work. This may include a deeper understanding of grace, the priesthood of all believers, and the relational and outward-focused nature of faith.

As James Scherer rightly noted, "For Luther, mission is always preeminently the work of the triune God—*missio Dei*—and its goal and outcome is the coming of the kingdom of God. . . . The rich but untested potential of Luther and the Reformation for mission practice comes down to the present, not as definitive guidance, but certainly as inspiration and challenge for missiology today. It becomes a calculable 'benchmark' for testing today's missiological axioms."[43]

How can one engage the missional church conversation from a Lutheran perspective? The Lutheran approach to mission is closely connected to the church's apostolic nature as stated in the Nicene Creed: "I believe in one holy, catholic [universal], and apostolic church." This declaration highlights the church's unity, universality, and continuity with the original teachings of the apostles. The term *apostolic* confirms that the church's teachings about Christ, passed down by the apostles, remain

41. For more detail, see the next chapter of this book.

42. Warneck, *Outline of a History*, 9.

43. Scherer, *Gospel, Church, and Kingdom*, 55, 66; italics original.

unchanged over time.[44] Understanding the concept of an "apostolic church" in this historical and biblical context sets the groundwork for understanding the Lutheran mission ethos. However, the term *apostolic* can also be understood more broadly to include the church's missionary nature. Connecting *apostolic* and *mission* shows that the church's apostolic identity naturally includes its mission.[45]

A study of the Gospel of John reveals a profound insight into the missionary (apostolic) character of New Testament Christianity. The apostle John frequently uses the terms *apostello* and *pempo* to emphasize the divine sending of Jesus Christ and, subsequently, Jesus' commission to his disciples. In John 20:21, for example, Jesus says, "As the Father has sent me, even so I am sending you." Here, the word "sent" (*apostello*) underscores the continuation of the mission that began with God sending Jesus into the world, which Jesus then extends to his followers. This concept is especially evident in verses such as John 3:17 (NIV): "For God did not send his Son into the world to condemn the world, but to save the world through him."

Furthermore, John 17:18 offers another layer to this apostolic (missionary) framework: "As you sent me into the world, so I have sent them into the world." This passage reiterates the cyclical nature of the mission: the Father sends the Son, and the Son sends the disciples. John's repeated use of *apostello* implies a continuous and unbroken chain of sending that defines the very nature of the Christian church. This apostolic mission differentiates Jesus' followers from others—they are inherently missionary because they are sent into the world to continue Christ's work.

An apostolic church, therefore, is essentially a missionary church, committed to spreading the gospel. Yet, there are several key aspects that we draw from this Nicene Creed which are foundational for outlining a Lutheran approach to the missional church conversation. Firstly, staying true to apostolic teaching is crucial; the mission is firmly rooted in the pure and unchanged doctrine of Christ as passed down by the apostles. This ensures doctrinal consistency and prevents straying from core Christian truths. Secondly, evangelism is central not just as an activity but as a fundamental aspect of the church's apostolic identity. Recognizing this importance underscores the significance of making disciples and sharing the gospel.

44. Eph 2:20, 2 Pet 3:15–16.

45. Marthaler, *Creed*, 317.

In missions and missional endeavors, the kingdom of God is unveiled through the proclamation of the word, including both the act of preaching and the message of the gospel, not solely through presence. As Luther argues, "God has to speak in a different way. If God opens the divine mouth, and lets a word go forward, so it works. . . . Also God has grasped, with this short word, the whole of the gospel and kingdom of Christ, so that nobody can eradicate it."[46]

Luther presented the content of the gospel in a fivefold sense. The first one is oral delivery of the gospel message, which is foundational. Through sermons, the word of God is declared, interpreted, and brought to life for the congregation. The second is of visible and tangible rites that are channels of divine grace. Baptism signifies entry into the Christian community while the Eucharist represents communion with Christ. Thirdly, the church's structured ministry, which includes ordained clergy, ensures that the teachings of the gospel are maintained, doctrinal purity is preserved, and pastoral care is administered. Fourth is engaging with the Bible, either through reading or listening, which nurtures and sustains personal faith and understanding of God's will. The fifth form of the gospel is known as "the mutual conversation and consolation of brothers and sisters."[47] This is considered an essential and necessary aspect of the gospel, in addition to preaching, sacrament, and ecclesiastical office.

Luther's inclusion of mutual conversation and consolation highlights the interpersonal dynamics within the Christian community. This form is essential for several reasons. Firstly, it ensures embodiment of Christian fellowship. Through mutual conversation and consolation, believers share their lives, encourage one another, and collectively bear witness to the gospel. It's through these interactions that the gospel becomes incarnate in the daily lives of Christians, manifesting in ordinary yet profound ways. Secondly, it becomes the means through which ecclesial offices provide formal pastoral care. Mutual consolation among believers offers immediate and personalized pastoral support. This informal care is vital for addressing the everyday struggles, doubts, and joys of Christian life. It allows faith to be a continuous, shared journey rather than a solitary or institutionalized ordeal. Thirdly, engaging in mutual conversation stimulates spiritual growth by encouraging critical reflection, mutual learning, and accountability. Through dialogue, believers challenge and

46. Luther, *In Genesin Declamationes*, 390, 27v; my translation.

47. SA 3.4 (*BC*, 319).

inspire one another, deepening their understanding of the gospel and its implications for everyday life.

The relevance of Luther's fifth form of the gospel remains significant in contemporary Christian practice. In a world characterized by rampant individualism and digital connectivity often devoid of genuine interaction, the need for mutual conversation and consolation is more pronounced than ever. This gospel form encourages the cultivation of deep, authentic relationships within Christian communities, moving beyond superficial engagement. As a missional community, churches and faith communities can take Luther's insights to heart by fostering environments where gatherings provide platforms for mutual support and spiritual growth.

In the journey of faith, Christians often find comfort and strength in embracing the message of the cross and cultivating fellowship with other believers. However, amid the solace of community and the richness of spiritual nourishment, there lies a vital calling that believers are called to heed—the mission of sharing the good news with the lost. The essence of the gospel is not merely in the embrace of its message within the walls of a church but in the transformative impact it has when shared with those who have yet to hear and accept it.

As believers dwell in the warmth of Christian fellowship and engage in the rituals of faith, it is essential to remember that the true power of the gospel lies not in containment but in dissemination. The message of salvation, hope, and redemption that Christians hold dear is meant to be shared with the world, reaching out to those who have not yet experienced the transformative love of Christ. It is through the act of showing and then telling the good news that the message truly becomes good news to those who hear and embrace it. The good news of the gospel is a powerful and life-changing message that has the potential to bring healing, restoration, and redemption to all who encounter it. However, its impact can only be fully realized when it is shared with others, when believers step beyond the boundaries of familiarity and proximity to engage with those who have yet to experience the transformative power of Christ's love.

CONCLUSION

While the *missional church* conversation offers many valuable insights, some certain limitations and concerns warrant critical examination. One concern is the potential for a theological and ecclesiological imbalance. The emphasis on mission, while essential, should not overshadow other aspects of Christian faith, such as worship, discipleship, and theological reflection. It is important to maintain a holistic understanding of the church's identity and purpose rather than reducing it to a solely missional framework.

Additionally, the missional church conversation sometimes faces challenges when it comes to practical implementation. While the call to be engaged in local communities is laudable, there is a need for careful discernment and accountability to ensure that missional actions align with biblical principles and ethical standards. Without a reflective and critical approach, there is a risk of inadvertently perpetuating harmful or misguided practices in the name of mission.

Seminaries play a crucial role in shaping and equipping individuals for ministry within the Christian church. Traditionally, these institutions have focused on teaching church doctrine, Bible studies, and church history, providing a solid foundation for theological understanding. However, despite the growing importance of missiology in today's globalized world, there is a noticeable gap in the recognition and integration of missiological teachings within Western theological education. Missiology often remains overlooked or treated as an elective course with limited prominence. This marginalization perpetuates an incomplete theological education and fails to fully address the practical realities of mission within the church. By not recognizing missiology as an integral part of theological training, seminaries inadvertently neglect the responsibility of preparing ministers to engage effectively in cross-cultural missions and engage in meaningful dialogue with diverse communities.

5

From Reform to Outreach

Navigating the Evolution of Protestant Missionary Work

THE PROTESTANT MISSIONARY MOVEMENT has been extensively studied by academics, not only for its theological significance but also for its sociopolitical context and worldwide influence. The pivotal moment for Protestant missions can be pinpointed to the Protestant Reformation, spearheaded by figures like Martin Luther. Luther notably acknowledged the significance of the Great Commission, which urges Christians to spread the gospel to all nations (Matt 28). In his writings, Luther underscored the importance of sharing the Christian message with a variety of cultures and backgrounds.[1]

This chapter aims to explore the historical evolution of Protestant missions, examining how theological, social, and political factors have influenced their trajectory. It will discuss the transition from inward-focused Reformation efforts to outward expansion in the following centuries, placing these developments within the broader context of global Christianity and colonial interactions. By doing so, the study will shed light on how Protestant missions navigated the opportunities and challenges presented by diverse cultural terrains and shifting geopolitical landscapes. The main questions addressed in this chapter are as follows: What factors led to the establishment of Lutheran churches in the non-Western world? Can Protestant mission history be understood as

1. Öberg, *Luther and World Mission*, 1.

colonial expansion or mission as translation (a term borrowed from Lamin Sanneh)?[2] What is the role of Indigenous missionaries in the expansion and shaping of Lutheranism in their context?

Understanding the complexities and transformations within Protestant missions provides crucial insights into the overall story of Christian missionary work. It emphasizes the relationship between faith, power, and cultural exchange, offering a detailed perspective on how religious movements adjust and transform over time and location. This paper aims to contribute to this continuing conversation by exploring the historical origins, development, and future possibilities of Protestant missions, enhancing our understanding of their lasting influence on global Christianity.

PROTESTANT MISSION

It is important to note that Martin Luther himself acknowledged the Great Commission, which called upon believers to preach the gospel to all nations (Matt 28). In his writings, Luther underscored the significance of sharing the Christian message with people from diverse cultures and backgrounds.[3] However, despite this recognition, Luther and his contemporaries seemed to prioritize their efforts on establishing and reforming churches within their immediate context.

One possible explanation for the limited emphasis on cross-cultural missions during the Protestant Reformation could be the social and political upheaval that accompanied the movement. The Reformation unfolded in a context of intense conflict and opposition. Protestant Reformers faced severe resistance from the Catholic Church, leading to a series of religious wars and political confrontations across the continent. These internal struggles, combined with external opposition from the Catholic Church, constrained their ability to focus on expanding their missionary endeavors beyond their own regions.[4]

Other factors include their theological priorities. Martin Luther, John Calvin, and other prominent Protestant leaders were mainly concerned with addressing what they saw as corrupt practices and doctrinal errors within the Catholic Church. Their focus was on purification of

2. Sanneh, "Gospel and Culture."

3. See the next chapter of this book.

4. See James, "Post-Reformation Missions Pioneer," 251; and Stolle, "How Lutherans Have Done Mission," 128.

doctrine, rediscovery of biblical truths, and reforming personal piety and church governance. This self-focused approach meant that their energies were mainly directed toward reforming European Christendom internally rather than engaging in outward missionary efforts.

Additionally, unlike the Catholic Church, which had created a well-structured missionary system led by orders such as the Jesuits, Protestant movements in the sixteenth century were divided and did not have comparable organizational frameworks.[5] The emerging Protestant denominations had few resources and were still working to build their theological, educational, and institutional foundations. Due to their ongoing development, coordinating and maintaining cross-cultural missions were challenging tasks that many Protestant groups were not yet ready to handle.

It is worth noting that while the Protestant Reformation seemed to lack an active engagement in cross-cultural missions during its early years, this dynamic would gradually evolve in the centuries that followed. For example, when the Lutheran churches gained official recognition as state churches in various German states, there were concerted efforts to initiate missions to the Jews. In Strasbourg, for example, Elias Schadaeus (c. 1540–1593) took on the task of reaching out to the Jewish community. Similarly, in Hamburg, Esdras Edzard (1629–1708) dedicated himself to this mission.[6] Yet, before the sixteenth century, Protestantism did not show much interest in engaging in cross-country missions like the Catholic countries of Spain, Portugal, and France. Instead, Protestants were more focused on establishing their own independent national churches under the authority of European Protestant rulers. The international expansion of Catholicism carried out through the establishment of colonies and missions in Africa, southern Asia, and the Americas was viewed by Protestants as oppressive and a form of imperialism under the supervision of the pope.[7]

The cross-cultural Protestant missionary movement first emerged in the 1600s when Holland and England embarked on overseas exploration, challenging the trade monopolies of Catholic countries. During this time, the Dutch set sail to conquer Portuguese colonies in Taiwan, Brazil, and Indonesia, among other places. It was the Dutch East India

5. James, "Post-Reformation Missions Pioneer," 252.

6. Stolle, "How Lutherans Have Done Mission," 131.

7. Thorne, *Congregational Missions*, 23. Also Robert, introduction to *Converting Colonialism*, 6.

Company, established in 1602, that played a significant role in promoting Protestant missions. Pressure from Dutch churches led the company to allocate funds for chaplains who not only served the military and colonies but also engaged in mission work among Indigenous populations.[8] The involvement of chaplains in both military and missionary activities showcased the intertwined nature of religion and commerce during that era. These chaplains, who were often Protestant ministers, were tasked with the double duty of providing spiritual guidance to the soldiers and settlers while simultaneously spreading the Christian faith among the native inhabitants.[9]

This was followed by the colony of New Sweden in 1638, which was established along the Delaware River, within the territories that today encompass Delaware, southeastern Pennsylvania, and New Jersey. This initiative marked Sweden's first attempt at establishing a presence and claiming territory beyond Europe. The concept of venturing to America was primarily driven by Samuel Blommaert and Peter Minuit, former employees of the Dutch West India Company (WIC), in collaboration with prominent figures in the Swedish government, including Chancellor Axel Oxenstierna and Admiral Claes Fleming.[10] The first expeditions embarked from Sweden in 1637 and 1639. Under the leadership of Peter Minuit, the first governor of New Sweden, the colony purchased a substantial area on the western side of the Delaware River. Here, they established a fort and a trading station near the Delaware River and Minquas Kill. The fort was named Fort Christina in honor of the Swedish monarch.

In the 1670s, King Frederick IV of Denmark (1671–1730) was interested in expanding the cultural and spiritual horizons of his realm. This interest extended beyond the borders of Europe, seeking to bring Christian teachings to distant lands. Among his far-reaching colonial enterprises was the Danish colony of Tranquebar (now Tharangambadi) on the southeastern coast of India. However, when it came to finding Danish volunteers willing to embrace the challenges and uncertainties of missionary work in such a remote locale, the king faced an unexpected hurdle: a complete dearth of willing participants.[11]

8. Robert, introduction to *Converting Colonialism*, 7.

9. Robert, *Christian Mission*, 41.

10. See Dahlgren, "New Sweden," 1–43; Ekengren and Naum, "Sweden in the Delaware Valley."

11. Robert, introduction to *Converting Colonialism*, 20.

Undeterred by the absence of Danish candidates for this noble mission, King Frederick IV looked beyond his kingdom's borders for suitable emissaries of Christianity. His search led him to learn about the German "Pietists," a movement known for its deep spiritual fervor and commitment to missionary and charitable work. Pietism, which originated in Germany in the late seventeenth century, emphasized personal piety, heartfelt religious experience, and a deep sense of devotion to God. It sought to instill a more heartfelt and personal approach to Christian faith focusing on Bible reading, prayer, and charitable outreach. This group was comprised primarily of German Lutherans and Moravians, who were collectively known as Pietists.[12] They were motivated by a strong sense of religious fervor and a desire to spread the Christian message to the furthest corners of the globe. As Stephen Neill contends, "The history of missions supported by the church on the European continent begins only with the emergence of the movement called Pietism."[13]

King Frederick enlisted two missionaries from the University of Halle in Germany, both of whom were Pietists. These missionaries were Bartholomäus Ziegenbalg (1682–1719) and Heinrich Plütschau (1677–1752). The Halle Mission was named after its connection to the University of Halle in Germany, which played a key role in its establishment and support. Between 1706 and 1856, the mission was staffed and financially supported by students from this prestigious university.[14]

Ziegenbalg and Plütschau arrived in the Dutch colony of Tranquebar in 1706.[15] Their mission aimed to spread Protestant Christianity among the local population, particularly focusing on reaching out to the Tamil people. They played a crucial role in establishing relationships with Indigenous peoples, learning their languages, and adapting to their customs, ultimately paving the way for future trade and commerce. They also served the purpose of exploring new markets and securing economic advantages for the Dutch.[16] They also established schools and orphanages and translated the New Testament and Luther's catechisms, prayers, and

12. Robert, introduction to *Converting Colonialism*, 7.

13. Neill, *History of Christian Missions*, 194.

14. Robert, introduction to *Converting Colonialism*, 7; see also Jeyaraj, "Mission Reports," 42.

15. Robert, introduction to *Converting Colonialism*, 7; See also Stolle, "How Lutherans Have Done Mission," 131; Sundermeier, "Gensichen"; Gensichen, "Plütschau, Heinrich"; Lehmann, *It Began at Tranquebar*; Ziegenbalg, *Genealogy*.

16. Singh, *First Protestant Missionary*, 11. See also Jeyaraj, *Beitrag*, 41–56.

hymns into the Tamil language, making the teachings of Christianity accessible to the people.[17] This way, the two Pietists missionaries became a model that inspired other Protestant mission societies in the following centuries. Their emphasis on education, language study, and cultural understanding shaped the approach of subsequent missionary endeavors.

In addition to learning the local language, the other most significant contributions of the two missionaries and other Pietist missionaries of the time was their emphasis on literacy and translation. As Dana Robert rightly states, "They completed the Reformation began by Martin Luther because they embodied, on a grassroots and personal level, the cultural shift towards literacy and spiritual self-direction."[18] They believed that every individual should have access to the sacred texts in their own language and thus undertook the monumental task of translating religious texts into various languages. Their tireless efforts in this area ensured that people could engage with religious teachings directly and in a way that resonated with their cultural and linguistic context. This emphasis on literacy and translation left an indelible mark on the missionary movement, inspiring generations of missionaries to follow in their footsteps and build upon their invaluable work.

Moving to the eighteenth century, which Kenneth Scott Latourette refers to as "the great century" in his classic work *A History of the Expansion of Christianity*,[19] a remarkable phenomenon emerged within Protestantism known as the "voluntary society." This society operated on the premise of receiving regular donations from ordinary church members in order to send dedicated missionaries abroad. These missionaries were tasked with a wide range of activities, including translation work, establishing new churches, and even founding schools. The voluntary society played a pivotal role in the expansion of Protestant missions during this period, facilitating the spread of faith and enabling the engagement of missionaries in various crucial initiatives.[20]

At a time when global exploration and trade were increasingly connecting different parts of the world, the voluntary society recognized the need for a concerted effort to bring the message of Protestantism to distant shores. Inspired by a strong sense of religious conviction, the society

17. Robert, introduction to *Converting Colonialism*, 7. See also Gensichen, "Bartholomäus Ziegenbalg."

18. Robert, *Christian Mission*, 42.

19. See Latourette, *Great Century*, 7.

20. Robert, *Christian Mission*, 45.

rallied church members to contribute financially to the cause. These voluntary donations provided the necessary means to fund missionary endeavors and promote the values and teachings of Protestantism beyond the boundaries of the local church.

The voluntary nature of the society and its reliance on the contributions of ordinary church members exemplified the grassroots nature of the movement. It demonstrated that individuals from all walks of life could make a meaningful impact by actively supporting missions and sharing their faith beyond their local communities. The collective efforts of the voluntary society and its missionaries led to significant advancements in translation, church planting, and education, leaving a lasting legacy in the history of Protestant missionary work.

One of the most notable figures in the history of the voluntary society and Protestant mission work was a missionary named William Carey (1761–1834). Carey is often hailed as the father of modern missions.[21] In his published essay, *An Enquiry into the Obligations of Christians to Use Means for Conversion of the Heathens* (1792), he urged all Christians to participate in the Great Commission, the biblical mandate to spread the Christian faith to all nations, and he was a fervent advocate for its application in the modern-day context.[22] Recognizing the need for financial support to carry out his mission, Carey devised a unique approach: he urged Christians to invest in shares of what he called a "missionary" enterprise. This innovative concept allowed ordinary believers to contribute financially to Carey's missionary endeavors. Carey's relentless determination, coupled with the financial backing of ordinary Christians, resulted in the establishment of the Baptist Missionary Society.[23] Other mission societies also came into existence, such as The London Missionary Society (1795), the Anglican Church Missionary Society (1799), the Religious Tract Society (1799), and the British and Foreign Bible Society (1804).

In the early nineteenth century, a wave of enthusiasm for Protestant mission work swept across various countries, leading to the establishment of voluntary mission societies. These societies emerged in the United Kingdom, the United States, Germany, Switzerland, and several other countries. Lutheran examples include the following:

21. Webber, *William Carey*, 7–11.

22. Carey, *Obligations of Christians*; see also Tucker, *From Jerusalem to Iran*, 123.

23. Robert, *Christian Mission*, 45; see also Tucker, *From Jerusalem to Iran*, 123.

- The Dresden Mission, established in 1836 under the leadership of Johann Georg Wermelskirch (1803–1872). Later, in 1848, the mission was relocated to Leipzig under Karl Grail (1814–1864). The Dresden Mission focused primarily on mission fields in India, Australia, and eventually expanded to East Africa. Their objective was to spread the teachings of Lutheranism to these regions, sharing the gospel and establishing Christian communities.
- The Neuendettelsau Mission, which was started in 1841 by Wilhelm Lohe (1808–1872). Initially involved in mission work among Native Americans, the organization later expanded its activities to Australia and New Guinea in 1886. The Neuendettelsau Mission aimed to evangelize Indigenous populations and provide them with spiritual guidance and support.
- The Hermansburg Mission, founded in 1849, was spearheaded by Ludwig Harms (1808–1865) and his brother Theodor Harms (1819–1885). This mission initially focused on South Africa and later expanded to Ethiopia. The Hermansburg Mission aimed to bring Christianity to the African continent, establish churches, and provide education and support to local communities.
- In 1871, Leipzig became home to the Evangelical Lutheran Central Society for Mission Among Jews. Led by Franz Delitzsch (1813–1890), this organization was dedicated specifically to mission work among Jewish communities. The society worked toward promoting dialogue, mutual understanding, and conversion among Jewish individuals, emphasizing the theological connections between Judaism and Christianity.
- Lastly, the Breklum Mission, established in 1876, was focused on mission activities in India. While specific information about the organization is limited, it would have shared the common goal of spreading the Christian faith and establishing a Christian presence in the region.

These mission organizations within the Lutheran tradition represent the broad reach and diverse approaches taken by individuals and groups seeking to share their faith and establish Christian communities during the nineteenth century. Each organization operated in unique geographical areas and addressed specific target populations. Despite the challenges and limitations faced, these missions for the most part played a significant role in shaping the spread of Lutheranism and the Christian faith during this time. They sought to mobilize Christians and harness their collective efforts to advance the cause of missions on a global scale.

In the United Kingdom, the birthplace of the Industrial Revolution, the enthusiasm for missions was fueled by a changing social and economic landscape. As industrialization brought newfound wealth and opportunities, many Christians felt a sense of responsibility to share their blessings with those in need. The British Empire's growing influence and colonization efforts also provided both the means and the motivation for spreading Christianity to far-flung corners of the world.

The United States in the twentieth century, similarly experiencing rapid social and economic transformation, witnessed the rise of voluntary mission societies during this period. Americans, driven by a strong sense of religious zeal, sought to establish a Christian presence in regions beyond their own borders. These societies, often associated with specific denominations, galvanized support and resources to send missionaries abroad, reflected the country's growing influence on the world stage.

Across continental Europe, notably in Germany and Switzerland, the establishment of voluntary mission societies reflected a desire to engage in global mission efforts. These societies allowed individuals to channel their fervent religious beliefs into practical action, sending missionaries to remote lands and cultures. Inspired by the Protestant Reformation's emphasis on individual responsibility and faith, these societies aimed to spread the gospel message to all corners of the earth, guided by the principles of the Great Commission.

When it comes to the establishment of Scandinavian Protestant mission societies, organizations like the Danish Mission Society (1821), the Norwegian Missionary Society (1842), the Norwegian Lutheran Mission (1891), the Swedish Lutheran Mission Society (1835), the Swedish Evangelical National or Fatherland Society (1856; later renamed as the Swedish Evangelical Mission), and the Lutheran Evangelical Association of Finland (1873) played pivotal roles in disseminating the Christian faith and undertaking missionary endeavors within Scandinavia and globally. These societies became instrumental in advancing the message of Christianity and expanding its reach across different parts of the world during this era.[24]

24. Schulz, "Nineteenth-Century Lutheran Missions," 53–55.

The twentieth century was a transformative period for many global movements, including Christian missionary efforts. This era was characterized by significant political upheavals, social changes, and ideological shifts that deeply influenced various aspects of society, including the religious sphere. Kenneth Scott Latourette encapsulates this turbulence by referring to it as "the new day of confusion [in which] many have lost a sense of direction and purpose."[25]

The early to mid-twentieth century was dominated by two world wars, the Cold War, and a series of decolonization movements. For example, in 1945, 99.5 percent of the non-Western world was colonized by Western powers. However, by the end of the 1960s, 99.5 percent of these nations had gained their independence.[26] These events reshaped national boundaries, realigned global power structures, and fostered a climate of uncertainty and instability. For missionary organizations, these shifts posed significant challenges and opportunities. In many regions, the spread of communism limited religious activities, while the collapse of colonial empires opened new avenues for evangelism. However, this new global landscape often led to a loss of direction, as traditional missionary approaches were no longer applicable in many contexts.[27]

Simultaneously, the twentieth century witnessed profound social changes driven by the civil rights movement, feminist movements, and increasing secularization. These transformations compelled missionary organizations to adapt their strategies and reconsider their roles within rapidly evolving societies. Latourette's assertion of a "new day of confusion" is evident as mission movements grappled with maintaining relevance amid changing societal values and expectations.

Similarly, the approach of Western Protestant missions in the Global South during this century underwent notable changes. Recognizing the importance of collaboration, mission organizations and churches began to emphasize the value of working in partnership. The establishment of various international bodies aimed at fostering cooperation among churches worldwide, such as the International Mission Council in 1921, the World Council of Churches in 1948, the Lutheran World Federation formed in 1947, and confessional federations such as the Lutheran Foreign Missions Conference of North America founded in 1919, played

25. Latourette, *Missions Tomorrow*, 213.

26. Winter, *25 Unbelievable Years*, 12.

27. Norrish, "Great Century."

significant roles in shaping the landscape of Protestant missions during this period.

MISSION AS COLONIAL EXPANSION VS. MISSION AS TRANSLATION

Protestant missions from the sixteenth to twentieth centuries were deeply interested in cross-cultural missions for a variety of reasons. One major motivation was the belief in the universality of the Christian message and the desire to fulfill the commandment of Jesus to "go and make disciples of all nations" (Matt 28:19). Protestants believed that it was their duty to share the gospel with people of all cultures, regardless of their background. However, it is important to acknowledge that this missionary endeavor was often connected to the wider goal of colonial expansion pursued by Western powers in the Global South, also known as the Third World. During the era of European colonialism, missionary efforts often coincided with and supported the broader agenda of Western powers aiming to establish political control and exploit resources in non-Western regions. In many cases, missionaries were backed, and at times even sponsored, by colonial powers with the intention of "civilizing" and "Christianizing" Indigenous populations.[28] As James Dennis documented on the practice of Christian missions in the nineteenth century in his three volumes titled *Christian Missions and Social Progress*, the missionaries had understood their mission as not only evangelizing others but also leading the third-world countries toward "civilization." As Scott Sunquist also rightly noted, the Jesus mission, "making people like Jesus," was often confused with the other mission, "making people like [the Europeans]."[29]

Missionaries played two distinct roles in this intricate situation, as they functioned both as advocates of religious conversion and as tools of colonialism. On one side, they sincerely believed in their objective to spread their faith to individuals who were not Christians. They dedicated themselves to establishing educational institutions, medical facilities, and social organizations that offered crucial services to native communities. However, their endeavors were often shaped by the prejudices and

28. Historians such as Arthur Schlesinger Jr. and William R. Hutchison have identified missionaries and their mission goals as "cultural imperialism." See Hutchison, "Moral Equivalent for Imperialism"; Schlesinger, "Missionary Enterprise."

29. Sunquist, *Unexpected Christian Century*, 13.

presumptions of the colonial period, as they endorsed Western cultural standards, imposed European languages, and eroded local customs and beliefs.[30] For instance, as E. W. Fashole-Luke contends, conversion for these missionaries was often "a radical breaking away from the past and being set in a new pattern of life though the cultural and social situatedness remains unaltered."[31]

Within the intricate web of interactions between mission organizations and Indigenous people, the political maneuvers undertaken by Western countries cast a significant shadow. However, it is crucial to avoid sweeping generalizations when exploring the dynamics of these relationships. The multifaceted nature of these interactions demands nuanced examination, taking into account the local context and the distinct approaches adopted by each mission group as they navigated encounters with both colonial powers and local communities.[32]

While it is true that some historians and theologians may attempt to simplify these relationships, reducing them to a monolithic perspective would be a disservice to their complexity. One notable divergence in approaches among Western missionaries was their varying focus and priorities. As Paul R. Spickard and Kevin M. Cragg argued, certain missionaries directed their attention primarily toward the overseas European population, perhaps disregarding or underemphasizing the needs and concerns of the local people they were meant to serve.[33] This skewed focus, rooted in a colonial mindset, hindered genuine engagement and understanding between missionaries and Indigenous communities. Conversely, some missionaries actively aligned themselves with the Indigenous people, valiantly advocating for their rights and striving to safeguard their dignity. These missionary individuals and groups emerged as allies, working alongside Indigenous communities in their struggles against oppression and marginalization. Their collaborative efforts sought to address the systemic injustices perpetuated by colonial powers while advancing the cause of equality and empowerment for the Indigenous population.[34]

30. For more discussion on mission and Western colonialism, see Song, *Tell Us Our Names*; also Comaroff and Comaroff, *Christianity*.

31. Fashole-Luke, "Quest for an African Christianity," 261.

32. Robert, introduction to *Converting Colonialism*, 4.

33. Spickard and Cragg, *Global History of Christians*, 304.

34. A good example for this is the work of the Swedish Evangelical Mission in Ethiopia.

When it comes to the Lutheran missions in particular, they were largely influenced by the theological doctrine of the "separation of the two kingdoms." This doctrine posits a distinction between the earthly or civil realm (the kingdom of the left hand) and the spiritual or ecclesiastical realm (the kingdom of the right hand). In this framework, the earthly realm pertains to the temporal, secular, and political aspects of human society, including governance, law, and societal structures. It is concerned with matters of this world and the practical affairs of daily life. The spiritual realm, on the other hand, deals with the spiritual and religious aspects of existence, encompassing matters of faith, salvation, and the church's role in guiding believers.[35] This theological framework led them to maintain a certain level of independence and distance from the imperial governments that wielded power over the colonies. By adhering to this theological principle, Lutheran Christians in missions sought to navigate their roles within colonial contexts while upholding their distinct mission and values, often opting to operate autonomously and maintain a degree of separation from the colonial administrations that governed the territories in which they were active.[36]

It is therefore essential to recognize that the relationships between mission organizations and Indigenous people were often characterized by a blend of these contrasting approaches. Within any given society, the attitudes and actions of mission groups varied, shaped by the specific historical context and the unique dynamics between different missionary organizations and the Indigenous populations they encountered. Consequently, it is imperative to examine the intricate details and examine each case individually, avoiding broad generalizations that fail to capture the nuanced realities of this complex interplay.

Nevertheless, as argued by scholar Lamin Sanneh, the "colonialism paradigm" that often dominates scholarly discussions tends to silence the voices and agency of Indigenous agents in the spread of Christianity. Therefore, in understanding mission history, it is crucial to move beyond such a paradigm because it overlooks the vital role these agents played in "translating" the gospel into their own cultural contexts.[37] Indigenous agents played a crucial role in translating the gospel message into their respective cultural contexts. They bridged the gap between Western

35. For details on Luther's theology of the two kingdoms, see Kolb, "Two Realms"; Biermann, *Wholly Citizens*, 2–3; also Deressa, "Luther on Two Kingdoms."

36. Stolle, "How Lutherans Have Done Mission," 133.

37. Sanneh, "World Christianity," 7.

Christian theology and Indigenous beliefs, practices, and languages, creating a distinctive and contextually relevant expression of Christianity. These agents drew upon their intimate understanding of their own communities and cultures, adapting and appropriating Christian teachings in ways that resonated with the values and traditions of their people.

According to Lamin Sanneh, one of the key factors that significantly contributed to the expansion of Christianity was the missions' unwavering commitment to translating the Bible into local languages. Sanneh emphasizes that this act of translation played a pivotal role in fostering the growth of literacy within diverse cultures, while simultaneously empowering Indigenous leaders. By prioritizing the translation of the Bible, missions effectively bridged the gap between Christianity and various local communities. This linguistic endeavor not only allowed for a deeper understanding of Christian teachings but also provided access to religious texts in a language that resonated with individuals on a personal and cultural level. As a result, it facilitated a sense of ownership and relevance among the local populace, fostering engagement and active participation in the Christian faith.

According to Sanneh,

> Christian missions are better seen as a translation movement, with consequences for vernacular revitalization, religious change and social transformation, than a vehicle for Western cultural domination. . . . Even the nationalist point of view that came to dominate such historical writing about the new Africa was to a large extent molded by the missionary exploration of indigenous societies.[38]

The implications of this translation effort extended beyond religious practice, however. In their pursuit of linguistic adaptation, missions inadvertently became agents of social and intellectual progress, particularly in societies where written language was scarce or nonexistent. Through the translation of the Bible, literacy and education were catalyzed, igniting a transformative process within these communities. Sanneh contends that this act of translation opened doors to intellectual development, enabling individuals to engage with a written language and harness its power for personal, social, and economic advancement.

Furthermore, the translation of the Bible also played a critical role in empowering Indigenous leaders. By making religious texts accessible

38. Sanneh, "Christian Missions."

in local languages, missions effectively dismantled linguistic barriers that had previously limited participation and leadership opportunities for Indigenous individuals. This newfound accessibility allowed for the emergence of endogenous leaders who were able to articulate Christian teachings within their own cultural contexts, thereby cultivating a more contextualized and inclusive expression of the faith.

MISSIONARIES AND THE INDIGENOUS CHURCH

One of the main challenges for the early Lutheran mission organizations was how to consider their relationship with the established churches in the Global South. Reflecting on this conundrum, a foundational teaching among Lutherans comes to light, encapsulated in article VII of the Augsburg Confession: "It is also taught that at all times there must be and remain one holy, Christian church. It is the assembly of all believers among whom the gospel is purely preached and the holy sacraments are administered according to the gospel. For this is enough for the true unity of the Christian church that there the gospel is preached harmoniously according to a pure understanding and the sacraments are administered in conformity with the divine Word. It is not necessary for the true unity of the Christian church that uniform ceremonies, instituted by human beings, be observed everywhere."[39]

This directive was interpreted diversely within Lutheran circles. Some Lutheran churches saw it as a green light to give autonomy to the local churches and forge unity with their counterparts in the Global South, fostering partnerships in mission endeavors. However, not all shared this viewpoint. Wilhelm Löhe, the visionary behind the Neuendettelsau Mission, staunchly advocated a more stringent approach. He contended that the *Confessio Augustana* should underscore an infallible, normative delineation of Christian doctrine as the cornerstone for unity and collaboration in mission.[40] Following Löhe's approach, Neuendettelsau Mission emphasized the *Confessio Augustana* as the main framework through which their relationship with Indigenous churches is defined.

Johannes Hoekendijk, a reformed theologian, argued on the contrary that merely adhering to the doctrinal formulations of the past is not sufficient to effectively fulfill the mission of the church in a rapidly

39. AC 7.1–2 (*BC*, 42).

40. Löhe, *Drei Bücher*, 141.

changing world. He suggests that a more holistic and dynamic approach is needed, one that takes into account the cultural and social contexts in which mission work is carried out. By viewing mission as an educative process, Hoekendijk highlighted the importance of engaging with and educating people in their own cultural and social contexts supplemented by word and sacrament, which he believed is foundational for creating unity and partnership with the Indigenous churches.[41]

Additionally, Hoekendijk emphasizes the need to build churches on the basis of homogeneous ethnic groups, a concept influenced by German romanticism. By organizing churches in this way, he argues, it is possible to create stronger and more cohesive communities that are better able to support and sustain each other in their faith journeys. Hoekendijk's approach challenged traditional understandings of mission and called for a more nuanced and culturally sensitive approach to spreading the word of God. By embracing these ideas, he believes that the church can more effectively fulfill its mission in a rapidly changing world.[42]

When examining the relationship between Protestant missions and Indigenous churches, it is important to note how Henry Venn, a distinguished figure and secretary of the Church Mission Society (CMS), addressed a pivotal and pressing issue of his time. During the eighteenth and nineteenth centuries, as European missionaries embarked on journeys to far-flung lands, they encountered diverse cultures and societies with deeply entrenched religious beliefs and practices. The interaction between these missionaries and Indigenous communities raised crucial questions about cultural assimilation, the role of native leadership, and the preservation of traditional customs and identity. It was a formidable conundrum that demanded careful consideration and nuanced solutions.

It is in this context that Venn made a compelling argument regarding the role of the European element in native churches. Venn aptly described the question surrounding the interplay between Indigenous churches and European missionaries as "involving the great missionary problem of the day."[43] Within these words, Venn captured the complex dynamics and challenges faced in the mission field during his era. He contended that this foreign influence could become a significant stumbling block, impeding the growth and progress of Indigenous congregations.[44]

41. Hoekendijk, *Kirche und Volk*, 60–105.

42. Hoekendijk, *Kirche und Volk*, 60–105.

43. Quoted in Williams, "Church Missionary Society," 86.

44. Shenk, *Henry Venn*, 34.

Venn boldly proposed that maintaining a clear separation between native and European churches, complete with their own hierarchies of bishops, priests, and deacons, would facilitate a more robust and rapid development for the native churches. He argued that "the European element in a native church is the great snare and hindrance to its growth: and that if native churches were kept separate with a complete organization of bishops, priests, and Deacon they would exhibit a more firm and rapid development."[45]

Venn's perspective challenged the prevailing notion that European missionaries should play a leading role in the establishment and governance of Indigenous churches. While acknowledging the valuable contributions of missionaries in introducing the Christian faith to new regions, Venn emphasized the importance of giving autonomy and agency to native believers. He believed that entrusting the responsibility of leadership and organization to the local population would foster a stronger sense of ownership and enable more dynamic growth within the native church.[46]

By advocating for the complete organizational structure of bishops, priests, and deacons within native churches, Venn aimed to ensure a self-sustaining and self-propagating spiritual community. He envisioned a system that respected and upheld the cultural and religious identities of the native believers while providing them with the necessary structure and support for their spiritual development. Venn believed that this approach would empower the Indigenous churches to flourish at their own pace and according to their unique contexts.

Venn's groundbreaking ideas regarding the establishment of genuinely Indigenous churches faced a significant shift within the CMS during the 1870s and early 1880s. Unfortunately, during this period, it appears that the CMS began to weaken or even abandon Venn's principles.[47] One reason for this is that the CMS leadership followed the principle of having "complete control over the indigenous church" rather than supporting Venn's idea of fostering independent self-governing churches.[48] This shift in perspective reflected a top-down approach in which Western missionaries sought to maintain authority and influence over the religious and administrative affairs of Indigenous congregations.

45. Williams, "Church Missionary Society," 86.

46. Shenk, *Henry Venn*, 34.

47. Williams, "Church Missionary Society," 93.

48. Williams, "Church Missionary Society," 106.

How could the CMS shift its position after Venn? External factors, such as evolving political landscapes or changes in the perspectives and priorities of the CMS leadership, may have also played a role in this transition away from Venn's vision. The pressures of colonial governance, shifting missionary strategies, and evolving theological frameworks may have influenced the CMS leadership's decision to prioritize control over Indigenous churches rather than promoting their self-determination and self-sufficiency.

However, it was the persistent insistence of Indigenous churches for self-control and self-support that ultimately catalyzed a shift in the approach of Western Protestant churches. Indigenous believers demanded greater leadership and autonomy in their congregations, prompting Western churches to transfer authority and decision-making power to Indigenous leaders. It was also the unprecedented growth of Christianity in many countries, especially in Africa, which brought about a significant shift in the relationship between Indigenous churches and missionaries. As Christianity took root in Africa, local believers began to take charge of their own spiritual progression. African evangelists emerged, passionate individuals who were driven by their deep faith and desire to share the gospel with their own people. They preached in their native languages, effectively bridging the cultural gap and resonating with their fellow Africans.[49]

This transfer of leadership marked a significant turning point in the history of Protestant missions, as Western churches began to recognize and respect the agency and dignity of Indigenous churches in their mission endeavors. Historians and missionaries alike have come to realize that the true catalysts of African Christianization were the Africans themselves. It was the efforts of African evangelists, catechists, native agents, and Bible women that truly propelled the spread of Christianity on the continent.

LESSONS LEARNED FROM THE HISTORY OF PROTESTANT MISSION AND THE WAY FORWARD

The history of Protestant missions from the seventeenth to the twentieth century offers profound insights and valuable lessons for contemporary missionaries and believers. This period is marked by notable achievements, particularly in the realms of translation and education, but it also

49. Deressa, "What Can the West Learn."

underscores significant challenges and missteps that modern practitioners must heed.

One of the hallmark achievements of Protestant missionaries during this period was their commitment to translation and education. The translation of religious texts into local languages played a crucial role in making the Christian message accessible to Indigenous populations. By translating the Bible, catechisms, and other religious materials into vernacular languages, missionaries ensured that the teachings of Christianity could be understood and embraced by a broader audience. This not only facilitated religious education but also demonstrated a deep respect for local cultures and traditions, fostering inclusivity within the Christian community.

Education was another cornerstone of Protestant missionary efforts. Missionaries established schools and educational programs aimed at empowering Indigenous populations and promoting social development. These institutions provided practical skills and knowledge, enabling local communities to improve their living conditions and participate more fully in society. Education, therefore, served as a catalyst for long-term social and economic progress in many regions.

Despite these positive contributions, the history of Protestant missions is also marked by significant challenges, particularly in the realm of cross-cultural engagement. Many missionaries struggled to navigate and respect the cultural norms and practices of the communities they served. Often approaching their work from a Eurocentric perspective, they prioritized Western values and beliefs, leading to misunderstandings and conflicts with local populations. This lack of cultural sensitivity and humility not only hindered effective communication but also undermined the trust and receptivity of Indigenous communities to the Christian message.

Another critical issue was the unequal power dynamics inherent in the relationship between Western missionaries and Indigenous churches in the Global South. Missionaries often held positions of authority and influence, exerting control over the religious and social practices of Indigenous believers. This paternalistic approach disenfranchised local leaders and undercut the autonomy and agency of Indigenous churches, perpetuating a sense of dependency and inferiority among Indigenous Christians. These power imbalances exacerbated the challenges of cross-cultural engagement and perpetuated harmful stereotypes and colonial legacies that continue to affect relationships between Western churches and Indigenous communities today.

MOVING FORWARD: A CALL FOR HUMILITY AND PARTNERSHIP

The lessons from this history are clear: modern missionaries and believers must learn from the mistakes of the past and adopt a new approach centered on humility, respect, and genuine collaboration. Moving forward, there are several key principles that can guide more effective and equitable missionary work:

Cultural Sensitivity and Respect

In the complex and interconnected world of the twenty-first century, the role of missionaries has evolved significantly from the colonial frameworks of the past. Today, cultural sensitivity and respect stand as pivotal principles for effective and meaningful missionary work. Cultural sensitivity involves recognizing and respecting the differences and commonalities that define various cultures. It requires missionaries to approach their work with humility and an open mind, willing to learn from the rich tapestry of local traditions and practices. For modern missionaries, understanding and honoring the cultural norms, traditions, and values of the communities they serve is not only a matter of ethical conduct but also a cornerstone for building genuine relationships and fostering mutual trust.

This sensitivity is crucial for several reasons. Firstly, *it helps to build trust and relationships.* Respecting cultural norms is essential for building trust. When missionaries demonstrate genuine interest in and respect for the local culture, they signal that they value the community's identity and heritage. This fosters a sense of mutual respect and opens the door to deeper, more meaningful relationships. Secondly, *it aids effective communication.* Understanding cultural nuances aids in more effective communication. Misunderstandings and conflicts often arise from cultural misinterpretations. By familiarizing themselves with local customs, missionaries can navigate interactions more smoothly and convey their message in ways that are more likely to be well-received. Thirdly, *it enhances receptivity.* When missionaries respect and incorporate local traditions and knowledge into their work, they make the Christian message more relatable and relevant to the community. This approach can enhance the receptivity and engagement of local populations.

Reflecting on Historical Legacies: Addressing Colonial Injustices in Missionary Work

As discussed above, the legacy of missionary work, particularly from the seventeenth to twentieth century, is inextricably linked with the history of colonialism. This association has left a complex and often fraught inheritance that continues to shape relationships between Western churches and Indigenous communities. Acknowledging and addressing these colonial legacies and historical injustices is essential for fostering justice and reconciliation in contemporary missionary activities.

As modern missionaries and church leaders seek to continue their work, it is imperative to engage critically with this legacy, striving to rectify past wrongs and promote equitable and respectful partnerships through honest reflection. This can be done by acknowledgment of wrongdoing. Public acknowledgment of past wrongdoings, including apologies and statements of repentance, is a vital step toward healing. This acknowledgment should not be merely symbolic but accompanied by a genuine commitment to making amends.

Beyond reflection and acknowledgment, concrete reparative actions are necessary to address the enduring impacts of colonial missionary activities. This can be done through (a) *creating partnership on equal terms*. Modern missionary work must prioritize partnerships on equal terms. This means recognizing the agency, wisdom, and leadership of Indigenous communities and approaching collaboration with humility and respect. Partnership should be based on mutual goals and shared governance. And, (b) *creating a platform for ongoing dialogue and accountability*. Establishing forums for ongoing dialogue between religious institutions and Indigenous communities is crucial. These forums should facilitate continuous reflection, feedback, and accountability, ensuring that missionary practices evolve in response to the needs and insights of Indigenous partners.

CONCLUSION

In this chapter, we explored the history of Protestant missions, with a particular focus on Lutheran missions from the seventeenth to the twentieth century. Throughout history, Lutheran missions have been marked by a dual commitment to spiritual proclamation and practical service, encompassing evangelism, education, and community development.

This dedication echoes the teachings of Martin Luther and the mission mandate laid out in the Great Commission, underscoring the importance of faith in action.

The history of Protestant missions provides many valuable lessons that are still relevant for modern missionary efforts. Initially, there was hesitation to participate in cross-cultural missions due to societal, political, and theological reasons. However, over time, a more organized and inclusive approach emerged. The focus on education, literacy, and translation laid the groundwork for meaningful interactions with different cultures, and the emergence of voluntary societies demonstrated the strength of grassroots involvement. Managing the complex relationship between missions and colonial expansion highlighted the necessity of cultural sensitivity and respect for native identities. Lastly, the ongoing discussion about Indigenous church leadership and independence emphasizes the importance of empowering local communities in their spiritual journeys. These lessons together contribute to a more comprehensive and successful understanding of missionary work in a globalized world.

Section Three

Contextual and Cultural Challenges in Mission

6

Mission and Barriers to the Gospel

Contextualization and Worldview

"The European missionaries brought the right gospel, they just brought it inappropriately." So remarked, the then-director of mission and theology of the Ethiopian Evangelical Church Mekane Yesus (EECMY)[1] to this author some years ago. The gospel message is universal and for all. God uses us as his people to proclaim that message to others through words and actions. But sometimes we proclaim inappropriately, and, despite our good intent, the gospel is just not heard by those to whom we seek to proclaim.

The missiological paradigm of mission as proclaiming the good news of God's salvation into the world poses the question, If one proclaims the gospel but no one hears, has the gospel been proclaimed? This question forms the basis for this chapter for mission into other cultures and contexts. We examine the process of gospel proclamation and identify the part we play in raising or lowering barriers to others hearing the message.

THE GOSPEL IN MISSION

More than one perspective emerges when one examines how the spread of Christianity has occurred, each perspective dependent upon the

1. Presiding President Rev. Dr. Yonas Yigezu; used with permission. Note, the EECMY is the numerically largest evangelical Lutheran church body in the world with reportedly over twelve million members (as of 2023).

whom and where, "Which forms of Christianity are appropriate in today's world?" or "Who decides which are the most proper?"

Answers sometimes seem expressed—at least to this author—through the myth that one's own expression of Christianity—Christ proclaimed—has wound its way through history and context into one's most pure understanding and institutional church forms of today. As a whole, Christianity ponders over the origins of denominational dogma and expends energy over questions like, Just how are Christians to be baptized? Or, What music is proper in the church setting? It is not a wonder that some observers are put off by disagreements both within and outside the world of Christians.

Yet this need not be. The foundation for living life in Christ is found through Scripture, and only Scripture (*sola scriptura*), a precept to which many forms of Christianity agree. Scripture provides a firm foundation to why we serve in mission—pointing others toward the saving grace of the gospel given through Scripture. The question must be asked, If most within Christianity find agreement within the same foundation, how did Christianity arrive at multiple expressions as the gospel has been carried into the world?

We acknowledge God at work using his people, the church, to carry the gospel into the world. But not everything commanded or instituted by those within institutions which define themselves as church has been of God. By the fifteenth century, the institutional church in Europe had devolved into practices where the gospel was obscured behind rituals, religious specialists, and language not understood by most. The natural consequence was that lay people and their religious specialists—priests—made their own assumptions. Martin Luther, a then-Catholic monk, studied such as Rom 1:17 in Scripture and understood the scriptural message that belief and faith in Jesus' death on the cross and his resurrection provides the free gift of salvation within Christianity. He challenged the practices and belief systems which over time had crept into the institutional church and obscured this underlying message. By 1522, he had translated the New Testament from Latin into common German. The invention of the printing press allowed mass distribution. The result was that it was no longer necessary to depend upon holy opinions formed within the institutional church for salvation. Rather God communicated directly through his word in a form congruent to understanding. Luther noted that "boulders and clods"[2] must not hinder understanding of the word, rather "the Word may have free course."[3]

It is within the word's *free course* that we acknowledge the power of the gospel message and the message communicated through Scripture as universal. God gives his gift of salvation as a free gift to *all* who believe. Jesus said, "I am the way, and the truth, and the life. No one comes to the Father except through me" (John 14:6), and, "For God so loved the world, that he gave his only Son, that whoever believes in him should not perish, but have eternal life" (John 3:16). As Christians, we acknowledge that mission, in its universality, is derived from God's nature, a concept termed as the *missio Dei*, or God's mission/sending. Our Triune God is the initiator and foundation for mission—God the Father sends his Son (John 10:15, 17:18, 21), God the Father and Son send the Holy Spirit (John 14:26, 15:26, Luke 24:49), and God the Father, the Son, and Holy Spirit send those called as the people of God (the church) into the world (John 17:18–23, 20:21) to announce this good news. In this way the Holy Spirit works that others might know the story of their salvation and be called into his kingdom with us. Mission is our Triune God calling us back to himself through his means. None are excluded, either by location, age, ethnicity, or any other form of differentiation. We are to share with all: "Go therefore and make disciples of all nations, baptizing them in the name of the Father and of the Son and of the Holy Spirit, teaching them to observe all that I have commanded you. And behold, I am with you always, to the end of the age" (Matt 28:19–20).

And that is where the cracks begin to appear—through our part in the process. The gospel may be universal and for all as "the power of God for salvation to everyone who believes, to the Jew first and also to the Greek" (Rom 1:16), but we as God's called people are less than universal. The apostle Paul describes the difference between the message and messengers in 2 Corinthians: "For God, who said, 'Let light shine out of darkness,' has shone in our hearts to give the light of the knowledge of the glory of God in the face of Jesus Christ. But we have this treasure in jars of clay, to show that the surpassing power belongs to God and not to us" (2 Cor 4:6–7).

The light shines in us, for us, but we—fragile vessels chosen to be its messengers—are less delightful, rather segmented by languages,

2. Luther, *On Translating*, 188, 193.

3. Luther, *Order of Public Worship*, 14.

ethnicities, cultures, and geographies. Our misperceptions and lack of universal perfection create barriers to our gospel communication. We add nothing to the process, yet God calls us to be a part anyway.[4] He makes us integral to the process in his mission, even as we can add nothing, in order that others understand that the surpassing power belongs to God and not us (2 Cor 4:7).

Our intentions in mission may not be incorrect. But our limitations distort the gospel message to which we serve as messenger. Understanding just where and how our human limits erect barriers to others hearing the message helps us to lower those barriers so that we do not serve proclaiming a gospel not heard.

WORLDVIEW AND THE GOSPEL MESSAGE

Humans observe and perceive events in their surrounding world through a limiting lens defined as *worldview*. A child is born into the world with an uninformed worldview lens and begins to observe. A learning process occurs, and values are formed (see chapter 7). The learning process may be positive or negative, partial or whole, but with each observation the child's worldview lens incorporates additional information, modifies, and reforms. That lens both conditions how we observe and the assumptions we make. One cannot know what one does not know. Rather one seeks to fit the meaning of what is seen or heard through the lens of what is already known—until something new is learned. Such learning then further modifies our worldview lens. Our worldview continues to broaden with time and experience, and it continues to inform the way we look at the world and apply meaning to what we see at specific times in our existence.

Each person's worldview is unique since it depends upon individual experience, but each also has general similarities to others within one's own culture and context. For example, a villager raised in a rural location in Southeast Asia will have a more similar worldview match to others raised in that location than with someone who has been brought up in a Western nation's urban setting. It is helpful to think of worldview effect as on a sliding scale. At one end there is much relevance toward mutual

4. Matt 28:18–20: "Then Jesus came to them and said, 'All authority in heaven and on earth has been given to me. Therefore go and make disciples of all nations, baptizing them in the name of the Father and of the Son and of the Holy Spirit, and teaching them to obey everything I have commanded you. And surely I am with you always, to the very end of the age.'"

understanding. At the other, worldview lenses differ so widely that they infuse action and understanding with such difference that alternate meaning is determined.

The story was told, by the then-president of the EECMY, of a visiting Western short-term mission team. The team members handed out trinket crosses created as an activity in their home church. However, in Ethiopia's cultural contexts, one gives a gift equal to the value of relationship in order to express the value of the giver's relationship to the receiver. If one cannot give a gift of value, it is better not to provide a gift. A gift of low value, such as the trinket crosses, sends a subtle unintended message of non-valued relationship.

Such worldview clash is sometimes humorous. A visiting pastor from the US was leading devotions at a primary school in South Africa. He told an illustrative story and indicated his own child height with his palm down. The children all laughed. The hand held with palm down indicates the height of an animal in that southern Africa context. Palm upwards indicates the height of a human. That differed from the pastor's Western culture where the height of both animals and humans is indicated the same way—palm down. The pastor was momentarily confused. He did not intend humor but communicated it without knowing.

Sometimes worldview clash is less humorous and may even provide a negative effect in the process of gospel communication. An example occurred in northern Liberia where, within the Bandi ethnic group, modesty is assigned as the responsibility of the beholder—one is not to look at another person who may be urinating or bathing within view. Western missionaries entered in the area. They perceived through a different lens, one which valued modesty as the responsibility of the one urinating or bathing. Several missionaries were in a vehicle. They drove by a group of young local women bathing in the river. They couldn't help but stare. Both groups complained. The local community noted that the missionaries were looking directly at the young women as they bathed. The Western missionaries were affronted at the lack of decorum next to the road.

Discussed elsewhere within the concept of translatability, the effort to maintain surface form, whether linguistic, action, event, or ritual, does not avert clash. Local translators and their Bible translation advisor were discussing a first draft of 2 John 1:12 into the local language. They were consulting an English translation as their mutually understood source: "I hope to come to you and talk face to face, so that our joy may be complete."

The next step was more intensive review discussion, and the review group wondered why John was so angry. He seemed joyful at the beginning of the chapter but not at the end. The discussion revealed the idiom *face to face*, in that culture, was used when people are angry at each other. The literal maintenance of *face to face* in their draft translation would preserve a surface form but change the deeper level meaning (to those from that culture) from a close relation to an angry one. What makes this example of more interest to a cultural linguistic discussion is that the original Greek idiom expresses the intended close relationship literally as *stoma pros stoma* (mouth to mouth). Most English speakers would not understand that surface expression being used to represent a friendly relationship. Rather, English versions preserve the deeper meaning by discarding the idiom's surface form and expressing it as *face to face* instead.[5]

Miscommunication and misunderstanding cause meaning-clash. Knowing which concepts differ and must be negotiated becomes integral to mission. It also must be acknowledged that accessibility to the internet and worldwide use of social media for wider communication comes with misunderstanding often not noticed. It is possible to observe speech and event from afar and use one's own worldview to apply one's own meaning. Those serving in cross-culture mission should be aware. The community they serve may not always perceive images and social media communication meant for those in the missionary's home culture the same as the missionary intends, thus distorting local relationship.

CONTEXTUALIZATION AS MISSIOLOGICAL PROCESS—LOWERING BARRIERS TO THE GOSPEL

When faced with worldview clash and communication distortion in mission, one in mission has two choices—either correct others toward perceiving as we intend, or determine how receivers use their worldviews and then use their forms to communicate the message. The first would be a nice step toward universal communication but, considering the vast numbers of diverse languages, conceptual perspectives, and peoples in the world, degenerates into not-possible. Rather the imprecise inventory of underlying meanings to even the same surface forms indicates that eliminating worldview clash and communication distortion by teaching others to perceive our intent cannot be the case even where we speak the same languages.

5. Narrative as told by Lutheran Bible Translators' personnel.

By default, we are left to understand others in order to lower the barriers which may cause worldview clash as we carry the gospel to others. This process is labelled as *contextualization* in missiological studies.

But consistent with the theme of miscommunication and misunderstanding, not all understand the process similarly. Rather, there are multiple understandings of *contextualization*, and its definitions have undergone meaning shift as those in different contexts applied their understandings.

The term was first brought to modern theological prominence by a 1972 education report for the World Council of Churches where it was defined as the "capacity to respond within one's own situation."[6] The report goes on to claim that encounter with the word "is always prophetic, arising always out of a genuine encounter between God's Word and His world, and moves toward the purpose of challenging and changing the situation through rootedness in and commitment to a given historical moment."[7] In this use of *contextualization*, gospel meaning is determined by the response of the hearer, at their moment in history, to whatever the hearer determines God is saying within that moment. This understanding often serves as motivation for liberation and justice activities seen as encounter between the word and world.

Meaning-shift occurred when those with other suppositions picked up the term. Early evangelical definitions express *contextualization* as "making concepts of ideals relevant in a given situation."[8] Hesselgrave and Rommen write, "[*Contextualization* is] the attempt to communicate the message of the person, works, word and will of God in a way that is faithful God's revelation, especially as it is put forth in the teaching of Holy Scripture, and that is meaningful to respondents in their respective cultural and existential contexts. Contextualization is both verbal and non-verbal and has to do with theologizing; Bible translation, interpretation and application, incarnational lifestyle, evangelism, Christian instruction, church planting and growth, church organization, worship style—indeed with all of those activities involved in carrying out the Great Commission."[9] Darrell Whiteman expressed *contextualization* as "attempts to communicate the Gospel in word and deed and to establish the church in ways that make sense to people within their local cultural

6. Theological Education Fund, *Ministry in Context*, 20.

7. Theological Education Fund, *Ministry in Context*, 20.

8. Kato, "Gospel," 1217.

9. Hesselgrave, *Communicating Christ Cross-Culturally*, 202.

context, presenting Christianity in such a way that it meets people's deepest needs and penetrates their worldview, thus allowing them to follow Christ and remain with their own culture."[10]

These evangelical definitions are comprehensive in describing the tasks included for contextualization, but one notes that the focus shifts subtly from the action of the hearer to the action of the messenger. This provides the impression that the gospel needs help to be all it can be. This is not the case. Rather the model for contextualization is Jesus, the Son of God, the Word made flesh and living among us—God's sending his Son to humankind that he be made known to us in all of his glory (John 1:14, 18). God's message is for all people (Gal 3:28), universal in its gifting, not a human message (Gal 1:11) needing help (whether through human response or improved presentation).

But though the gospel is universal, it is not magical. Succinctly captured in *The Book of Concord* as the confessions of the Evangelical Lutheran Church, "No one has written or suggested that people benefit from the mere act of hearing lessons they do not understand, or that they benefit from ceremonies not because they teach or admonish but simply *ex opere operato*, that is, by the mere act of doing or observing."[11]

From this we conclude that the gospel proclamation process includes communication and contextualization, not as the process of somehow helping the gospel out but of lowering barriers erected through our sinful human condition. The following expresses this as a Lutheran confessional worldview understanding of the missiological process for contextualization in mission:

> The Gospel message is universal and for all. God has chosen us not only as receivers of this message, but also as its messengers. True contextualization, therefore, springs from the action of the Gospel message upon the heart of the messenger and preserves God's universal message to others through such scriptural means as the messenger has at his disposal. It is initiated and accomplished by the power of the Holy Spirit through discovering and lowering the barriers to the Gospel that man erects through his sinful self and sinful world. . . . Contextualization is God's action in the world through Jesus by the power of the Holy Spirit's calling and involving us in His purpose and using us as means to call others. It is God and His Word, involving both messenger

10. Whiteman, "Contextualization," 2.

11. Ap 24.5 (*BC*, 258).

> and hearer, who, in faith given, preserve and express that Word throughout the world's many peoples and cultures. We proclaim and hear the Gospel imperfectly. Yet God calls us anyway and works in our hearts and minds, and so we witness to what He has done for us through His Son. As messengers, we understand ourselves as integral to the message, but also as its corruptors. Thus, we constantly seek, by the wisdom of the Holy Spirit, to remove barriers and corruption and preserve that message so that the Word may have free course.[12]

Summarized, we acknowledge worldview differences in mission. Contextualization is the process of discovering and lowering barriers so that others are not inadvertently pointed away from the fullness of the gospel message and God's story of salvation to the world through Jesus. When the messenger is not intentional toward lowering barriers raised by culture and context, the version of the gospel proclaimed may be not be heard, or distorted by the recipients of the message.

CONTEXTUALIZATION IN SCRIPTURE: PAUL IN THE NEW TESTAMENT

Not all perceive the same. An event, ritual, action, or linguistic form may be the same, but underlying meanings may be assigned differently through alternate worldviews. Our intention is good. But our actions, words, observations, and assumptions raise barriers which distort meaning. Understanding barriers erected is necessary to removing them—that the word might be free. In this way, the Holy Spirit works to bring faith wherever the hearer may be.

The Christian missionary journey is one of learning—one's unfolding sanctified life in Christ, not without mistake. The apostle Paul in Acts provides a descriptive example in Acts 14—an early attempt to proclaim the gospel message outside the Jewish context. He and Barnabas came to Lystra with a bold confidence in God's power exhibited through a healing event. Paul and Barnabas had been a part of "sign and wonder" events through God's power in the Jewish context (Acts 14:3), but this was a foreign context, as evidenced by the local use of a language that Paul did not understand. All did not go as expected. The act of healing was not perceived as God at work. Rather the Lystrans concluded Paul and Barnabas

12. Rodewald, "Barriers to the Gospel," 60.

were gods and determined to sacrifice to them. What Paul and Barnabas failed to understand was the difference of context into which they proclaimed. A local Lystran legend, as recorded by Ovid in *Metamorphoses*, told of two gods, Zeus and Hermes, rebuffed by local citizens until an elderly couple took pity on them and slaughtered a goose for them. The inhospitable citizens were punished and the elderly couple rewarded.[13]

It is not a wonder that the local Lystrans concluded Barnabas as Zeus and Paul as Hermes. The local population did not want to make that mistake again. Even an excellent explanation toward correction (Acts 14:15–17) did not change perspective for most. Rather, the barriers of language and context caused the locals to supply their own meanings, which were then used by Jews from Antioch and Iconium to incite them. Paul was stoned and left for dead.

Paul survived his mission experience in Lystra. It did not stop him proclaiming the gospel message. However, it is significant to note that he approaches gospel proclamation methods different later in Athens (Acts 17)—another foreign context. He takes time to reason both in the synagogue and in the marketplace with local philosophers. When provided the opportunity to share on Mars Hill, he utilizes the Athenians' unknown god as a point of contact to present the God who made the world and everything in it. His presentation lowered barriers to those who heard. Some rejected, others were curious and wished to learn more, and some believed. He was not stoned this time.

We observe Paul's approach to gospel proclamation and mission in a foreign environment changed. His bold but rather naive early approach to proclamation in a foreign context transforms as he gains mission experience in new contexts. He summarizes during his third missionary journey, writing from Ephesus, "To the Jews, I became as a Jew, in order to win Jews. To those under the law I became as one under the law (though not being myself under the law). . . . I have become everything to everyone in order to save at least some of them" (1 Cor 9:20, 22). Paul's experience and writing presented in Scripture provides a powerful affirmation that the gospel is equally at home in every language and culture and is for all people no matter through which approaches they hear the fullness of the gospel for themselves.

13. See Tenney and Longenecker, *John and Acts*, 435; Ovid, *Metamorphoses*, bk. 8.

CONCLUSION

The words of Scripture through Paul in 1 Corinthians provide direction for mission method today. Our part in gospel proclamation mission method is not proclaiming through our own foreign forms, languages, or preaching, under which the gospel is distorted or not perceived. Rather, we understand mission, and thus define *contextualization*, as removing barriers to the gospel message. We serve in mission, becoming "all things to all people," that the knowledge of what Christ accomplished for us is understood in a manner through which the Holy Spirit works to produce faith—a process succinctly captured by Martin Luther as removing "boulders and clods" that "the Word may have free course."[14] Such is the confessional scriptural Lutheran Christian way of proclaiming the gospel to others within God's mission.

The process of learning and growing in Christ (sanctification) within the missionary journey is not without err. The positive is that even through one's mistakes one learns more about the universal gospel message given for self and for the world. It is a joy to observe God at work in ways that many from a missionary's home context may never see or understand. But a note of caution when reentering one's home context. The worldview of the sojourner in mission builds as one experiences God at work in another context. Such may expand his/her worldview in ways not present within the worldviews of those within the missionary's home context. When the missionary returns "home," new insights into God and his word at work in the world may be perceived as threat rather than informing insight. Thus the missionary sojourner finds it an integral part of the missionary journey to extend the same grace and patience to those from his/her home church body or congregation (with its own limiting set of worldview values) as the missionary sojourner extends to those to whom the gospel message is carried within a different cultural context.

14. See Luther, *On Translating*, 188, 193. Also, Luther, *Order of Public Worship*, 14.

7

Mission and Culture Clash

Worldview Value Components

A PERSON APPLIES MEANING to events, objects, and words dependent upon the experiences and learning from the contexts which formed his/her worldview. Preventing worldview clash and incorrect assumption is found by identifying those value components within a worldview which supply meaning. An example of how value components provide meaning can be seen in linguistics. The surface form *dog*, in English, has a number of value components which in totality become how a person views a dog. A person from the US context may apply values such as "animal," "canine," "pet," "companion," "family member," "spiritual being," etc. These components, in their total, supply how that person perceives a dog. A person with a worldview developed in a different context may apply different value components and perceive *dog* as "enemy," "scavenger," "object of ridicule," "demonic," "food source," or "fearful." Even those with worldviews developed within a similar cultural context may perceive *dog* with difference based upon the components applied.

Cultural worldview clash occurs when one assumes another perceives the surface form—*dog*—in a similar manner. Some Muslims consider dogs as ritually impure and thus to be avoided since one invites demonic danger when interacting with a dog. Through their worldview, if a wet dog touches a person, that person becomes impure (*mutanajjis*) and cannot pray until purified.[1] A Western Christian seeking witness to a Muslim while maintaining a dog as a pet or member of the family risks

1. Some Muslims feel differently; see Haider, "Dogs in Islamic Culture."

clash and distortion of the message he/she wishes to impart. And *dog* is only one surface-word-noun out of the eighty thousand nouns or so recorded for the English language.[2]

Culture clash occurs also on the linguistic phrase level when alternating values create alternating assumption. A group of Western seminarians approached a Kenyan student studying in the US and said, "Let's go out and get something to eat." The hidden underlying worldview assumption is, "Who pays?" The Kenyan student was aghast when he finished eating and found he was expected to pay for his own food. He had to borrow money from another student. From his worldview context with a high-value component of hospitality, the one who invites is expected to pay. That is not the case in a Western seminary student community whose worldviews contain a low-value component for hospitality and a high individual component—students assume that each person will pay for one's own food.[3]

One notes the possible culture and worldview clashes and distortion of message as we communicate through linguistic form. Not only may we have different components of meaning, but those components may be expressed differently, resulting in misunderstanding. Non-linguistic form clashes similarly. Two people may observe the same surface action or object but arrive at different meanings depending upon how value components are assigned to that form. A local pastor from South Africa related a story about early Western missionaries. The missionaries established church services and translated the words of European liturgical services into the Zulu language. They changed the linguistic forms but maintained other form within the services. They taught their Zulu congregants to stand during the reading of the gospel lesson in order to indicate respect for the gospel as it was read. However, according to the pastor recounting with a chuckle, no Zulu person was permitted to stand in the presence of their king—Zulu culture required them to sit in order to respect the king's presence. The act of standing or sitting at the reading of the gospel lesson in that context was not neutral. It indicated either respect or its opposite depending upon how the value component was assigned and expressed within the worldview of observers.

2. Study.com, "How Many Nouns."

3. Rodewald, "Outside Look," 264. Unless otherwise specified, the mission examples throughout are from the personal experiences of the authors or from conversations had with others serving in cross-cultural mission.

At times, there may be no mutual concepts in which to express a concept present in one cultural context but not the other. For example, there is no concept of being *bored* in the ethnic cultures within Ethiopia. There are just no words or phrases to express the concept of *bored* within local languages since "to be bored" is a conceptual component not present and not possible to communicate—there is always something to do. That is not the same in a Western context such as the US, where being bored is a commonly expressed mood.

Serving as a cross-cultural messenger of the gospel is not an intuitive task. The mere presence of the missionary outsider seeking to proclaim the gospel may provide distortion no matter the intent as others assign meaning and make assumptions through their worldviews. A Western missionary (the author) with Lutheran Bible Translators had been living in a remote town in the high-bush of Liberia for almost two years. He devoted time to learning the language and culture as the first step toward developing a writing system in order to translate the Bible into the local language. He ate the local food and learned by intent (and trial and error) the appropriate ways of acting within that culture. He was open about his purpose, and the people in the town were friendly. Two years in, one of his local friends asked, "Why are you really here? Some people think you are here to look for gold in the hills around here, others think you are just trying to learn bush-society secrets."[4]

Just the fact that the Western missionary was present as a unique outsider created assumption. The local people saw the missionary's presence through the values of their worldviews. His purpose did not make sense to them. There had to be another reason. Later in the same location, a Western short-term missionary intern hiked on a nearby mountain. It caused an uproar. Some local people claimed that he had disturbed the spiritual powers that the locals claimed were on that mountain. They demanded restitution, a sacrifice of a black bull. For others, it affirmed their suspicions. The missionaries had come to look for gold. After all, who goes walking on a mountain for fun?

Similar disconnect may occur when short-term mission teams from a Western context visit a cross-cultural mission context without troubling to acknowledge the differences between their own worldviews and the ones from those they visit. They often perceive themselves as sharing the gospel through the gifts they provide while locals see wealth and fail

4. From Rodewald's personal experience.

to perceive the visitors' gospel intent. What one intends while serving in the cross-cultural context is not always what is perceived, as actions are scrutinized and meaning applied through the values of contrasting worldviews.

WORLDVIEW VALUE COMPONENTS—A SPECTRUM OF CONTRASTING STRENGTHS

There is no universal worldview lens shared by the varied peoples of the world. Rather, multiple value components combine to form the cultural worldviews of its members. The strength of each component and how it exhibits provides understanding, which then allows us to reduce the barriers to sharing the gospel across cultural boundaries.

While it is not possible to provide an exhaustive list of worldview value components which create culture clash, a discussion toward some is helpful to understand just how clash occurs. A high-value component in one worldview may find itself in a clash with a low value of the same present in another worldview. Alternately two different components, each held in high value, may clash. Eugene Nida, in his classic *Message and Mission*, discusses society orientations that affect the gospel message in the mission context, suggesting that societies can be ordered into three types—tradition-oriented, inner-directed, and outer-directed.[5] Lingenfelter and Mayers use other contrasting orientations—time/event, dichotomist/holistic, crisis/noncrisis, task/people, role status / achievement status, and willingness to express vulnerability—to describe how societies differ.[6] These and similar serve as value components applied within worldview. Some are stronger; some are weaker. Different values and/or strengths cause incorrect assumptions which then distort perception and communication, at least until one becomes conversant with how others communicate and act within their worldviews.

The accompanying chart (figure 5) shows a hypothetical but possible clash in values between two worldviews using relational-component values and task-component values. The reader notes the difference between the values held by each. Culture 1 has a strong relational value component in contrast with culture 2. The opposite is the case with the

5. Nida, *Message and Mission.*

6. Lingenfelter and Mayers, *Ministering Cross-Culturally.*

task value. Interactions between members of those two communities will be distorted by the difference in values as assumption occurs.

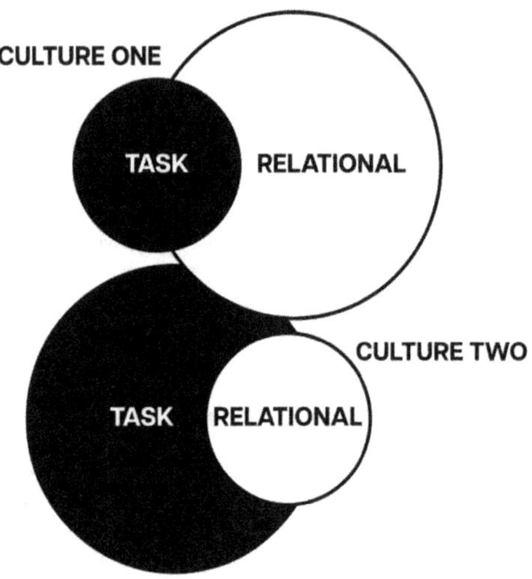

Figure 5: Value Components and Worldview Clash

Note that communities with similar strength values are not free from distortion. Rather, as noted previously, there is the ever-present potential distortion caused by interpreting differently the surface form that exhibits value in that culture, even where value strengths are similar.[7]

The following contrasts examples of differing value component strengths so the reader may note the culture clash and results which occur as perception of the same object, words, or event differs.

Time–Event

Some worldviews place a high value on *time* and time's effect on events. *Event*-oriented people tend toward the opposite. The event, and accomplishing of it, takes priority over time. Worldview clash occurs where wide differences occur.

7. Strength comparisons in the chart are for illustration. Ascribing value strength to a culture-component is more art than science, and as such strength may of necessity be assigned through observation of those within a cultural context rather than trying to access the overt knowledge of practitioners unaware that their values differ from others. In other words, if asked directly, most people of the world may say they value time, but in the observation, one will determine the strength of that value.

Church services were at ten o'clock. Members of the short-term mission team from the US showed up a bit early to make sure they were on time. They were surprised. No one was there except for two ladies sweeping the church floor with straw hand brooms. A young man showed up a few minutes later, apologized, and rushed to beat a stick on the old car tire rim which served as the church bell. He invited the visitors to enter the church and sit in the front row. Several ladies of the community entered and started singing and clapping in the local language. The pastor arrived. He put on his gown behind the church and handed the visitors several copies of the hymnal in the national language. Children began peering in through the windows. Some entered and joined the singing. Others arrived, each finding a place to sit on the benches inside the church. The singing became louder and louder as participation grew. Finally the pastor came to the front of the church and raised his hands. The service began. Three hours later the visitors walked out of the church. They were hungry and tired. They couldn't wait to get back to their much-delayed lunch and a bit of rest before the next scheduled event.

Note the difference in action between those with worldviews from a culture with a high value placed on *time* versus those with a high value placed on the *event*. Both may also have time or event values with lower value, but priority happens between components of high value. Culture clash occurs when those from time-cultures expect events to be constrained by *time*, while those with high *event* values implement when all is ready and finish when all has been accomplished. For those with strong event-oriented worldviews, time is often less important than making sure that everything is accomplished. The value of *time* against the value of *event* and how each is expressed often creates misunderstanding through cultural differences in values.

Task–Relationship

Members of societies whose worldviews hold high values toward *tasks* (doing) often clash with members of other societies who prioritize *relationships* (being).

A short-term youth mission team from the US visited the southern Africa nation of Botswana. They wished to use miming (body motions) as a way of expressing Bible stories and the gospel message to the local people in rural towns and villages. They partnered with youth from the local Botswana diocese to do so. They accomplished mutual training and camped as a group using rural church buildings as their base. Each day they woke early, studied the Bible together, had a time of prayer, and then went as a group to mime the gospel. They returned to base in order to prepare food and wash clothes. Then—exhausted—they fell asleep. The youth groups separated after a week of outreach—local youth to their homes and the US youth to a game park and then back to the US. Debriefs were held. The comments from the US youth tended to reflect failure. Only one new person had come to church on the Sunday following their activity. The Botswana youth had a different take. One girl remarked, "Another church youth group come from Germany. They were with us but they were more interested to see the animals. But these youth, we watched them. We prayed with them, we studied the Bible with them and we lived with them every day. We know they are real Christians."

Africans tend to give up tasks to maintain relationships, while North Americans and Europeans tend to give up relationships to accomplish tasks.[8] The US youth viewed their purpose as the task and results of the short-term event. The youth from Botswana experienced differently. They observed the relationship and its value as their takeaway.

In such as North American worldviews, doing and accomplishing tasks toward results has a high priority. In such as African worldviews, tasks are necessary, but it is maintaining the relationships in order to accomplish tasks which is of higher value. The worthiness of an idea/task is less important in accomplishing the task than that relationships are present. Events such as the sharing of food, visiting and honoring family, lay the ground for the completion of tasks. Where relationship is not accomplished, accomplishing a task has a high chance of failure. Misunderstanding can occur between short-term mission initiatives originating within the US for implementation with African partners. Relationship may begin with enthusiasm between partners but later degenerate into disappointment through failure to build and maintain the necessary relationships for accountability and goals. African partners are disappointed that US partners did not respect relationships. US partners may feel that African partners deceived them.

It is worth noting that in the debriefing outlined above, the US youth and leaders expressed that they were exhausted by the week-long

8. Note that this is a general example in that not all cultures in Africa have an identical relationship-component strength, but most have a stronger one than those from North America.

twenty-four-hour communal living with the Botswana youth. They just weren't used to that amount of scrutinized relation. Living and serving with those with different worldviews is not simple, but when one's service is accomplished in ways that those within another cultural context perceive as positive, differences are minimized and both relationship and task-oriented goals are more easily accomplished.

Group–Individual

Those in some cultures have worldviews with a strong *group* value component—the individual exists because the group exists. Individuals are inextricably bound through the group. The Bantu cultures of southern Africa express this understanding through concepts such as *ubuntu*—"a common bond between us all and it is through this bond, through our interaction with our fellow human beings, that we discover our own human qualities."[9] In such worldview, the purpose of the perceived group supersedes the purpose of individual members. Success and reward, as well as happiness and contentment, rests upon others in the group not being unhappy or discontent. Conformity is desired and perceived to bring harmony and happiness as illustrated in the following story.

The Western missionary lived and served in a small town in West Africa. A young girl helped her with chores around the house, so the missionary shared one of her prized candy bars as a thank-you reward. There were other children present, so the girl divided the bar into small portions and gave each a piece of the bar. She shared all with those present, even though she had done the work and earned the reward. The missionary was curious and explained to a local friend. The friend told her that one cannot be happy at the expense of others. Keeping the candy bar for herself might cause others to be unhappy—an example of a worldview with a strong group component.

Other worldviews have a strong *individualist* component. The individual, individual success, and individual possession is prized. The Western missionary was fuming. He had loaned his hammer to a member of the town in which he was residing. It had been three weeks, and the hammer was still not returned. He asked his friend what he should do. The friend was surprised. "Go and get it when you need it," he said. For the missionary, the hammer was his, and the borrower should return to

9. Boudreau, "Ubuntu."

the lender. For the town member, the hammer was to be used as needed. The borrower could come for it at any time.

The *individualist* value component assumes each person as unique and defined by one's emerging perception of self. In such worldview, the girl given the candy bar in a previous narrative would *not* have been wrong to keep the rewards of her labor for herself. She may or may not share with others, but the assumption is that the candy bar is hers since she earned it. So with the missionary who owned the hammer.

The relative strengths of *group/individual* values emerge in language. The Bandi language in northern Liberia uses a single pronoun form to refer to all individuals, whether man, woman, child, or animal. That is not the same in English in the United States, which uses separate pronouns—he, she, it—and a recent proliferation of other pronouns attached to one's own preference, which is indicative of a high individualist component value.[10]

Charitable–Hospitable

Africans place a high value on *hospitality*. Americans tend to value being *charitable* over hospitable. This does not mean that Americans are not hospitable. Rather, the American strength value of being hospitable is weak compared to the African value component. And vice versa for the charitable-component value.

The Western missionary lived in a rural part of Liberia (West Africa). He and his team had great initial success proclaiming their versions of the gospel message to the people. Many had appeared at gatherings, and the beginnings of a local church body formed. But now the crowds were smaller, and few seemed willing to come to Sunday church services. "What happened?" he wondered. He asked someone from another mission agency who was more proficient in the language and culture to find out the cause. That missionary visited several of the locals and queried them discreetly. There were a number of telling comments, but one of the most telling was, "That missionary only waves at us as he drives by on his motorcycle. He never stops and greets us."[11]

Those from many cultures place a high value on hospitality and relationship toward neighbors and visitors within their context. Relationship

10. Andrew, "Guide to Neopronouns."

11. Rodewald's personal experience.

is enhanced through ritual, such as unique forms of handshaking, as well as long and frequent greetings. They honor and treat guests with food and lodging and make sure that guests feel comfortable for as long as needed. They are less prone to providing help outside their context, such as sending a donation in response to a plea from another continent.

Those with worldviews formed in Western cultures tend to place a high value on charity—extending help to others at a distance rather than close proximity. Giving gifts is preferred. Inviting recipients of gifts into one's home is less preferred. Guests may be welcomed in the home, but the time period of welcome is different than those with worldviews formed in high hospitable-value cultures. The result is that Westerners prefer to visit those needing development or evangelism, help, and then return to their own homes, rather than helping someone with a similar need in close proximity and a longer expected relationship.

Short-term visitors from the West may feel honored by the hospitality of African cultures as church officials make it a priority to gather, eat together, and make sure that the guests feel welcomed. The same African church officials are somewhat surprised when they visit in Western cultural contexts. Busyness of tasks and life contribute to a weak hospitality value in Western worldviews which then provides a different sense of priority for attending events held to honor visiting church officials from other countries.

Spiritual Holism–Dualism/Pluralism

Holism seeks comprehensive connection. Dualism and/or pluralism is the fragmentation that occurs as individual pieces are perceived as separate from connection to other pieces.

A dualist/pluralistic-oriented culture splits the fabric of the universe into smaller parts—spiritual/physical, good/evil, good/bad, eternal/temporal, sacred/secular, right/wrong. Each part is defined and examined by comparing or excluding other parts. Pluralism finds its path with variations on a theme—multiple limited interests seeking validation or even advantage over others. The following definition attempts to capture the best of those who hold pluralistic worldviews: "Specifically, pluralism is social tolerance for individuals or groups who have different backgrounds, views, or beliefs. It also provides space for them to express views and practice their beliefs without reprisal—even when they conflict with others."[12] For the purpose of discussing spiritual worldview, one notes both the focus on conflict and the fragmentation which emerges. Dualism/pluralism by nature creates conflict desiring resolution. Passionate Christian denominationalism may be the result of positions held by those with a high dualist value in their worldviews.

Those with a high holistic value in their worldviews see the spiritual/physical fabric of the universe as comprehensive in connection. A West Africa proverb, "Nothing happens for nothing," captures the concept of no coincidence in the world. Rather *all* physical events, nature, and people are connected to the spiritual world, as illustrated in the next story.

A local pastor and missionary were driving to the capital city. They drove too fast, and the police pulled them over. The driver was issued a ticket. The local pastor said, "Satan caused us to get a ticket. Someone did something to cause this. Let's pray!" The missionary said, "We were driving too fast." Note the holistic connection between spiritual and physical present in the local pastor's comment. For the local pastor, every physical event is tied to the spiritual. There had to be a spiritual reason for the event, either good or bad, and thus cause and effect had to occur. For the missionary, the spiritual had nothing to do with it. He was just driving too fast and got caught.

Those with a high holistic spiritual value in their worldviews often tend to be less judgmental since without dualist/pluralist fragments at odds with each other, one cannot be expected to know which behavior is right or wrong. Rather, one knows that harmony is not in order when a result is not as one would desire. The following oral story is told among the Kalanga people (Botswana) concerning *Mwali*, the identifier name by which the Kalanga people call *Ndzimu*, their historical Kalanga spiritual power / creator god.

A hunter went to hunt on a mountain. He killed a *duiker* (small antelope) and began walking home with his prize. But he could not get off the mountain no matter how much he walked. He propitiated *Mwali*. *Mwali* said, "You killed my duiker without asking. To propitiate, you must sacrifice when you reach home." The hunter promised to do so. He was able to come off the mountain, go home, and make his sacrifice.

This narrative illustrates how harmony is broken and restored in worldviews formed in contexts with high holistic value. It was noted by local speakers with whom the author reviewed the story that wrong

12. Walsh and McKenzie, "Pluralism."

occurred against Mwali, but the hunter could not know he "missed the mark"[13] intended by Mwali until something negative happened, in which case propitiation was necessary for spiritual harmony to be restored.

High values of dualism/pluralism and high values of holism each have a positive and negative side. A dualist/pluralist value allows one to determine right versus wrong. However living out life in Christ may digress into the things one does—attending church, Bible study, reading the Bible, evangelism—not always connected to other parts of one's life. Those with a high holistic value in their worldviews are enviable in acknowledging connection with the spiritual world but may use connection for their own self-centric purpose, as occurs through spiritualist religions such as African traditional religions and New Age practice.

Holistic unity in Christ for ALL things in the fullness of time is promised—the perfect holism desired (1 Cor 1:10).

Shame–Guilt

Shame occurs when a member of a community acts in a manner which causes others, and even perhaps one's self, to perceive an action as hurting someone in the community or damaging community norms. Communities with high *shame* value perceive such action as bringing shame upon the community, group, or family. An action itself may not be judged as right/wrong. If one is not caught, no shame can occur. Rather it is the perception of others which is of import. The severity of an action is supplied by the amount of shame brought on self, family, group, or community, and the restitution which must be negotiated. An example is provided in the next story.

The Western missionary from Lutheran Bible Translators was driving in a four-wheel drive on back roads in Botswana. He was unsure whether he had taken the right turn to get to the rural area he was seeking. He asked an elderly man on the side of the road, "Is this the road to Mapoka?" The man applied in the affirmative. The missionary continued. It was only after several more kilometers that he realized that it was not the road to Mapoka. He turned around. The man in his answer dodged the shame of not knowing the answer to the question. The missionary

13. Note the Kalanga traditional word for indicating infraction is *khuta* (LL tone), which means "to miss the intended target." This is similar to the Hebrew understanding of *sin*. A connection between the Kalanga language and people with Hebrew origins is presented in Rodewald, "Understanading Mwali," and Rodewald, "Mwali."

would have been more effective if he would have stated his problem differently, such as, "I am lost. I am looking for Mapoka." The man then could have been free to determine a solution to which he did not feel shame, perhaps even entering into the problem by taking him to someone who would know how to get to Mapoka.

Guilt is different than shame. Guilt is a feeling of responsibility, anxiety, or remorse for transgressing a law or rule. Those with a high-value *guilt* component within their worldview operate differently than those with high values of *shame*.[14] The rules governing guilt may be informally learned or formal in application, but when one breaks the rule, guilt occurs in the offender. Accountability is to authority and restitution required for the one who breaks the rule.

Shame and guilt may exhibit similarly, but they are not the same. Underneath it all, there lies a different sense of application. One sees this while applying God's law as provided through Moses on Mount Sinai. In worldviews with a high-value *shame* component, living out the law is desirable as God's people—together as community. Not accomplishing the law brings consequence which brings shame to others and to God. God's law is applied with different reasoning by those with a high-value *guilt* component. The law shows where we err from God's purpose for us. Guilt is determined through breaking his law. The approaches may be different, but in both, *shame* or *guilt*, restitution is desired. Jesus brings us into relationship with God and others through forgiveness of our wrongs no matter whether seen through high-value *shame* or *guilt* worldview components.

Crisis–Noncrisis Orientation

Some cultures have a high *crisis-oriented* value toward future crisis. Crisis causes learning. Through such lessons, preparations are made so that a similar crisis may not occur in the future. The opposite occurs for those with high *noncrisis-oriented* value worldviews who defer reaction until a crisis occurs. Effort and energy is spent upon the current crisis. Less is spent preparing for a future crisis. After all, who can predict the future?

The leader of the Western short-term mission team was puzzled. He had contacted the leader of the African church diocese which he and

14. A high-value guilt component often is present alongside high-value right/wrong and direct/indirect components within worldviews.

others planned to visit. He had laid out his expectations of what might be accomplished but received only vague answers in reply. It was time to get on the plane. He was still unsure if any concrete plans were in place for the visit. The church leader met him as he arrived and quickly called the local youth group together. He told them what he expected of them and made sure that logistics were available. It was chaotic and the beginning of a whirlwind of activity. Much activity was reactive rather than planned, from the Western short-term group perspective, but all was accomplished. The visit was less planned than accomplished.

The opposite example of *crisis-orientation* value in a worldview is seen in the Western world seeking to avert similar problems in the future. The following paragraph provides an example of Mississippi River flooding (US) and a crisis-orientation toward "the next high water event."

> The corps identified where repairs to levees and other parts of the system are needed and is using $802 million approved by Congress. . . . to make critical and non-critical fixes "to prepare for the next high water event."[15]

An exhibited feature of a high value toward crisis-orientation is the presence of an insurance industry seeking to cover future contingency. There is a large part of the world with a high-value *noncrisis-orientation* in their worldviews, as noted by the UN in that "half the world is not prepared for disasters."[16] The reasons may be listed as poverty, lack of education, or even fatalism, but those with *noncrisis-orientation* use resources when crisis occurs rather than preparing for a potential crisis which may or may not happen.

Future–Past Orientation

Language reflects culture and the worldviews of those within that culture. The Bandi community lives in a remote part of Liberia in West Africa. The Bandi language does not have a strong future tense, rather they have what is best described as a *potentive* tense—a future event that may or may not happen.

The Western missionary was fuming. This was not the first time someone had told him they would come to his house on a certain day. He

15. Sainz, "Mississippi River Flood."
16. World Meteorological Organization, "Not Prepared for Disasters."

had waited patiently. They never showed up. These people are just liars, he thought.

The missionary didn't understand the culture. He was still learning. Even when translated into English, "I will come to your house tomorrow" had an underlying cultural meaning of "I may come to your house tomorrow." The local people weren't lying. The missionary was just making an assumption by applying his high value toward certainty in the future to statements of *potentive* action. The Bandi language has three different past tenses—recent, medium, and long—indicating a higher value for the past than for the future. Other language groups reflect similar traits.

Western societies have a low-value *past* component in their worldviews. This value is seen when reading the first chapter of Matthew—the genealogy of Jesus. Western readers tend to skip over the list of generations and names in the first chapter of Matthew. It is not the same in cultures where worldviews have a high-value *past* component, such as in Africa where the genealogy in the Matthew text is read with interest and even memorized. Scripture establishes Jesus with the authority of past generations. The implication is clear. Jesus is not just a mythical figure made up by Western missionaries for their own mysterious purposes—Jesus is real. This value is seen in the following example.

A Western missionary and short-term mission group were visiting in Tanzania. The father of the local diocesan bishop asked the missionary to name his ancestors. The missionary named three. Each member of the Western group could name from two to four generations of grandparents and great-grandparents. The father of the local bishop named seventeen. His identity was determined by those relatives from the past.

Prescriptive–Functional–Traditional

Some with worldviews formed in Western cultures tend toward a high *prescriptive* value component—implementing the correct or proper form or action. Results matter less than proper form or process. For example, those with worldviews formed in European society tend to have a high-value *prescriptive* component. Implementation is accomplished with much confidence since the norms are its own, and inner security is derived from being right. Information is systematic—organized and taught. Those with high-value prescriptive components take the position, "We ought to do it this way because it is the right way." Structure is based upon rules. Respect is allocated by operating within prescriptive norms. A high-value *prescriptive* component often seems to pair with high-value components for *judgment* and *guilt*. Judgments are applied according to specific criteria. Inner guilt is felt when departure from norms occurs. Mission method by those with high *prescriptive* values is often implemented by transplanting through proper form and method, as defined by those in mission.

Others, such as those with worldviews formed in North America, have a high *functional* value component. The formative question is, What is the best way to accomplish the purpose? If a process or plan doesn't get results, change is justified. Those with a high-value *functional* component in their worldviews gather around ideas, principles, and goals and modify action toward desired results. There may be doubt in implementation because the rules are not as clear as in those with high prescriptive values, but they move forward with statements such as, "Others are doing it, so it must be okay." Mission method toward those with high *functional* values is often initiated through questions such as, "What is the meaning of life?" or through intentions of "making a difference." The gospel in *functional* value mission method is presented toward resolving man's dilemmas. Expository proclamation is preferred over systematic presentation. Discipleship and learning is valued over the correctness of instruction. A high-value *functional* component often pairs with high-value *judgment* and *achievement* components—achievement is judged and respect allocated accordingly.

Those with a high *traditional* value component approach the present as in the past. This honors those from the past and informs members of the community how the present is to be maintained. Life and its problems are less questioned than accepted. Physical and spiritual life are integrated. The future is less anticipated; rather, living out the present and honoring the past is prioritized. Change comes slowly and most often occurs only after a communal challenge or disaster forces change. African societies generally tend to have such high *traditional* values in their worldviews. They prioritize maintaining the traditions of their identifying histories. They see the world and its patterns as holistic, each piece relying on the other. A high traditional value often pairs with strong *nonjudgmental*, *role*, and *relational* value components. Judgments are open-ended and consider the whole person and circumstance rather than a specific action or statement. Security comes from multiple relationships throughout society. Personal achievement is sacrificed for group relations. Learning is accomplished through mentoring as one observes how he or she is to fit within the whole. Mission method to those with such worldview uses the historicity of Scripture and God's relationship to man to fill in the blanks of what has not yet been known of God, the history of the world, and man's transitioning into a new and meaningful whole through Jesus Christ. Filling in the blanks of the past lowers barriers to spiritual worldview change for those in the present.

Clash between these three worldview components is seen in the following example.

The Lutheran Church in Southern Africa (LCSA) was formed by German missionaries from Europe. These missionaries tended to be prescriptive in mission method. They translated the words of hymns and liturgies from their sending church body into local languages but maintained melodies and liturgical forms as those proper for worship services. The words were not without error and meaningless literalness, but the local church members accepted. They implemented those worship forms in Sunday services, and they became tradition. But now the youth, with a less strongly formed attachment to their culture than the elders, were disappearing to other churches. The elders were worried. They met with the German missionaries and some American missionaries that were a part of the mission of the church. What could they do? The Americans, considering their strong functional component, suggested trying something new—perhaps some different songs? The Germans, using a strong prescriptive component, clashed and noted that the songs and worship forms from the other churches were not proper for Lutherans. The local members, with a strong traditionalist component, acknowledged that their church forms had been instituted and maintained by those who had preceded them. No resolution occurred. The church continued to struggle with youth disappearing from Sunday morning services.

Those with a strong *prescriptive* value allow change only after acknowledging a form is no longer proper/correct, in which case change occurs and a new form becomes the proper one. A worldview with a high *functional* value component clashes with those holding high prescriptive or traditional values by focusing on results and the changes needed to obtain the desired result. Those with worldviews with high *traditional* value allow change only when it is no longer possible to maintain a past tradition, in which case a new tradition forms. This more often happens through a perceived calamity event of larger magnitude, which then forces a new tradition to be formed, rather than voluntary small changes.

Prescriptive and *functional* values often seem to clash with *traditional* worldview values as mission partnerships are formed. Well-meaning Western partners with prescriptive/functional values initiate with financial support, expecting the need for their help to decrease as the local church or mission initiative gains independence. Research by Wayne Allen demonstrates that such subsidy method slows the growth of the local church when salaries are paid by outsiders and concludes, "Wisdom suggests that we limit our financial subsidy to areas other than pastoral support,"[17] an example of dependence with consequence toward undesired result. The intentions may be good, but initiating dependence can form a tradition which resists change despite the intent of those with high *functional* or *prescriptive* values to move partners with high *tradition* value to independence.

Role–Achievement

Value components which assign respect differ in alternate cultural contexts. In worldviews with high-value *role* components, respect and status are accorded by position held. Status is described with titles like chief, judge, president, bishop. Competence matters less than the position—respect accorded not by how one fulfills the position but rather to the person in the position. Positions, and accompanying respect, may be handed down over generations, such as in the case of royalty.

Worldviews formed in other cultural contexts have a high-value *achievement* component—respect is given through competence and knowledge. The outcome of a high achievement value within a worldview is that of an expert. Experts lead and advise others how to best accomplish the roles needed to accomplish goals. Worldview clash may occur as in the following example.

The African bishop was complaining about meetings with a group of Western short-term mission leaders. In his culture, those with the lowest status were to speak first in meetings. Higher-status members spoke last. The bishop, in accord with his highest-status role, was to listen to everyone who spoke and then sum the discussion and make the decision. Consensus was thus reached and plans and solutions instituted.

But Western short-term mission leaders were not waiting to speak in positions expected by locals. Rather, they would begin speaking about

17. Allen, "When the Mission Pays."

their expectations and lay their ideas out first. Locals were confused. They perceived these mission leaders of high status, and yet they were presenting where those of lower status were expected to present. Some local members of the church council were afraid to speak following the high-status visitors—to speak out of order would conflict with status and dishonor the visitors. The visitors were met with silence, which they assumed to be agreement with their ideas and presentations of partnership for mission. For the visitors, all seemed good until implementation required local action. The locals did not perceive consensus since they had not played their part in decisions leading up to the implementation. The Western visitors were disappointed in the lack of local buy-in to their ideas. They blamed the bishop.

High *role/achievement* component values within worldviews create clash where respect and value for ideas and results differ from respect and value for position held. Negotiating differences makes for a partnership which accomplishes the desires of both.

Majority–Consensus

Those with worldviews containing a high-value component for *majority* decision-making tend toward a 50-percent-plus-one method of making decisions. Discussion occurs and a vote is taken. Democracy unfolds as the majority winner is decided, leaving a minority opposition which does not agree and may even be uncooperative toward implementation. A different decision is made only when a majority votes in favor of the new decision.

Those with worldviews containing a high *consensus* component differ. The outside event may be similar—discussion occurs and a decision made—but consensus occurs when those on the losing, less-majority side join with the majority to implement together. In this way unity, or at least its appearance, is preserved. This does not mean that the losing side agrees on the issues but rather that all agree to support the decision as the community making the decision. A strong *consensus* component sometimes pairs with a high-value *shame* component—voters determine which way an issue/candidate is swinging and join in voting for the side expected to win. In this way, the shame of losing does not occur, and the appearance of unity is maintained even as some may feel private dissatisfaction with the decision.

Judgmental–Nonjudgmental

Members of cultures with a high-value *judgmental* component in their worldviews tend to scrutinize their own and others' actions for mistakes as defined by the one who judges. The general outlook is critical of others and even self. Finding fault helps identify and eliminate problems. Critical thinking is used toward making a person, plan, situation, etc. better. Criticism may result in division as such is seen to disrupt harmony and self-esteem, in which case the perceived failure is not experienced in a positive manner. A high *judgmental* value often pairs with high *prescriptive*, *functional*, and/or *guilt* value components.

Members of cultures with a high *nonjudgmental* value component in their worldviews value harmony. Critical thinking expressed in public (and resulting solutions) is discouraged even when some may be dissatisfied with a person, situation, or group. This is in order to maintain cohesiveness within the community. Actions within the community are often not publicly criticized, but actions by those outside a defined community can be safely condemned.

The Western missionary was outraged. Two young men (West African) had privately told him that another man in the community was misusing community funds. They were adamant in their accusation. The missionary pondered how best to address the situation. He discussed with the two young men, and they came up with a solution. There was a town council meeting. He would bring it up, and with the backing of the accusers, the problem could be addressed. The council occurred that evening. The missionary gathered his courage and stood up. Everyone got quiet. The missionary stated the problem and proposed a solution so that it could not happen again. He turned to the two young men for support. They had disappeared. They did not want to be guilty of publicly acknowledging the problem. The issue was not discussed further, and the problem quietly disappeared. The missionary learned a lesson about judging in a culture where a non-judging component was more valued than his own.

The *judgmental* value component seeks to resolve problems at the risk of conflict. The *nonjudgmental* value component seeks to avoid shame. A high *nonjudgmental* value often pairs with high values for *shame*, *indirect*, and *role*.

Direct–Indirect

Some have worldviews with a high-value *direct* component toward dealing with confrontation. Problems are stated to another in a direct manner and solutions found. *Direct* confrontation risks fractured relationship when not resolved, but stating one's opinion publicly and clearly is considered desirable and healthy for society as resolution occurs.

Worldviews formed in other cultures prefer surface harmony over the disruption caused by direct confrontation. These cultures have a high-value *indirect* component in confrontation. A problem occurs and a third party provides the communication link toward a solution between the offended parties. Often a parable or proverb is used to indirectly correct an offender. Everyone may know the offender targeted by the parable, but the target's name is not mentioned publicly. In this way, shame is avoided and harmony maintained.

The Western missionary was angry. He had purchased limited medical supplies and gave them to those in need guided by a missionary medical manual, "Where There Is No Doctor." He was not a medical person, but there were no other options for the townspeople, so they appreciated his medical knowledge about headaches, intestinal worms, and malaria. More and more townspeople started coming for help. He instituted a minimal charge toward replacing medicines. Then he overheard two ladies talking. One claimed to the other that the missionary was getting rich by charging for medicines. The missionary felt misunderstood. The charge didn't even come close to cover the price he paid. He packed away the medical supplies and refused to listen to any more medical complaints. The town chief visited him and asked why he no longer was helping the town with medicines. The missionary explained. The chief called the town council to listen. The town council apologized on behalf of the community. The two ladies' names were never mentioned, but harmony was restored when the missionary, by now feeling rather sheepish, began again to treat those who had headaches, worms, and malaria.

Direct/indirect component values within a worldview often parallel high/low values for *guilt/shame* and/or *judgmental/nonjudgmental*. The *direct* value pairs with *judgment* to resolve the problem, while the *indirect* value seeks to avoid *shame*.

Low Knowledge Context–High Knowledge Context

Those with a high *high-knowledge* value in their worldviews rely on the knowledge of those within the context to navigate within the culture's context, as demonstrated in the following example.

The Western visitor was excited. It was his first time in the capital city, Addis Ababa. He purchased a map outside his hotel in the southern part of the city and found a taxi driver who spoke his language. He asked the driver to take him to St. George Cathedral in the north part of the city. "No problem," said the driver. Ten minutes later it was apparent the driver was lost. The Westerner attempted to help with his new map. The driver listened politely, but there were no road signs to affirm the map, so the driver pulled over and asked someone a question. That seemed to provide some clarity, so again they took off. Five minutes later, the driver pulled over again to query someone on the side of the road. He found his answer, and they continued. It took several more helpful answers from those on the side of the road, but they arrived. The taxi driver offered to stay with the visitor for the ride back. The Westerner agreed—he did not want to repeat the uncomfortable experience of not knowing where he was or if he would arrive at his destination.

Those with high *low-knowledge* value, such as the Western visitor above, depend upon resources outside of self and the community. It is possible to arrive at the airport in Johannesburg, South Africa, rent a car, and follow the signs on the road to arrive at one's destination by using a map. All without asking for directions from locals. With Google Maps, it is even easier. This is not the case where there are few road signs for outsiders; rather, only the high inner knowledge of those who live within the context.

Right/Wrong–Good/Evil

The roles of *right/wrong–good/evil* have application both within and outside theological approach. God's law shows us where we err in his purpose for us. The good news of Scripture announces God's grace of Jesus the Christ reconciling us to God (2 Cor 5:18) that we might live in his purpose. Scripture tells the story of this ongoing and eternal triumph of God's good over Satan's evil starting in Genesis and ending in the book of Revelation.

But these worldview components are also applied in varying strengths outside of this scriptural foundation, as worldviews formed within varying societies apply their values. For example, is abortion good or evil? Or, is abortion right or wrong? Answers may be the same viewed through component values formed with Scripture as primary foundation or by those within societies who value the addition of children to the family. In other portions of society, worldviews may have different components defining moral values. Such dissonance causes alternate answers to the same questions.

Events experienced through a high-value *right/wrong* component point to those judged as wrong or bad. There is a morality attached even where the judgments are provided by society rather than Scripture. Those who adhere to one position are labelled *right*. Those of another position are labelled *wrong*. Objective morality is the sought-after goal. *Right* versus *wrong* is judged by those that follow perceived rules, and those that don't. For example, using the abortion argument, some argue that the choice of the mother is *right* and to not acknowledge such in the context of abortion is *wrong*. Others argue that considering an unborn child first is *right* and to replace that rule with a mother's choice to eliminate the unborn is *wrong*.

The *good/evil* component plays also a role in broader human society—sometimes with scriptural basis and sometimes without—as moral judgments of good and evil for present-life actions are applied through human preference. For example, in some parts of Africa, good or evil is only determined by result: Did an action cause benefit (good) or harm (evil)? Judgments are subjective rather than objective. Again, using the abortion arguments, does someone benefit or is someone harmed? Answers are subjectively applied.

The dynamic between *good/evil* and *right/wrong* value components in life often plays out within God's people as the church. Some apply God's law through moral high-value *right/wrong* or *good/evil* components within their worldviews. This is not incorrect but, without adjustment, moves toward a focus on justice, morality, or action toward humanly defined good, rather than the freedom of the gospel which saves from evil and self.

CONCLUSION

What happens when those in a culture with high *hospitable*, *relational*, and *traditional* value components come together with those from a culture with high *right/wrong*, *prescriptive*, and *task-oriented* value components? Worldview clash!

An example of such clash occurs in church relations. Christians in both Ethiopian and Western Lutheran church bodies may have the same biblical understanding of real presence—Christ's body and blood within the elements of the Lord's Supper—but differing values within worldviews cause a clash in practice. In Ethiopia a high value for *hospitality* includes the sharing of food. The value for *hospitality* pairs with a high value for *relationship*. A refusal to share food is seen as serious and dishonors the relationship with those from whom food is withheld. These worldview values exist within the practice of sharing the Lord's Supper within the EECMY, the largest Lutheran church body in the world. Members from some Western church bodies visit Ethiopia with different value components in their worldviews, such as *right/wrong* and/or *prescriptive*.[18] Members of these church bodies practice the Lord's Supper to exclude those without an officially sanctioned relationship between their church bodies. Visitors from Ethiopia are surprised and fail to understand why they are excluded in some evangelical Lutheran churches in the Western world. Conversely, within Ethiopia, church members are not positively impacted by Lutheran visitors who refuse the fellowship relationship offered when sharing the Lord's Supper. The reasons may be passionate for each set of behaviors, but as exhibited without understanding the other's values, worldview clash occurs in practice and relationship is affected.[19]

The concept of worldview and value components within a single culture bears mentioning since value components also raise barriers and cause interrelational clash at a local level. For example, as worldviews are formed in childhood, the family context may include trauma, parental abuse, or other dysfunction as a consequence of a sinful human condition. In result, components such as *mistrust* and/or *abandonment*

18. As in, imposing of forms determined as correct.

19. The breaking of historical fellowship in 2013 by the EECMY with the Evangelical Lutheran Church of America (ELCA) and Church of Sweden over same-sex issues was quite momentous since it meant the sharing of the Lord's Supper would no longer occur. From the Ethiopian perspective, it meant they took the issue seriously. To not allow members of those churches to participate in the Lord's Supper equates with an acknowledgment of lack of valued relationship.

are formed with significant strength. One with such formed values will assume others are not trustworthy or supportive and will view them with suspicion. This causes clash affecting interpersonal relationships unless one modifies worldview discernment by adjusting or adopting value components through spiritual growth that reduces effects. As Jesus followers we are justified by faith (Rom 5:1) and enter into the process of sanctification and peace with God with the help of the Holy Spirit. Our model is Jesus: "Looking to Jesus, the founder and perfecter of our faith, who for the joy that was set before him endured the cross, despising the shame, and is seated at the right hand of the throne of God. Consider him who endured from sinners such hostility against himself, so that you may not grow weary or fainthearted" (Heb 12:2–3). Our values as those who know Jesus are found through Jesus, who considers us of value (Luke 12:7), rather than through worldview values formed outside our place in the story given by God through Jesus. Expanding one's own worldview through understanding our value components contributes positively and lowers barriers to relationships, which is integral to our life in Christ—the process of sanctification—whether for cross-cultural or interpersonal interaction.

Differing value strengths within worldviews pose barriers for relationship and communication of the gospel message we carry. Failure to identify and lower barriers to the gospel message results in worldviews which collide and clash. Misperception occurs and the gospel, though proclaimed, may not be heard through the barriers formed. The Holy Spirit calls, gathers, and enlightens the people of God as his people where we hear the gospel. Our actions, the forms we use, and the words in which we communicate bear examining into forms which lower barriers to those to whom we carry the message of salvation found in Jesus' death and resurrection on the cross—a message for the whole world.

8

Mission and Animist Worldview

The Spiritual Battle

THE CHRISTIAN FOUNDATION IS the word of God recorded through Scripture (the Bible). The Bible not only records God's relationship with his people written by multiple authors over many generations, it also provides description and comprehension of God's intent for all nations. It is the story of our salvation. God's good, Satan's evil, and humankind's place within are all present. The story starts in Genesis and ends in Revelation. Communicated through the varied languages of the world, one can only marvel at the reality of the story and the power of God's faithfulness to faithless people. We learn of our broken relationship with him. We see God sending his Son, Jesus, to die for humankind on the cross and be raised again so that relationship with him might be fully restored.

For those who trust Scripture, the narrative is one of truth and ultimate triumph of God's good over evil. We know the ending. That is a comfort. But we are still in the midst of the story, and the nature of evil seeks to point humankind away from the relationship God intends. We have the freedom of will—the ability to choose those things that God does not desire for us. That freedom has consequence. Evil as a choice cannot be minimized. Exploring the nature of spiritual warfare is essential for the follower of Christ. Additionally, and important for mission, one who understands how one's own communication, actions, forms, rituals, and symbols may be interpreted differently than intended can reduce barriers to others, allowing them to more fully understand the reality of the gospel message.

For the reader seeking accounts of demons and demon possession, this chapter will not meet that desire. This does not mean that such does not occur but rather that this author is not independently able to verify observations within as an underlying case of demon possession. They may have been, but maybe not, and this author's Western worldview affects interpretation of such events. The reader will have to visit different sources which claim authority over that aspect of the spiritual. Rather, this chapter seeks to bridge the gap in understanding between dualistic secular cultures and spiritually holistic cultures by presenting examples and conclusions through both. The unseen is mysterious, and we as authors choose to examine occasions of spiritual beings, evil, and such possession in two often opposing opposites: as revealed in Scripture, or everything else.

THE ROLE OF SCRIPTURE—FOUNDATION FOR TRUTH

The authors acknowledge the fervent faith feelings of those within the religions of this world, some with holy books and others not, but this chapter is based on the premise that Christian Scripture is the message of God's truth through which the power of the Holy Spirit brings faith.

Acknowledging such is less difficult today than in the past. Some tout contemporary Christianity as evolved from primitive religious form,[1] while others denounce Christian Scripture as a fantasy.[2] However the wealth of Mideastern archeological evidence unearthed in the last decade cumulatively affirms multiple events recorded in Scripture. Perhaps more reassuring, no evidence has been unearthed to date which proves its recorded data false. In the face of available data, we can state with confidence that it takes more faith to claim Scripture a fantasy than to believe it true. Even theory developed within the scientific paradigm points more toward the reasonableness of recorded events in Scripture rather than away. Professor of mathematics Peter Stoner, in his book *Science Speaks*, put some of his students on determining the odds of multiple biblical prophecies being randomly fulfilled. Together they deduced that if only eight messianic prophecies were fulfilled, and there have been more,[3] the odds of random fulfillment was one in ten to the seventeenth power

1. Ambrosino, "How and Why."
2. Robinson, "Bible Is Fantasy."
3. Bernis, "How Many Messianic Prophecies."

(10^{17}). It could happen but is a scientific improbability.[4] Science provides confidence from outside Scripture to those serving within God's mission. The scriptural foundation for Christianity and the nature of spiritual warfare described within is that of reality, not fantasy, even as it may be interpreted in variant ways through dissimilar human worldviews.

This chapter presents the nature and exhibition of evil in opposition to God's love for his people, then moves to the animist spiritual cosmos and precepts behind animist methods—ritual, possession, and use of names and numbers for supplication/propitiation. This in order for the mission-focused reader to better understand how the animist lens provides interpretation. It continues with a discussion on animist practice as it appears in different societies and religions throughout the world and ends with observations and insight gained from Old and New Testament texts viewed through the animist worldview lens. Through this look, we see our Trinitarian God as the consistent and unique God of grace who calls his people to follow and serve him because of who he is, not the other way around.

DECEPTION AND THE PEOPLE OF THE LIE

Scripture provides clarity toward understanding the nature of evil. Satan is described as the *deceiver of the world* (Rev 12:9)—the opposite of God's truth. The description of Satan and deception begins in Gen 3, recorded in a narrative often termed as "the fall." What God as creator has pronounced as good is presented in a manner that contains deception—if the woman eats from the tree of the knowledge of good and evil, she is told, "You will not surely die. . . . [Rather] you will be like God, knowing good and evil" (Gen 3:4–5). Human innocence within God's creation is traded for the lie of not dying and the dubious value of knowing evil.

We create our own worldview lenses within this fallen paradigm. The truth of Scripture, and knowledge of the promise of God to send Jesus as Savior, is not present through our own determinations of good/evil, right/wrong, etc. Conflict is inevitable. Christ-followers trust the promise that evil is defeated through Jesus, but in the meantime, all humankind struggles. Innocence is gone and human nature affected by deception through which evil then exhibits. Psychologist M. Scott Peck wrote *People of the Lie*, a classic tome which discusses psychological aspects of

4. See Stoner, *Science Speaks*, ch. 3.

good and evil. He thoughtfully acknowledges cases of probable demon possession and how such is exhibited through what he terms *people of the lie*.[5] Through untruth, humans are pointed away from God's purpose for us. The symptoms and details of action which point away from God and his desire for humankind may be myriad, but the commonality is deception—the lie. Where we succumb, we become implementing agents for evil's chaos within the world. Evil consequence may be the result of direct demon possession or our fallen human nature. It does not matter; it is evil consequence. The deceiving world has a goal, pointing humankind away from God's story of salvation and, in the doing, seeking to draw humans deeper and deeper into its effect, which may include demon possession.

We know the ending. God has already defeated death and Satan's effect on our lives (1 Cor 15:54–57). But that does not mean that a spiritual warfare battle is no longer present. And so we find ourselves watchful, acknowledging ourselves as not good within ourselves, while through the power of the Holy Spirit, we are both protected from evil and given the strength to believe God's truth and hold on to him through Jesus (Eph 6:10–18).

GOD'S LAW—POINTING US FROM EVIL

Lies and deception are the overt symptoms by which evil may be identified. Where lies exhibit, evil occurs in opposition to God's truth. In the chapter on worldview, we talked briefly about the differences between the *good/evil* and *right/wrong* worldview components applied outside God's law. Viewed through the *right/wrong* component within Scripture, God's law shows us where we miss the mark, why we need his gift of grace through Jesus. Viewed through the *good/evil* component formed within Scripture, God's law not only shows us where we miss the mark in what God desires for us but also is a gift which points us away from actions that have consequences affecting us into the evil paradigm. The human context is not spiritually neutral. It is not possible to gain God's good by following his law, but where we fail to follow, we open ourselves to evil and its consequence.

5. Peck, *People of the Lie*.

THE HUMAN ROLE IN SPIRITUAL WARFARE

Humankind has a propensity for seeking out the spiritual for one's own self-benefit, both in physical existence and spiritual world afterlife. In Exod 20:3 God declares his purpose for his people, "You shall have no other *elohim* [spiritual power(s) / god(s)] before Me." He additionally admonishes not to create carved images or any likeness of anything below the earth, above the sky, or below the waters for the purpose of worship and serving other spiritual powers. Left to ourselves, we create our own spiritual realities in opposition to God's purpose. It is our fallen nature. Even members of secular society who purport no religious or spiritual basis are innately challenged by the human propensity for spiritual effect. Iris Murdoch, a secular atheist claiming no spiritual basis, states her challenge—the only way to be good is to be good for nothing.[6]

Examining human approaches standing in opposition to God's story of salvation demonstrates the width of spiritual warfare deceptions through which the spiritual battle plays out. A universal term for such approaches is desired, and found, in the term *animism*.

ANIMISM DEFINED

The term *animism* is historically used as a label for religions practiced by societies described as primitive. One provided definition is, "The doctrine that all natural objects and the universe itself have souls."[7] Such description is misleading. While not untrue that primitive religion practice is a form of animism, it is a mistake to assume that animism is confined to primitive society. Noted by secular anthropologist Marvin Harris, "Animistic beliefs [are] to be found in every society, and a century of ethnological research has yet to turn up a single exception."[8]

Animism is defined observing its practice. Members of human society, whether holistic, dualist, pluralist, historic, or contemporary, are naturally tempted toward animist practice by our nature, not reason. Those who enter into animist practice have difficulty explaining. This author was questioning a local man within the Kalanga community in Botswana on the details of propitiating dead ancestors and ancestral

6. Murdoch, *Sovereignty of Good*, 71.

7. Vocabulary.com Dictionary, s.v. "animism," https://www.vocabulary.com/dictionary/animism.

8. Harris, "Why We Became Religious," 7.

relationship with the creator/high god (*Ndzimu*). The man said with a laugh, "It doesn't matter. What matters is if it works!" For the human end user, the import is found in the question, How effective was my action toward causing the supernatural to meet my perceived problem?[9]—a symptom of our fallen human-centric nature.

Animism occurs in traditional religions and neo-pagan practices. It can be identified within the world's major religions and occurs even under the guise of Christian practice. The gospel proclaimer who fails to understand its universal presence—however exhibited through surface form—fails to lower animist barriers to the gospel message. He/she may even raise barriers through mission methods casually observed by the intended receiver as just another form of animist supplication and propitiation.

SEEKING THE SPIRITUAL—ANIMIST PRACTICE

Animist practice has a basic underlying principle—the practitioner has a desire. He/she seeks to fulfill that desire by accessing the spiritual world in a manner sufficient to attain that desire. Lutheran Christian dogmatician Francis Pieper points to the big picture. He writes, "[There are] only two essentially different religions."[10] He defines those two religions: the first as the "religion of the Gospel, that is, faith in the Lord Jesus Christ, belief wrought through the Gospel by the Holy Ghost that we have a gracious God through the reconciliation already effected by Christ, and not because of our own works";[11] and the second, endeavoring to reconcile with God through man's own works.

Pieper's statement is based primarily upon a theological discussion of reconciliation of Christ's victory over death for human spiritual existence as it extends into the afterlife rather than the here-and-now self-benefit of much animist practice. But the statement is still universally valid—there are only two religions in the world: (a) our Trinitarian God providing his free gift of grace to us, to which we respond, and (b) everything else. There is simple contrast. Christian life is lived through God's grace. God's people are the result of what God does through Jesus and the power of the Holy Spirit. God's action is first. We respond through faith given, in gratefulness to what has been done for us (see figure 6). There is nothing we can do to

9. Rodewald "Observing Sacred and Profane," 73.

10. Pieper, *Christian Dogmatics*, 1:10.

11. Pieper, *Christian Dogmatics*, 1:10.

earn God's action in our lives. All is accomplished for us through Christ as a matter of God's grace. Ours is to believe and live out God's purpose by the power of the Holy Spirit. Accomplishment is not ours.

Figure 6: Christian Worldview

Animism and its approaches to the spiritual world are the opposite of that just described. It is the everything else. In animist practice, the practitioner initiates. The spiritual world is hoped to respond in the manner desired (see figure 7), whether for benefits in this world or perceived afterlife.

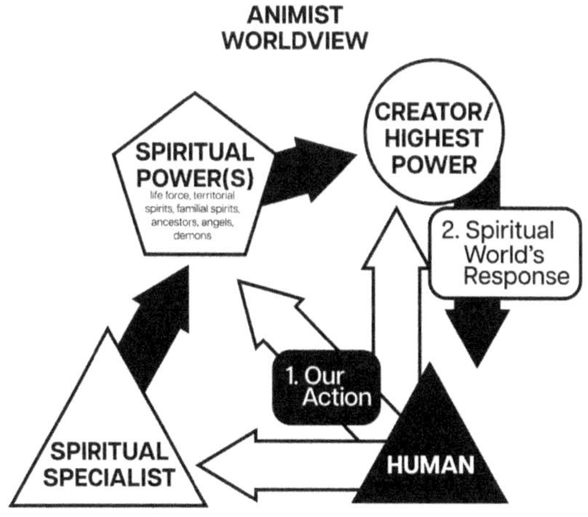

Figure 7: Animist Worldview

In its practice it points toward self and away from the true nature of a loving God and his purpose for humankind. There is a spectrum. If the animist practitioner does not perceive a desired result, temptation toward more and deeper animist supplication occurs—spiritual self-deception leads to more deception. Evil is awaiting.

PRECEPTS WITHIN ANIMIST PRACTICE

There are no primary animist religious texts with which to deduce a formal religious system. However, as a practice found in every human society,[12] it is possible to observe its details and derive underlying principles. Details may be different from society to society, but in their totality, common principle occurs.

Causal Link

The spiritual and physical worlds are considered mysteriously linked through animist practice. A proverb from Liberia (West Africa) captures this notion, "Nothing happens for nothing!" There is no coincidence in societies overtly involved. Actions in the physical world are felt to cause the spiritual world to respond and vice versa. At the other end of the animist spectrum are those in dualist societies whose members' worldviews relegate animist practice to individual or limited group activity, often dismissed as superstition. Yet the mysterious causal link is common to both.

This author was living in a town in West Africa existing within a holistic-oriented society. Members did not recognize coincidence, rather every physical effect was thought linked to the spiritual. One day, a crowd began to gather at the house next to the author's house. When the author went to see what was happening, a young man was laying on the floor writhing and foaming at the mouth. Someone in the crowd said that the man had traditional *medicine*[13] in the form of a charm to help get the wife he wanted. But the *medicine* had rules. The young man had broken the rules, and now the power behind the *medicine* had turned on him. Someone suggested that a local traditional doctor (*sowoi*) be visited, and I (the author) could take someone there since I had a motorbike. I agreed. When we came to the *sowoi*'s house, an old man sitting in front stood up before we could get

12. Harris, "Why We Became Religious," 7.

13. Spiritual power made available through an object.

off the motorbike. He did not ask any questions but rather said, "Go back. The problem is solved." When we returned, the young man was walking around. My Western worldview provided much rationalization, but in the local worldview, the spiritual world had been appeased.

Similar occurs in dualist/pluralist societies, as found in the West. Animist notion is in our human nature. An airplane passenger, Westerner Brian Morris, remarked of his ritual of touching an airplane as he boards, "It's funny how our minds work; I thought that this little act somehow warded off danger, even though, deep down, I knew it was just a superstition."[14] Fans of sports teams may wear specific garb in order to bring "luck" to the efforts of their team, with the underlying premise—even where not cognitive—that by wearing specific garb they *somehow* cause an undefined spiritual world to affect desired outcome. Often dismissed as harmless superstition, fans are persistent and continue to try to find ways to accomplish their desire even in the face of failure. Perhaps a different jersey? If that doesn't work, try something else—all in an attempt to manipulate the mysterious to affect the outcome! Note the similarity to sporting events in Africa, which include animist rituals such as fervent chanting or drumming throughout a football (soccer) match, hoping to affect outcome. If a loss occurs, the actions were not sufficient for the spiritual world to respond in the way wished. Or, perhaps the opposing team's rituals were just more effective?

The Created Spiritual Cosmos Within Animist Worldview

Scripture points to truth. Humankind creates its spiritual worlds outside that truth. Every culture and society has inputs which then affect the worldview lens of its members' interaction with the spiritual world.

The majority animist concept of the spiritual cosmos includes recognition of an ultimate spiritual power—a somewhat dimly defined creator spirit or high god. Such creator spirit may be viewed as responsible for all spiritual power through creation, but its current being is perceived as distant, diffuse, or not directly approachable. Rather, there are additional beings—ancestors, demons, angels, or other spiritual power types linked to religious, national, tribal, territorial, household/religious groups or individuals, and nature—through which to access more or less of the creator spirit's power. Since these spiritual beings are viewed closer to the

14. DiMella, "Flight Passengers' Ritual."

creator spirit than humans, they are sensed to be more readily available as intercessors for propitiation and supplication.

In addition to power accessed through spiritual beings, physical objects are felt to contain more or less of the creator spirit's power, provided or leftover from creation. Natural features such as mountains, rivers, large bodies of water, rocks, or trees may home specific spiritual beings but are also often considered natural repositories of diffuse spiritual power. Living objects such as animals and humans may also be felt to contain a mysterious spiritual aura/energy. Such created, mysterious, and diffuse power is labeled for use through a variety of terms; life force, mana, kismet, astrology, fate, and supernatural aura or energy, among others (see table 1).

Hiebert, Shaw, and Tienou dissect the details in their analysis of folk religion systems by dividing human perception of the supernatural into high (heavenly) and low (earthly) frames, organic (moral/immoral) and mechanical (amoral), unseen (supernatural) and seen (empirical/physical).[15]

The provided chart (table 1) expands upon Hiebert, Shaw, and Tienou's analysis to provide a wider paradigm of animist perceptions of spiritual power. The details concocted by the world's varied worldviews are not possible to list in a comprehensive manner, but in summary, there are two ways that amounts of spiritual power sourced to the creator spirit / high god become available: through (a) spirit-beings, and (b) a mysterious supernatural energy labelled variously as life force, fate, mana, karma, etc. Physical methods are used to supplicate, propitiate, and manipulate this power as available through specific spirit-beings or sacred objects. Successful propitiation is believed to empower one's own purpose.

Hiebert additionally calls out "the flaw of the excluded middle"[16] present in Western society, in which members in mission often actively exclude unseen spiritual activity within the physical (earthly) frame. In the doing, Westerners largely limit physical interactions to physical (empirical)[17] interaction while excluding the spiritual. This does not mean that animist practice and spiritual activity on the physical plane is not active in Western society, just that it is not overtly identified or acknowledged as in other societies and cultures.

15. Hiebert et al., *Understanding Folk Religions*, 49.

16. Hiebert, "Flaw of the Excluded Middle."

17. Knowledge based upon verification by observation or experience.

Table 1: Animist Spiritual Worldview Paradigm

<table>
<tr><td colspan="4">Creator Spirit / High God</td></tr>
<tr><td colspan="2">Organic Moral/Immoral</td><td colspan="2">Inorganic Amoral</td></tr>
<tr><td rowspan="2">Unseen, super-natural</td><td>Other-worldly spirit-beings, Satan, cosmic gods</td><td>Life force, fate, luck, kismet, destiny, super-natural aura, natural energy, karma, mana, diffuse spiritual power</td><td>Other worldly, consisting in other worlds or time</td></tr>
<tr><td>*Spiritual power as spirit-beings accessed as tribal, clan, family, or territorial spirits, local gods and goddesses, ancestors, ghosts, saints, angels, de-mons, jinn, genies, devils</td><td>*Spiritual power ac-cessed as life-force or supernatural energy present in or through physical objects, such as charms, amulets, relics, crystals, evil eye, lucky foot, images, shrines, graves, statues, features of nature (mountains, rivers/ waters, ancient trees, or ruins)</td><td rowspan="3">This world, consisting in present physical plane</td></tr>
<tr><td rowspan="2">Seen or em-pirical, observed directly through senses</td><td colspan="2">*Methods of access to spiritual power: rites, ritual, mantras, power identifiers by name or number, taboos, dreams/visions, divination, voodoo, posses-sion, witchcraft, magic, astrology</td></tr>
<tr><td>Human intellect, human affect and decision-making</td><td>Natural law, science</td></tr>
<tr><td colspan="4">Spiritual power activity as appears in the shaded center quadrant is often not cognitively attributed by the majority within societies affected by Western secu-larism and its worldviews. Rather, members of Western societies tend to ascribe physical cause and effect to either the empirical, superstition, or coincidence/ happenstance. Paul Hiebert describes Western missionaries' cultural failure to perceive direct spiritual activity perceived by members of other cultures they seek to reach as the "flaw of the excluded middle."</td></tr>
</table>

Spiritual Beings

Not every member of every society applies worldview in a way that includes a comprehensive total of the spiritual beings believed to exist in the spiritual world. It is only through observation of practice within a single society that its beings are described and through multiple societies that a totality can be approximated. Chul Hwan Kim presents data from Taegon Kim, a scholar of Korean folklore. He records 273 different types of spirits in Korean shamanism. These are classified into twenty-two nature categories (heavenly, earthly, mountain, road, water, wind, tree, stone, demon, animal, agriculture, etc.) and eleven human spirit categories (royal [king/queen], commander, ancestral, bride, Taoistic, etc.), as well as several miscellaneous spirits. This total is but one Korean perspective. Another, from a shaman located on one of Korea's southern islands, claims eighteen thousand spirits present in a house built for gods and spirits to repose.[18] Douglas Thomas claims more than seventeen hundred subordinate deities (*orisha*) of the high god *Olodumare* in Yoruba (Nigeria) society. One such is *Ogun*, the deity of iron and steel. *Ogun* is perceived as a war deity and resides on the top of hills. Sacrifices to him are made for protection from knives, guns, road accidents, and machinery accidents. He has many houses in heaven and places marks on individuals which are thought to keep them in good health.[19] The Kalanga ethnic group of Botswana historically accessed spiritual power in this category largely through ancestors. Ancestors were perceived to be the cause of trouble or have the power to help by making creator-spirit (*Ndzimu*) power available to those who propitiate. A specific ancestor's (*ndzimu*) presence would not be known until its name was divined. Some such ancestral spirits were discontent in personality (*kabah*) and as such caused problems. They needed to be placated for problems to go away.[20] In Western secular societies, members may acknowledge a mysterious force identified as "God" while "demythologizing" demons, angels, or ghosts. Some as atheists may not acknowledge the presence of *any* spiritual power. There is much uncertainty in the animist cosmos. It is only through mysterious animist methods of propitiation or divining that questions might be answered. Mystery answers mystery.

18. Kim, "Central Issues," 63–65.

19. Thomas, *African Traditional Religion*, 90–91.

20. Rodewald, "Observing Sacred and Profane," 29–30.

Supernatural Energy / Life Force

Life force is perceived as a diffuse amoral supernatural spiritual power or energy available for physical use. Among the Bandi ethnic group of Liberia, this diffuse power is acknowledged as sourced from *Ngalangi* (the high god), as power infused from creation,[21] a common if not always precisely stated understanding. Alternate terms used to describe this mysterious power are mana, essence of life, aura, or natural energy, among others. The concept behind the use of life force in animist practice is to harness power existing in one space and apply it for the benefit of the user in another space using physical objects through which more or less of this power is available *if* one knows how to access it.

A Western-worldview synonym for the mechanics of life force is the dimly defined concept of "luck." Energy provided through possession of a lucky rabbit foot is hoped to provide good outcome for the user—an underlying attempt to harness life force for one's own purpose. Animist practice may be found in varying degrees in attempts to harness the life force / energy of crystals, mountains, rivers, trees, animals, and even humans. Everyone has more or less access to life force, as in the case with a rabbit foot. But it is also possible to turn to a specialist who, it is hoped, knows how to harness such force for best effect.

Attempts to access life force and its mysterious power are viewed as harmless superstitions by some. But such attempts may also be made in a less innocuous manner. In some societies, the life force of a human being is forcefully accessed. The method is to murder an individual and harvest body parts for a specific purpose (love, health, wealth). The more a victim struggles, the stronger the life force is thought to be when captured in any portions of human flesh harvested.[22] Objects such as charms and amulets are imbued with such captured life force, which then works toward the purpose wished. The most efficacious human life force is thought to be that of a child since its force is believed to continue to grow in its ability to assist. Perhaps the most diabolical of all is the notion that the life force of one's own child is believed to harness most powerfully toward fulfilling *your* "need." Eileen Krige records the phenomenon among the Zulu of

21. The Islamic term *baraka* captures the notion of life force. Baraka is said to be given by God and may be transferred to other people or objects (Hiebert et al., *Understanding Folk Religions*, 69).

22. Rodewald, "Observing Sacred and Profane," 34–35. Also note that a number of these observations were obtained through conversation with T. M. Mbulawa who served in the Botswana Police CID and investigated such as murders.

southern Africa for the purpose of crop growing: "For making the best medicine for *sukula*'ing [growing crops], it is said that you must kill your child, your firstborn son. Certain parts of his flesh must be eaten with medicines, while others are mixed with the seed."[23]

The concept of using life force within the spiritual power paradigm is also practiced in the secular West, felt to be a harmless spiritual approach worth "a try" even where not supported by science. Note the following quote from healthline.com, a Western medical website, on the use of energy from crystals:

> "Crystals are made up of different elements or compounds, which our bodies react to in different ways," says Sonali Saujani, a crystal master healer. "Crystals are minerals that hold energy, and as we as humans are made up of energy, we can exchange energy with the crystal when we work with it." . . . Although science doesn't support crystals as a healing modality, *there's no harm in giving them a try* if you have realistic expectations about what they can and can't do.[24]

Life force as a supernatural energy or spiritual power is defined through its use. Though sometimes perceived as originating from a supreme being through creation, life force has no moral quality in itself. Rather it is through its use that good, bad, or evil occur, as defined by the user and felt by those affected.

Propitiation and supplication through life force as supernatural energy has rules specific to use and context. These rules may be known to the user. They may also be unknown, determinable only after breaking them and failing to achieve the desired result. The breaking of rules is failure of life force to perform as desired and may even bring negative effect. More supplication must occur in order to alleviate bad effect or in an effort to attain still unfulfilled desire. It is a slippery slope. The attempt to access life force, whether viewed as successful or not, opens the door to more attempts. The increase moves the practitioner toward evil's purpose through consistent invitation and further away from God's purpose.

It is appropriate to contrast animist notions of life force and spiritual beings toward the concept of demons presented in Scripture. Spiritual beings termed *demons* exist. They know Jesus as the Christ. Jesus has power over them (see such as Luke 4:41). They may even take possession

23. Krige, *Social System of the Zulus*, 192.

24. Rekstis, "Healing Crystals 101"; emphasis mine.

of a human's spiritual and physical life. But not every case of evil is determinable to direct activity of spiritual beings termed *demons*. Rather demons await as our human-centric nature seeks our own spiritual solutions through propitiating spirits or manipulating life force and, in the doing, creates invitation for deceptive "demons" to enter with their effect.

God calls his people to serve and follow in response to him. His love is provided not only through his law given to point us away from evil but also through his grace sending Jesus as Savior and the Holy Spirit as Helper to produce faith. In this way, he calls us into his kingdom and away from consequences that move us from God's desire into the realm of evil.

Ritual

Ritual is perceived as a key for accessing spiritual power. In the animist world, the practitioner contacts, propitiates, and supplicates the spiritual world through rituals, rites, and/or mantras. These are discerned as a method which sources spiritual power that can be used for protection, riches, success in love or business, witchcraft, spiritual blessing, evil, or other purpose of the user.

Rituals, rites, and their mantras may be simple. For example, some Muslims spit to ward off *jinns*.[25] At other times rituals are complex. Simple or complex, it is in correct practice that the key turns and unlocks spiritual power for the desired purpose. The spiritual world is not blamed where rituals do not accomplish its purpose. Rather, failure is considered that of incorrect performance—the key did not turn. Philip Steyne explains,

> A ritual is a formula for eliciting help from the spirit world and mastering nature to serve man's purpose. . . . If the devotee or officiant to the ritual says the right chant or mantra, performs the right sacrifice, or goes through a liturgy in a particular order, the god or spirit must do such and such. The efficacy of the ritual has nothing to do with the inner disposition or marital character of the officiant or recipient . . . the use of correct forms is indispensable in securing the desired objectives.[26]

Rituals are considered efficacious to bind spiritual power without subservience to the power beneath the ritual. As noted by Steyne, the

25. A lower-ranking spiritual power within the Islamic spiritual cosmos, thought able to possess humans or animals.

26. Steyne, *Gods of Power*, 93–94.

efficacy of ritual has nothing to do with the moral character of the practitioner. As example, religious specialists termed *pretsavan* of Haitian voodoo are said to imbed a Latin form of Catholic ritual into their rituals for invoking voodoo spirits.[27]

Some animist rituals involve sacrifice—even human sacrifice—in their attempt to influence the spiritual. In Ethiopia among the Kambata people group, a priest on the mountain was traditionally declared the manifestation (*magananch*o) of the Kambata's creator spiritual power (*maganno*, *maganacho*). This god-priest instructed child sacrifice to Kambata practitioners in order to ward off further calamity, sickness, and the death of other children in the family.[28]

The efficacy of animist ritual depends both upon correct performance and the presence and type of power invoked through ritual. It is a double-edged sword. If not performed correctly, an incorrect ritual is thought to cause unhappiness within the spiritual world. This brings negative result. When this happens, additional steps must be taken in what becomes a revolving cycle of disharmony. A narrative earlier in this chapter recounted a young man (in a largely animist context) writhing on the floor and foaming at the mouth. Upon query to a bystander, the author was told that the young man had a "charm" to cause a young lady to love him. But the "charm" had "rules" of performance attached which had to be followed. The young man had failed to follow them correctly. The power brought through the charm had turned on him. The only solution, according to a bystander, was to seek restitution through a *sowoi*, a local traditional doctor who as a religious specialist could play the role of intercessor.

Religious Specialists

If rituals are the key to unlocking spiritual power, the religious specialist is viewed as the holder of the keys. They provide intercessory services between the physical and spiritual worlds. Such specialists come in many different forms observed through titles such as shaman, sorcerer, medicine man, wizard, traditional doctor or priest, voodooist, conjurer, crystal gazer, fortune teller, soothsayer, and medium, among others (in

27. Brown, "Voodoo."

28. From a conversation with Dr. Bruk Ayele, July 8, 2024; see also Grenstedt, "Ambaricho and Shonkolla," 53.

English). Not all claim to access the spiritual world in the same ways, but, as noted by Steyne, they have one common purpose: "When all of a man's personal resources for securing life force have been exhausted, he can resort to a religious specialist who has means to capture it and put it at man's disposal—for a price."[29]

Religious specialists viewed through animist worldview have the ability to "help" but also the ability to harm. In Liberia (West Africa), a young man asked the author if he could stay in the missionary house for the day. When queried, he said that a *sowoi* (traditional medicine doctor) wanted to borrow his radio. It would be dangerous for him if he said no, so he was trying to avoid him, hoping that he would forget.[30] The animist worldview lens sees the religious specialist as a resource but is also aware that a dissatisfied religious specialist can use spiritual power to harm.

A religious specialist is viewed as having the knowledge to coerce the spiritual toward one's purpose. If a religious specialist fails, either his/her knowledge is insufficient or a stronger power is at work. A Loma traditional doctor was called to heal a young woman in the Bandi[31] town in which this author was living in Liberia. Traditional doctors (*zowoi*) from a neighboring related ethnic group (Loma) were locally renowned—considered able to do things that Bandi *sowoi* could not. I had mentally diagnosed the girl [*Mboway*, by name] as mentally ill, maybe schizophrenic? I asked if I could observe. The *zowoi* was accommodating, and we engaged in conversation. He mixed herbs with palm oil and put the concoction in a pint bottle. He set it in the fire and told me, "If it doesn't break, it will be strong enough to heal her." The bottle broke. He mixed another. It also broke. He announced failure after the third bottle broke in the fire. He packed up his things and acknowledged he did not have access to such power which could heal the girl.[32] The reader's underlying interpretation will depend upon the reader's worldview, but the local perception of power was that a stronger spiritual power was at work than any available to the *zowoi*.

Most religious specialists within animist practice are not accessed to make sense of a spiritual afterlife. That may occur, but the wider use of spiritual specialists is to propitiate and help within the here and now.

29. Steyne, *Gods of Power*, 91.

30. Rodewald, "Observing Sacred and Profane," 42.

31. A town in northern Liberia inhabited primarily by people from the Bandi ethnic group.

32. Rodewald, "Observing Sacred and Profane," 43.

Where sickness, envy, desire, or accident occur, the religious specialist is available to help, most often for payment. However, just as ritual has its double-edge, manipulating the spiritual world through a religious specialist also has its downside. Religious specialists must be kept happy or they may provide negative consequence through the use of such power to which they are believed to have access.

Power Words and Numbers

The animist's spiritual world contains much mystery. Human-centric approach seeks substance in order to better access and bind the mystery toward one's own purpose. One such way, as discussed previously, is ritual whose correct performance is thought efficacious toward causing the spiritual world to respond in the manner desired. Additionally, identifying spiritual power by name,[33] number, or symbol is used within ritual as a way of increasing likelihood toward access and success. There is an opposite side. Incorrect use of spiritual identifiers is thought to risk the spiritual unhappiness of the identified power, bringing unwished result.

The Old Testament narrative recorded in 2 Kgs 5 examined through an animist worldview lens provides a clear example. Outsider Naaman is afflicted with a serious skin disease. His actions reveal him an animist whose spiritual powers in his homeland have failed to heal him. In desperation and on the words of a slave girl, he heads to Israel with a large amount of riches to pay for successful healing. His search ends when he meets Elisha.

But Elisha, as prophet of YHWH, is different from other religious specialists Naaman may have used in the past. Elisha did not supplicate YHWH through ritual or power identifiers as evidenced by Naaman's words in verse 11, "Behold I thought that he would surely come out to me and stand and call upon the name of the Lord [YHWH] his God [*eloha*, "spiritual power"], and wave his hand over the place and cure the leper." Note Naaman does not view this ritual as anything tied to his own relationship with YHWH; rather, he expects Elisha to call upon Elisha's spiritual power (YHWH) for desired result. Elisha as the servant of God refuses to conform to actions required by Naaman's spiritual worldview. He rather sends Naaman with simple instruction—*wash* in the Jordan River seven times. Seven is a number used repeatedly in God's story

33. Van Rheenan, *Communicating Christ*, 224.

of salvation through Scripture to identify YHWH and witnesses to his power over other powers presented in Scripture.

But by this time in the narrative, Naaman has dismissed any spiritual power in the Jordan River. He contrasts with those within his own nation's rivers, "Are not the Abana and Pharpar, the rivers of Damascus, better than all the waters of Israel? Could I not wash in them and be clean?" (v. 12). But Naaman is persuaded into going into the river by his servants, despite his rage.

Naaman's contempt is seen in his next actions. Desired result in animist worldview depends upon correct performance. Incorrect performance risks spiritual anger. Naaman does not care. He follows Elisha's instruction to wash seven times but directly challenges any power within the Jordan River by lightly *dipping* (וַיִּטְבֹּל; v. 14) rather than *washing* (רְחַץ; v. 13). In the doing, Naaman defies the ritual and efficacy of any spiritual power in the river identified by the number seven—a direct insult.

But the unexpected happens. Rather than negative effect, Naaman is healed of his skin disease with flesh like a child's (v. 14). Naaman had never met a spiritual power like this. His previous spiritual paradigm is gone. He is healed, not because of his or Elisha's correct performance but because the spiritual power identified by name and number (YHWH, seven) provided him a gift through the waters of the Jordan. Naaman had met the God of grace. His confession in verse 15 exhibits this understanding. He does not confess meeting yet another powerful spiritual power, but rather he confesses Israel's spiritual power as different than all he had approached in his past, "Behold, I know that there is no God [*elohim*, "spiritual power(s)"] in all the earth but in Israel." Naaman had met the ONE God who calls through his own means and uses his people, as he did Elisha, for his purpose.

This narrative is a powerful missionary text in the Old Testament. It provides a focused comparison of our unique one true God of grace, unmistakable through name and number, providing his blessing and calling to respond because of who he is. This stands against human-centric purpose, which seeks to manipulate the spiritual for desired benefit.[34]

34. Rodewald, "Outside Look."

Charms, Fetishes, and the Part/Whole Concept

Objects, including charms and fetishes, are thought possible to be imbued with spiritual power by those containing the knowledge to do so. Using imbued power for one's own purpose is accomplished through the correct performance of ritual. In this way, it is surmised that protection from evil or other purpose may be obtained by association or close proximity to the object's aura.

Integrated into the use of imbued objects is the notion of part/whole—a piece is linked to the spiritual power contained by the whole. Members of the Bandi ethnic group in northern Liberia carefully gather cut hairs after a haircut so that others cannot gather and use the hair to create charms used to cause harm to the person who just received the haircut. Through the cut hair there is felt to be enough access to harm the whole person. The part/whole concept of accessing spiritual power through a specific object for one's own purpose can be seen in the following example from Botswana.

> A few months ago . . . a friend of ours found some "medicine" placed in the office where she works. This "medicine" was a concoction of substances put together by a witch. It was a little black ball about the size of a marble. Her fellow worker recognized the "medicine" for what it was because he has several family members who deal in witchcraft. They decided to go to a diviner who would throw bones to find out why the "medicine" was placed in the office. The diviner told them that the cleaning woman wanted our friend's job, so she put it in the office to make our friend ill so she would lose her job. Oddly enough our friend's leg had been having a terrible pain in it for a week and she was having trouble walking. He [the diviner] also told them they should get rid of the "medicine" and fire the cleaning girl, but they should not tell her why she had been fired or else she might get angry and do something bad. When this was done our friend's leg was fine.[35]

Interpretation of the details is again dependent upon one's worldview. But notice the attempt to manipulate the spiritual by using an object believed to connect with its power in order to harm another. Whether or not the process and effect is ascribed to coincidence, superstition, or reality, the act itself was intended to harm, evil in its motivation.

35. From Rodewald's *Mission Glimpses* newsletter, Lutheran Bible Translators (Jan./Feb. 1995).

The part/whole concept is also present in graves, shrines, relics, or other objects through which the mysterious aura of life force associated with a known ancestor or otherwise termed spiritual intercessor being[36] is considered accessible for familial, clan, territorial, or group adherents. Graves and shrines are to be venerated to provide health and protection for those nearby. Sacred symbols such as a cross or Bible may be perceived to give access to Christian spiritual power and revered as a method of protection or accessing power believed to be associated with the object. The members of some independent churches in southern Africa put Bibles under their beds for protection. Others use ritual to identify specific Bible verses as a means of accessing power thought to be contained within the verse.[37] Others reportedly cut Bible verses out and ingest them in tea as a way of gaining specific blessing toward their desire.

The part/whole concept through sacred objects also occurs in some who identify as being within the visible Christian church. In the years before the Reformation of the sixteenth century, laity and priests used sacred objects in ceremonies as protection from weather. Weather-protection ceremonies were most commonly held on April 25 (St. Mark's Day) and the week in which Ascension Day fell. These ceremonies were not an officially recognized act of the institutional church, but they were still practiced by its members. After Latin Mass there was an outdoor procession into the fields to invoke divine protection on crops and cattle. It was customary to carry elements of the Eucharist in a box around the priest's neck. Relics of the saints were also commonly carried.[38]

One notes the animist concept of accessing spiritual power for one's own purpose, protection, and/or benefit being practiced within institutional Christian churches. Identifying within a church is not protection from animist action in itself. Rather, human nature is insistent—one's own action seeks spiritual power toward one's own purpose.

36. As example, some faith tradition streams within Islam consider beings termed *wali* (variously translated as "protector," "friend of God," or "saint") available for intercession by virtue of close proximity to God (Allah). These spiritual beings are considered to have earned status through piety and deep connection with Allah. Adherents do not worship wali, their graves, or artifacts but show them respect and seek intercession and blessings through them. Some wali are considered capable of miracles. While details differ, there are also faith traditions which use similar approaches and institute or permit spiritual beings considered closer to God through which adherents might seek intercession and blessing (see such as Facts and Details, "Muslim Beliefs").

37. Born, "Worlds of the Spirit," 146.

38. Scribner, *Popular Culture*, 34.

Animist practice occurs even where the perceived source of spiritual power is within Christianity.

Totems and Taboos

Totems serve as a system to provide kin-group identification—family, clan, tribe—whereby the group is considered to be in close relationship with an animal or plant. Each totem has a specific set of taboos (proscribed rules) to be followed. For example the *Bakwena* clan's totem in Botswana is the *kwena* (crocodile). The Bakwena are prohibited from eating aquatic creatures. Bakwena ancestors are believed to be offended by those breaking this taboo, which then brings sickness and death through ancestral unhappiness.

Taboos as rules serve as governing laws within animist thought. Breaking a taboo is thought to break harmony with the spiritual world, which then brings a negative result. Taboos, as proscribed law, are functional rather than moral. Their purpose is protection from ill effect. Paul Hiebert records several taboos governing pregnancy in Taiwan: a pregnant woman must not eat ginger—or she will give birth to a baby with eye disease or with eleven fingers; a pregnant woman must not watch a puppet show—or the child will be born as a puppet with soft bones; a pregnant woman must not step over a rope dragging an ox—or her pregnancy will be extended twelve months.[39]

Taboos involving the spiritual world in secular Western society have been largely relegated to superstition. But they still remain. Stepping on a crack will break your mother's back, walking under a ladder brings bad luck, it is bad luck to open an umbrella indoors, among others. These are all examples of governing taboos exhibiting physical consequence as brought by a mysterious spiritual world in the secular United States context. Some within US society still seek to fulfill such taboos just in case . . .

Societal taboo systems tend to become more and more complicated and extensive as taboos are added. They may govern marriage, childbirth, hunting, agriculture, travel, and/or religion all within a group. Such may be dismissed as superstition or false belief, but regardless, the underlying animist system is apparent in the fear of not observing the taboo. When a human breaks a taboo (first step), the spiritual world sends retribution (reaction to the first step). Correct behavior as

39. Hiebert et al., *Understanding Folk Religions*, 159.

the first step is thought to influence the spiritual world by maintaining harmony (no negative reaction).

Possession

Possession is a means by which the spiritual world is thought to become accessible to the living—a means of direct communication mysterious in its working but understandable in content:

> If the rains fail, or if pests or wide-spread disease occurs, [Shona] people continue to approach the spirit mediums in large numbers in order to seek their advice. Falling possessed, the mediums then inform the petitioners in what ways they have offended the territorial spirits and what they have to do in order to make amends.[40]

Similar types of possession are claimed in Western societies under the New Age phenomena:

> Hear Lea Schultz speak with the voice of somebody called Samuel. . . . Samuel usually discusses problems he feels are present in the audience then takes questions.[41]

Identifying a spiritual power behind every case of contemporary claimed possession is not possible. The spiritual world is unseen and deception occurs. Charlatans provide answers purportedly through possession, while in reality they are deceiving their audience. In the secular West some who might otherwise be labeled as demon-possessed elsewhere are psychologically diagnosed with personality disorders, such as covert narcissism with its self-serving spirit. Distinction occurs but is not necessary for recognizing the spiritual warfare battle. Evil conspires with evil to create chaos within God's story of salvation through deception, false narrative, and other acts within the evil paradigm.

The murkiness of possession may serve to obscure it, but to ignore it is not wise for those with a Christian worldview. The apostle Peter writes in 1 Pet 5:8, "Your adversary the devil prowls around like a roaring lion, seeking someone to devour." The reality of demon possession is verified in Scripture in such as Matt 4:24. Not every contemporary human claim of demon possession is verifiable—demon possession occurring outside

40. Bucher, *Spirits and Power*, 49.

41. Friederich, "New Age Harmonies," 416.

of Scripture is not a scientific data-filled discussion. But it can be observed that the consequence of animist spiritual approaches lead further and further away from the truth of God's relationship with his people, which then hardens hearts and opens the door to direct possession by demonic spirit.

Some use animist approaches seeking to rid a possessed person of perceived demons. They are destined to fail. Their purpose may be worthy but their method not. An example is found in Acts 19 as the seven sons of Sceva seek to relieve a demon-possessed man using Jesus' name. It did not happen. Relieving the demon-possessed is possible where God's power and authority is witnessed but is not possible through animist method, no matter how well intended.

Dreams and Visions

Dreams, and/or visions, are thought to be a means through which the spiritual world makes the mysteries of its world known to the human world. They may be considered representations with meaning needing divination through a religious specialist. Or they may be considered a literal indication of reality. Among the Bandi ethnic group in northern Liberia, if someone dreamed they were a witch, that person should tell someone as soon as they awoke so that the appropriate supplications could be made. If they did not do so, it was feared they would find themselves a witch in reality.[42]

Dreams are also viewed as a guide providing information not accessible in another manner. A traditional *Annang* (Nigeria) doctor describes how he sometimes determines ingredients for his traditional medicines:

> During such dreams *Ibok* leads me into the bush and shows me certain leaves, and what I must use them for. When I wake up I will go into the bush I was led into and will discover the leaves just as I saw in that strange dream.[43]

It is not only religious specialists that access special information through dreams. "Gambian President Yahya Jammeh announced he had discovered a cure for the disease [AIDS] . . . telling them the treatment was revealed to him by his ancestors in a dream."[44] God used dreams and visions to communicate at times, as recorded in Scripture. Today, many

42. Rodewald, "Observing Sacred and Profane," 49.

43. Unwene, "Some Annang Christians Revert," 155–56.

44. Koinange, "AIDS Cure."

Muslims who have become Christ-followers point to dreams as their initiating moment away from Islam. One cannot downplay the reality of these moments. Yet not every dream originates with God as source. The spiritual source of a dream is only derived from result—does the dream point to God's truth or away? That question is answered by agreement with the truth of God's salvation provided in Scripture. Human-centric desire and a misleading spiritual world conspire to point humankind away from God's truth, and any other conclusion about dreams or visions as communication from the spiritual world is bound to mislead.

Witchcraft

The term *witchcraft* conjures up images dependent upon worldviews within a society. In Western societies, its primary use is to refer to those who access malevolent spiritual beings for their own evil purposes. In other places, it has a different meaning.

To those with strong holistic-oriented worldviews, there is spiritual cause where there is a calamity. The process of arriving at the calamity or its result may be pronounced as "witchcraft" within such societies. Those with secular Western worldviews may observe the same event and assign meaning differently, as in the following event. Here, one worldview attributes causal result to witchcraft, another to intoxication:

> No sooner had Paul's son finished his university studies than he was killed in a car accident. His sister, who had never gone far in school, admits to having killed him by witchcraft, out of jealousy. The fact that he was intoxicated at the time of the accident is not considered important [among the *Adioukrou* of Cote d'Ivoire].[45]

Practicing witchcraft is sometimes considered involuntary within animist perspective. A person may not know that he or she is guilty of witchcraft until divined so by a religious specialist. In involuntary witchcraft, a witch is determined through cause found—jealousy, greed, hatred, or envy. Religious specialists use confession, ritual, and/or sacrifice to divine cause. Societal restitution is required. In some societies, to be divined as a "witch" was to be sentenced to death.[46]

Witchcraft may also be intentional in purpose. This occurs when a practitioner successfully supplicates the spiritual world in a manner

45. Hill, "Witchcraft and the Gospel," 324.

46. Krige, *Social System of the Zulus*, 226.

which is viewed by society to harm someone else. For example, life force in itself is considered amoral—neither good or bad. But when another is harmed in its use, evil is considered to occur. Such is the case when life force is "captured" through ending the physical life of a person and harvesting flesh or organs, especially with the belief that the more one struggles in death, the more powerful is the captured life force within the harvested object. Captured life force is then put to use for one's own purpose—health, wealth, fertility, etc. These goals may be felt "good" by the practitioner, but the methodology used—harvesting human flesh—is pronounced evil by societal norms and often labelled as witchcraft.

Table 2: Four types of witchcraft overtly acknowledged as not-good or evil within animist thought

Unintentional: caused by unknown envy, jealousy, or greed; must be divined.	Intentional: caused by envy, jealousy, or greed.		
Spiritual world reacts to moral lapse (as defined by society) with negative consequence. An unaware witch is the cause of the problem. Responsibility is determined through divination. Restitution is made to restore harmony with the spiritual world.	Spiritual world is actively accessed to help obtain desires. Societal evil occurs as victim is harmed by the method (of harnessing life force or spiritual power).	Spiritual world is actively accessed to help obtain desires. Victim is harmed through the manipulation of the spiritual for physical consequence.	Spiritual world is actively accessed to help obtain desires. Spiritual powers identified as evil are intentionally used to accomplish purpose.

Another form of intentional witchcraft occurs when a religious specialist manipulates life force or spiritual powers to bring about sickness, accident, calamity, or death for others' advantage. Embedded within this method is the part/whole concept in which it believed that access to a part gives access to the power of the whole. Practitioners use articles of clothing, cut hair, or use other objects in order to supplicate spiritual power and bring negative result to the owners of those objects. The power behind such witchcraft may be claimed as neither good nor bad, but society experiences evil as others are harmed by others for another's purpose.

A last type of witchcraft is that which fits among those with a primarily Western worldview—a witch practitioner accesses evil spiritual powers through ritual and supplication for their own purposes, including to harm others.

A comment is appropriate for Western readers who have heard the term *Wicca*. Wicca, as a neo-Pagan religion which (re)emerged in the West in the mid-twentieth century, is often casually perceived as the equivalent to the last description of witchcraft. There may be similarities, but this does not state the reality. A deeper dive into Wiccan approaches[47] reveals parallel precepts to the animist approaches presented in this chapter. Practitioners identify themselves as witches who practice "magic"/"magick" to access their spiritual cosmos of gods and goddesses and universal natural energy.[48] Wiccans themselves view their use of magick as beneficial unless practiced to harm others.

The reader can note that for all its self-profession of good, Wicca is but another religious form bundled under the animist paradigm which seeks to point the user away from the truth of God and his story of salvation through Jesus.

WITHIN THE "EVERYTHING ELSE"

The previous sections outlined precepts deduced from practices observed in holistic societies termed "primitive" in their approach to religion. But combining the claim of anthropologist Marvin Harris, "animistic beliefs [are] to be found in every society,"[49] and Francis Pieper's observations, which claim only two religions in the world,[50] it is possible to conjecture that one only has to dig a bit within a society or religion to discover animist practice.

This is certainly true within the secular West, apparent in sport. Some fans wear specific jerseys in an attempt to effect the outcome of a game. Other rituals are more complicated. Note the ritual behavior of animist practice by professional baseball player Mike Griffin toward causing the mysterious spiritual world to positively respond and affect his game:

47. DEOMI, "Wicca."

48. Berger, "What Is Wicca?"

49. Harris, "Why We Became Religious," 7.

50. One that trusts the story of God's salvation through Jesus as a gift of God's grace; and one that is "everything else."

> A 17-game winner last year in the Texas Ranger organization, Mike Griffen, begins his ritual preparation a full day before he pitches, by washing his hair. The next day, *although he does not consider himself superstitious*, he eats bacon for lunch. When Griffen dresses for the game he puts on his clothes in the same order, making certain he puts the slightly longer of his two outer, or "stirrup," socks on his right leg. "I just wouldn't feel right mentally if I did it the other way around," he explains. He always wears the same shirt under his uniform on the days he pitches. During the game he takes off his cap after each pitch, and between innings he sits in the same place on the dugout bench.[51]

Animist practice is also found in religions termed as "major" in the world, such as Islam:

> *Dhikr* (remembrance of *Allah* by recitation) can take place with the tongue, for which the one who utters it receives reward. It is not necessary for this that he understand or recall its meaning, on condition that he not mean other than its meaning by its utterance.[52]

Also in the same encyclopedia of Islamic doctrine,

> Abu Hurayra reported that the Prophet said, Whoever says, *la ilaha illalallahu wahdahu la sharika lah, lahu al-mulku wa lahu al-hamd, wa huwa ala kulli shayin quadir* (there is no god but Allah, alone, without partner. His the sovereignty, and His the praise, and He has power over everything) a hundred times a day will have a reward equivalent to the reward for freeing ten slaves. In addition, a hundred good deeds will be recorded for him and a hundred bad deeds of his will be wiped off, and it will be a safeguard for him from satan that day until evening, and no one will be better in deeds than such a person except he who does more than that.[53]

Again, animist practice is seen in correct performance upon which one receives reward from the spiritual world. Man's action of remembrance-by-recitation is first, to which the Islamic concept of the spiritual world is promised to respond.

The Hindu system of religion is also one of such reciprocity. The supreme spirit-god Brahman is unknowable, but personified lesser gods and

51. Gmelch, "Baseball Magic," 298; emphasis mine.
52. Al-Asqalani, *Fath al-Bari*, 11:251, quoted in Kabbani, *Remembrance of Allah*, 9.
53. Kabbani, *Remembrance of Allah*, 33.

goddesses are considered more accessible. When one prays for healing or success, a promise is made to give a specific gift to the deity *if* the wish is granted.[54] This author visited a Hindu temple in Chicago as a part of an observation group in order to learn more about other religious practices. A woman was praying as she repeatedly walked around one of the divinities symbolized in the temple. The temple guide explained that the woman did so every day at the same time. When we asked why, the guide replied, "Because she does not know on which round the deity will grant her request." Note the approach. Human action is first, hoping that the spiritual world would respond to faithful repetitive human action. One notes the underlying precept of animist practice.

Buddhism as a religion sees humans as a part of a universal force of existence. The practitioner has a goal of being one with that universal force. Eternal truth (*dharma*) is available only through practice.[55] There need not be understanding—the goal is to separate one's self from one's own thoughts since thinking keeps one from *dharma*. Rather, the correct practice of ritual brings benefit: "He who is fully learned in *mantras* [sacred utterances] and has mastered the Secret Altar; burns away for his disciple all his sins in accordance with the rules."[56] Spiritual enlightenment and the removal of sins which hinder that enlightenment is accomplished only through correct practice—a concept synonymous with that of animist approach.

Christians are not immune to animist practice. Christians are, after all, humans with a human nature that tempts to put one's own self-centric purposes before that of following God through Jesus. By the time of the Reformation in Western Europe, much animist practice existed in the institutional church. The gospel message in Scripture was obscured behind foreign language, opaque rituals, and objects from which the lay people believed that God's power could be accessed to deal with daily problems. Priests as their religious specialists conspired to create sacramentals—blessed candles, herbs, and other objects believed to give access to spiritual power. Objects laid under the altar were believed to be imbued with healing powers. Priests held the Eucharist to the heavens with the sign of the cross to ward off the effects of storms and hail.[57]

54. Huyler, *Meeting God*, 59.
55. Parrinder, *World Religions*, 271.
56. Giebel, *Varocanabhisambodhi Sutra*, 167.
57. Scribner, *Popular Culture*, 11.

While the Reformation era did a great service for Christians by questioning non-biblical forms of Christianity, it did not protect against animist practice. Some leaders of the emerging Lutheran church body propagated the thought that Bibles, beds, images, and buildings associated with Luther were "incombustible."[58] In the doing, the "incombustible claim" tacitly put Luther on the same holy level as the saints of their opponents and implied that God was smiling on their side as they emerged into the first centuries after the Reformation.

But animist practice by those within institutional churches is not confined to history. Contemporary Christians are also tempted into animist practice. Emerging independent Christian church bodies in Africa struggle in blending old approaches to the spiritual into their new understanding of God. The First Apostolic Church of St. John in Botswana holds the following position:

> The church does not allow its members to honor the ancestors and any other power other than God according to Exd. 20:1–2. But the church does not forbid people from praying through their ancestral spirits because [*sic*] is a strong connection between members of the church and their ancestors as a community or family of God.[59]

There is a subtlety to the animist practice evidenced in this statement. God is added to the animist cosmos rather than their relinquishing the practice of praying to a mysterious high god through ancestors.

Such churches are derided as guilty of syncretism. Yet syncretism can be a label provided by others. Animist practice, and thus syncretism, can be found even in those who consider themselves not-syncretistic. "'When you give to God,' [TBN evangelist Paul] Crouch said during a typical appeal for funds, 'you're simply loaning to the Lord and He gives it right on back.'"[60] Again we note the animist approach of binding the spiritual for our own purpose. If one gives to the spiritual world, the spiritual world gives it back—our action first, followed by spiritual reaction thought to reward.

In another contemporary example, a pastor of the Word of Faith movement states, "The effectual fervent prayer of a righteous man achieves results. And if someone didn't achieve the result they were after, something

58. Scribner, *Popular Culture*, 352–53.

59. Amanze, *Botswana Handbook of Churches*, 100.

60. Lobdell, "Pastors Empire."

was done incorrectly."[61] Again, we note animist precepts in play—it is through correct performance that the spiritual world shall respond.

Another statement gleaned from an online Bible study exhibits the same on the mode of baptism: "Sprinkling is just as vain as if it had never been done. Since sprinkling is without God's authority, if you were sprinkled or poured, then you have not been scripturally baptized, and you still have every sin that you have committed and are still lost."[62] According to the author, baptism is only efficacious if accomplished through immersion, a conclusion based upon interpreting Scripture outside of God's command and purpose, which then transfers into an animist notion of effecting the means through which God gives his grace to his people. Correct practice is again proposed as the causal link between sin and forgiveness in the spiritual.

Animist statements can be found in the belief systems of even those who have determined their forms to be the most proper within Christianity: "Christ will judge believers, rewarding them for acts done while living on earth."[63] The statement points to truth. God's gift of grace to us *is* the cause for thankful response. Any acts of service which witness to him, originate in him; and any "reward," however speculated, is fulfilled in the continuation of spiritual life in Christ through God's grace, not something motivating us to gain additional heavenly reward. But as stated, the quoted statement subtly misleads toward an animist approach. It motivates toward acts of Christian service as a human means by which one gains additional, but undefined, spiritual reward. Again, human action is seen as the key to achieve this reward. In such presentation, one observes the subtlety by which animist approaches can appear.

Another example comes from some who might consider themselves more orthodox in their practice of Christianity:

> When we touch the relic of a saint, the object itself isn't healing; rather, God's intercession through the object performs the blessing.[64]

Note again the subtlety of animist approach expressed as holy action. Human action is first said to bring the blessing of the spiritual world through the object. The part/whole notion of animist thought is exhibited

61. Jarvis, "Defending the Word-Faith Movement."

62. Boatwright, "Baptism Is Immersion."

63. Fairchild, "Southern Baptist Beliefs."

64. House of Joppa, "Relics of Saints."

as the user seeks to access God's intercession through an object mysteriously connected to power within the spiritual world.

Another example of animist perspective happened at a Lutheran congregation in Botswana. Visiting members gathered and filed away from the altar of the Lord's Supper in a counterclockwise manner. Local members claimed that the efficacy of ritual was disturbed. The proper ritual within that congregation was to gather and file away in a clockwise manner. Some might dismiss this example as an issue from another continent, but some clergy in the West argue over the efficacy of ritual which excludes the sign of the cross—an action not deduced from Scripture but treated indispensable toward properly consecrating God's gifts given through sacraments.

The title of Christianity is no barrier to animist propensity. It is our human-centric nature to be animist in our approaches to the spiritual. Some within pray fervently and attribute their lack of perceiving an answer as a lack of faith or effort. Some blame themselves or wonder how disaster can happen if they have been so faithful in their church. But God is merciful. He gives opportunity to all to repent and change the way we think and follow our own desires. He calls us to follow him into his purpose in witness to the God with whom we are in unique relationship, not as one who reacts to us but whom we follow.

SPIRITUAL WARFARE IN SCRIPTURE

We now take a look at Scripture and observe events within as observed by those who see through an animist worldview lens that assigns meaning as described above.

It is beyond the scope of a chapter to dissect all examples of spiritual warfare recorded in Scripture. Some, usually those with worldviews formed through the secular West, categorize spiritual warfare into a mystical otherworldly fight, but the picture of spiritual warfare as seen through animist precepts is valid for building additional understanding in one's study of biblical text. Missiologist Andrew F. Walls writes, "It is the primal religions, so often called primitive, which underlie all the other and frequently gives the clearest models of religion."[65] Peering through others' religious lenses allows us to consider questions formed outside our own backgrounds. How did those who worship other "gods"

65. Walls, "Building to Last," 10.

see YHWH as the spiritual power of the Israelites?[66] How did YHWH maintain relationship with his people? Douglas E. Thomas coins the term *religio-cultural* to describe the life-integrated quality of African religious practices.[67] Physical life events are connected to the spiritual world, no exception. The events recorded in Scripture contain the same religious holisticity. Behind every nation, tribe, territory, culture, clan, or family is perceived spiritual power. Leaving one's nation, tribe, clan, etc. is felt to leave the protection of and access to one's own spiritual power(s), instead entering into another's.

Scripture unfolds the underlying spiritual battle through its historical events. The spiritual world is omnipresent, and viewing events in Scripture through such a precept allows us to observe the underlying spiritual battle in ways not present for those in cultures without such a spiritually integrated worldview. We see the LORD God (YHWH *elohim*) contrasted different from all other supernatural power(s) within the animist perception of the spiritual. He calls his people not to attempt to use him for our own purposes but to respond and serve. The following examples demonstrate this.

2 Kings 3

Author Baruch Margalit notes that events in 2 Kgs 3, culminating in verses 26–27, have not had a clear explanation.[68] But viewed through an animist precept, additional understanding is gained. Here is the text: "When the king of Moab saw he was losing the battle, he took 700 swordsmen to try to break through to the king of Edom. But they couldn't do it. Then he took his firstborn son, who would have succeeded him as king, and sacrificed him on the wall as a burnt offering. There was bitter anger against the Israelites. So they went home to their own country" (2 Kgs 3:26–27 GW).

Margalit anthropologically records the practice of Canaanite nations and their child sacrifice to Baal. It was not uncommon. Child

66. A note on English translation: English translations have continued the Jewish tradition of not directly using God's name, spelled as YHWH/Yahweh, rather substituting "LORD" in a manner of respect. Also the term *elohim* in Hebrew may be translated as "God," "god," "gods," or "spiritual power(s)." All are correct, but we choose to translate more directly at times using "YHWH" instead of "LORD" and "spiritual power(s)" instead of "god(s)" so that English readers may "eavesdrop" a bit closer to the meaning of the original text.

67. Thomas, *African Traditional Religion*, 7.

68. Margalit, "King Mesha of Moab."

sacrifice still exists in forms of propitiating the spiritual world today (see previous subsection, "Supernatural Energy / Life Force"). But this is only the last act of the underlying spiritual battle exhibited in previous verses. In summary, King Joram, son of Ahab, had previously torn down Baal's altars but did not turn away from evil or the sins that Jeroboam had led Israel to commit (2 Kgs 3:1–3). The state of faith within Israel and its king is apparent when he decides to attack the Moabites with the help of the kings of Judah and Edom. The campaign does not go well, and the king of Israel suddenly fears YHWH. He sees their disaster as evidence that YHWH has put them at the mercy of the Moabites (2 Kgs 3:10). The kings seek spiritual help through Elisha the prophet of YHWH. YHWH guides them and witnesses to his power through the prophetic words of his prophet as recorded in 2 Kgs 3:16–17. Everything Elisha proclaims through prophecy becomes true . . . until the last city where the king's son is offered as a burnt offering on the city walls. The Israelites shrink away.

Western commentary tends to focus on Moabite anger as the result and motivation for Israelite retreat.[69] Other Western commentary surmises the sacrifice as appeasing and invoking the supreme power of the Moabites, *Chemosh*.[70] But such assumption misses much. A word comparison of the Hebrew construction *qe·ṣep̄* (קֶצֶף; alternately appearing in English translations of 3:27 as "anger"/"fury"/"indignation") shows its concept not referring to human origin, feelings, or response. It rather conceptualizes a "supernatural force" sourced from outside the physical world.[71]

The Israelites had not been defeated by Moabite feelings or any associated spiritual being up to this point. They had followed YHWH and his promises up to the last Moabite city. The results were as predicted. They even defeat a desperate last gasp counterattack by the seven hundred swordsmen led by the Moabite king. But now they believe a powerful supernatural force has been unleashed, antagonistic, through child sacrifice. This spiritual force is not one associated with a Moabite god in competition with their own, and such is not attributed so in the text. Rather, in animist precepts, supernatural energy is believed available to be propitiated and bound, and it is most powerfully efficacious for one's

69. See such as Henry, "2 Kings 3"; Guznik, "2 Kings 3"; and New Song Church, "Why Did the King Sacrifice."

70. For an overview of commentaries that interpret the passage this way, see StudyLight, "2 Kings 3:27."

71. See such as Num 1:53; 18:5; Josh 9:20; 2 Kgs 3:27; 1 Chr 27:24; 2 Chr 19:2, 10; 24:18; 29:8; 32:25–26; Isa 34:2; 54:8; Zech 7:12.

purpose through sacrifice of the firstborn child.[72] The Israelites and their leader exhibit the underlying state of their faith. They fail to follow into YHWH's promise as instructed within the prophecy. Additionally, they do not acknowledge YHWH as their One God ascendant above *all* other notions of spiritual power (*elohim*). It is apparent, at least as examined through animist worldview, they have experienced YHWH's faithfulness and power, but in retreat they remain within the paradigm of spiritual powers that Israel's leaders had allowed to become the state within the nation of Israel.

This narrative exhibits the stark reality of the underlying spiritual battle of our God calling his people to trust him exclusively and follow into his blessing without fear of any other spiritual power. Israelite failure to follow is not God's failure to act—a powerful witness to God's guiding not because of human faithfulness but because he is faithful to those he calls, even when underserved, as is seen again in the next example.

1 Samuel 4–7

Humans failing to follow into God's purpose is a consistent theme in God's story of salvation as recorded in Scripture. But what happens when his chosen people attempt to access his power in an animist manner for their own purpose, similar to surrounding nations and their powers?

God tells his people as recorded in Deut 5:7, "You shall have no other gods [*elohim*, "spiritual power(s)"] before me." Immediately following, he commands not to create images or worship them, the consequence of which is to not be under his protection. Deuteronomy 5:11 continues, often appearing in English with such verbiage as, "You shall not take the name of the LORD [YHWH] your God [*eloheka*, "spiritual power"] in vain [*lassaw*]." Western English readers often supply a meaning of not using the name of God disrespectfully.[73] This is not incorrect but does not complete the concept. A word study comparing passages with the Hebrew word *lassaw* provides additional components of meaning—"uselessly,"

72. This spiritual force is variously labeled as life force, natural energy, supernatural energy, or aura (see subsection, "Supernatural Energy / Life Force") available for one's own purpose if one knows how to access it.

73. "You shall not take the name of the LORD your God in vain [that is, irreverently, in false affirmations or in ways that impugn the character of God]; for the LORD will not hold guiltless nor leave unpunished the one who takes His name in vain [disregarding its reverence and its power]" (Deut 5:11 AMP); brackets original to the translation.

"emptily," "for no good purpose," "vanity," "evil," "selfishly," or "for self-focus." Each provides wider understanding beyond disrespect, such as, "Do not use the name of YHWH your spiritual power for self-purpose." In animist precepts, names and symbols serve as power identifiers which are used to propitiate and manipulate specific spiritual power—power, name, and/or symbol are considered inexorably linked (see previous subsection on "Power Words and Numbers"). God commands his people not only to not use his name with disrespect, but also to not attempt to use his name and power for our own purposes.

The Israelites were surrounded by peoples linked through animist precept to their spiritual powers. But YHWH is not to be approached the same. Where the Israelites fail to follow into his leading through his commandments as expressed in Deut 5, the results are not what can be defined as success. This is seen in the biblical narrative recorded in 1 Samuel, chapters 4–7.

The condensed version of this example is that the Philistines defeat the Israelites. The Israelites lose about four thousand troops (1 Sam 4:2). The leaders of Israel wonder why YHWH did not protect them from defeat. They decide to carry the ark of YHWH's covenant into battle to empower their purpose against the Philistines. This animist approach to using YHWH's power did not go well. Israel suffers a major defeat, this time with thirty thousand casualties and the ark captured (1 Sam 4:10). But the Israelite failure in battle was not a failure of YHWH's power. In the next part of the narrative, the Philistines witness YHWH's power through negative result (1 Sam 5). In the end, they return the ark to the Israelites with propitiating gifts of gold (1 Sam 6:10).

This text provides a powerful example of the LORD God being unique and different than spiritual power(s) within the animist perception of the supernatural. Shown through his commandments, he is the One to be followed above all others and not to be used to empower our own purposes.

Acts 19

A last example observed through animist precepts is seen in the New Testament record of Ephesus in Acts 19. When this author was living overseas on the continent of Africa, a friend provided a letter received from the US. It contained a paper handkerchief. The letter promised that if the receiver sent a contribution, he/she could put the handkerchief under their bed and blessings would occur. It referenced Acts 19:12.

The letter piqued my interest. I had never really paid much attention to anything about Paul's handkerchiefs in the Bible, but when I referenced it, sure enough, God was accomplishing great miracles in Ephesus through "handkerchiefs and aprons" that had touched the apostle Paul. My family and I were living and serving at the time in a society that used objects thought to provide access to spiritual power. The thought hit me, "How did this biblical reference fit into such practice?" A study through available Western commentary was descriptive but did not provide deeper insight on handkerchiefs. My local friends were happy to explain the details of the narrative as they understood them. A whole new appreciation emerged.

The awesome nature of Scripture is in truth, even where we may not perceive its totality. The tendency of modern Western society toward the spiritual world is to dismiss it or understand the message of Scripture through worldviews modified by its secular enlightened context. The spiritual theories created within New Testament society were no different. The Ephesus of Acts 18–19 was famous for its silver idols. Ephesians had developed their own practices and links to the powers of their spiritual world. They could assign their understanding to the results coming through Paul and the handkerchief/aprons which touched him. The method was familiar—not a far reach within local worldview. But such was to be challenged.

Itinerant Jewish exorcists began using Jesus' name, saying, "I adjure you by the Jesus whom Paul proclaims!" (Acts 19:13). In animist practice, identifying and calling on the name of a power is thought to invoke that power to your will (see previous subsection on "Power Words and Numbers"). The invoking has nothing to do with the faith of its practitioners; rather, it seeks to use a specific power for one's own purpose. The seven sons of Sceva, a Jewish high priest, invoke Jesus' name in verse 14. Animist precepts dictate that the power affiliated with the name of Jesus would respond to the command and throw out the evil spirit. But that did not happen. Rather, the spirit inside the man beat the seven sons and sent them packing naked and wounded, saying, "Jesus I know, and Paul I recognize, but who are you?" (Acts 19:15).

The result is the reason. Everyone in Ephesus heard about it. They knew the method but not the power. The witness was massive. This Jesus was different, someone to be followed, as Paul was setting the example. The impact was not small. The name of Jesus was extolled. In Acts 19:17–20, even believers got off the syncretistic fence by divulging secret practices. Former magic arts practitioners burned literature to a worth of fifty thousand pieces of silver. And the word of the Lord continued to increase.

Not all were happy, especially the silversmiths who made the idols (Acts 19:24–27). But through the result, many, both Jew and Greek, were pointed to faith through Jesus. And that is the point. This event is not about healing, magic, or handkerchiefs. That may have been familiar method to the animists of Ephesus, but this power was different, not to be used but followed. Many were pointed to their Christ, a Savior different than any spiritual power they had experienced before.

Scriptural Narrative Summary

Such scriptural narrative exhibits God's nature, power, and truth as not ours to manipulate for our own purpose. The message of Scripture is that we are given the gift of eternal life, not because we are faithful, wise, or great but because God reaches to us and offers his gift of salvation right where we are: "While we were still sinners, Christ died for us" (Rom 5:8). Our Triune God uses his power not to fulfill our desires through our actions but that humankind might witness his power and turn away from ourselves and other spiritual powers to be his people under his blessings. There is no other purpose.

There is nothing we can do or accomplish to receive his gift to us through Jesus. It is a gift. Its opposite—using God's name without belief or within animist practice for our own purpose—deceives and has consequences leading us into evil, which God does not desire for humankind. Our failure to follow is not God's failure to be faithful. This is as true today as it was yesterday. Even where we fail, God remains steadfast that we might again follow him.

CONCLUSION

Christians find spiritual truth provided through the words of Scripture. This is a great comfort as the Holy Spirit works through means—the word proclaimed to us through the words of Scripture, the waters of baptism, and the bread and wine of the Lord's Supper, as promised in Scripture. Understanding the holistic link between spiritual and physical opens up new appreciation for those God calls into his story of salvation as his people. He calls us to follow from the beginning of time. He calls yet today and into the future. Nothing is changed. He remains our Triune God: the Father sending his Son, Jesus, as the Savior of humankind; God the Father and Son sending the Holy Spirit empowering us to faith and following him; and God the Father, Son, and Spirit calling and sending his people into the world to witness to him (see chapter 1, on the *missio Dei*). There is no other purpose. Our Trinitarian God is for all nations, families, and societies through his blessing. No one is excluded.

Human-centric approaches to the spiritual world seem endless, practiced through centuries of time with imprecise understanding. What was described by Luther and others as works-righteousness interlocks within the paradigm of animist practice—human action first. Whatever the goal, the animist practitioner somehow hopes that the details of their spiritual world, whether god, spirit, ancestor, life force, or other notions of spiritual power, will somehow meet desire. Perceiving the consequence of an animist approach to the spiritual helps us more fully appreciate and be grateful for the blessings freely given us in our salvation. We recognize evil within God's story of salvation, but we are not bound by it.

There is One spiritual power who is different—our Trinitarian God—Father, Son, and Holy Spirit. God sent his Son, Jesus, that we might be free from evil and human failure. Father and Son send the Holy Spirit that we might be empowered into his purpose. Where we as God's people follow him into his purpose, we follow into his blessing. This is spiritual warfare. The spiritual battle is on. The spiritual battle is won.

Section Four

Collaboration and Practical Engagement

9

Mission and Translatability

INTRODUCTION

Some pastors were complaining.[1] The New Testament had been completed in their local language, but pastors had completed their theological training through English. They read English-language Bibles and preached in English, or, as the occasion determined, they interpreted on the fly into the local language. But now, previously illiterate women were learning to read Scripture through their own language. They had been excluded from discussion, but that was changing. They were growing in faith and even challenging pastors as they preached their interpretations. Some pastors did not like the challenges, but one ruefully realized how limited his scope was when he used English in his sermons: "I was just preaching to myself." The word proclaimed, through language understood, reduces barriers to what the word has to say and to growing the faith that follows.

The nature of Christianity is captured in the concept of translatability—capable of being understood through alternate languages and forms of worship. This premise is grounded in God's sending his Son, Jesus, to the world not as opaque mystery but in human form, a form through which we could relate and understand the story of God's salvation to us. Jesus as true God, and yet also true man, is a paradox not fully

1. The following is from a report to Lutheran Bible Translators from Sierra Leone, West Africa.

understood but a mystery accepted within Christianity. God in human form is more relatable to us than that of a distant creator-spirit to which we make our own approach. Rather, God gives us Jesus the Word (John 1:1) through Scripture so that we might glimpse the glories and wonders of God even through the limits created by our human boundaries.

The apostle Paul writes that the good news of God's story of salvation through Jesus is not a human message (Gal 1:11–12). But the act of proclaiming that good news within Scripture does not operate magically—that is, without understanding. As recorded in the historical *Confessions of the Evangelical Lutheran Church*, "No one has ever written or suggested that people benefit from the mere act of hearing lessons that they do not understand."[2] Where the good news of Jesus is proclaimed and the message understood, God calls to faith, gathers, enlightens, and sanctifies through the power of the Holy Spirit. God's desire and relationship with us is translated through Jesus into a relationship which changes us as we grow in the knowledge of him through the work of the Holy Spirit. The result is that through faith given, we serve in God's kingdom and proclaim this good news so that others may understand their relationship with God through Jesus too.

Translatability finds root in God's sending of Jesus. A foundational understanding within the Christian faith is that *all* are given the gift of salvation through Jesus' death and resurrection, and the translatability concept and processes extend into methodology as the gospel message is carried into the world. Salvation is a gift of grace and becomes ours through such faith as given by the power of the Holy Spirit. There is nothing we do to gain that gift; it is only ours to *believe* and respond by faith in gratefulness for the gift given, no matter in which language or form one "hears," believes, and lives out life in Christ.

Other religions differ. History allows us to compare the notion of translatability—foundational and inclusive within God's kingdom—with precepts of Islam, one of the world's major religions that does not contain the concept of translatability.

There are some similarities between Christianity and Islam. Both religions point to a single creator and acknowledge Jesus. Both claim revealed Scriptures, including elements from the Hebrew canon. But it is in the comparison that we note that the underlying precepts are more different than similar. Christians approach God and Jesus as revealed

2. Ap 24.5 (*BC*, 258).

in Scripture different than Muslims approach Allah, Isa (Jesus), and the Qur'an. Islam dispenses with human understanding in order to respect the original historical words of Allah. This precept seeks to preserve the words of its holy book, the Qur'an, as revealed by Allah through the angel Gabriel to the prophet Muhammad in its original forms and rules (*tajweed*). While those historical Arabic words may technically be translated into other languages, the underlying precept is that translation as a human act can only provide an approximation of the original.[3] Thus the product of human translation cannot be considered a legitimate expression of Allah's words nor is the original language of the Qur'an fully understood. The follower of Islam cannot know the extent of the salvific mercy of Allah. Rather, they earn rewards toward entrance into paradise through orthopraxy (correct conduct/practice) which may, or may not, earn sufficient mercy to allow entrance to paradise.

Some years ago this author visited a mosque and observed classes of young men praying, memorizing, and reciting the Qur'an. The author asked the imam how one could be certain that Allah heard their prayers. He answered by saying that proper prayer was the only prayer that Allah would hear—one must void one's mind and recite the Qur'an without thought. If one provided one's own thought, one might supply incorrect meaning, and the prayer would not be heard. Understanding is not necessary.

Christianity is not the same. The late Lamin Sanneh, Gambian missiologist and professor at Yale, expresses Christianity's defining feature as being able to be "equally at home in all languages and cultures, and all races and conditions of people."[4] Christians study Scripture not to maintain original form but to understand relationship with God through Jesus. We acknowledge Jesus as God coming to us right where we are. We have a relationship with God through Jesus no matter what language or form our prayer and supplication. It is through belief, not practice, that one becomes a follower of Christ within God's kingdom. Non-salvific conclusions (doctrines) and practices may differ from one context to another, but understanding the word and living it out lies at the center of Christianity. The power of God is benefited through understanding[5]—no matter which language, symbols, or form are used to communicate the message.

3. Majestic Quran, "Can the Quran Be Translated?"

4. Sanneh, *Translating the Message*, 51.

5. Ap 24.5 (*BC*, 258).

TRANSLATION OF SCRIPTURE

Nowhere within Christianity has the premise of translatability been more widely applied than in the field of Bible translation. The contemporary Bible translation movement claims over 7,000 languages in the world, of which 776 have full Bible translations. In addition 1,798 have completed New Testaments, and 1,433 have portions of Scripture in their own languages.[6] Yet many language groups remain without access to Scripture, especially those within who do not have sufficient language skill in a wider language of communication. The process of reaching others through their own language is not a simple challenge. Remaining language groups are isolated or small and may require development of a writing system before translation can even begin. Governments and location may limit access. Some can be reached with oral versions of Scripture, but the control or nonavailability of technology and media tends to limit the overall effort.

But the effort is not without result. Where the word of God in Scripture comes through one's own language, the word comes with lowered barrier, and a solid foundation is formed as faith occurs. The results are apparent—translations of Scripture create foundations for Christian church bodies throughout the world, even in some of the most remote places of the earth.

The same does not happen where the word is proclaimed through foreign form. Such effect can be seen, again in comparison. Northern Africa experienced mass conversion to the Christian faith in the third century and produced great church fathers—Athanasius of Alexandria in Egypt, and Tertullian, Cyprian, and Augustine in North Africa. Scripture was translated into the language of the people of Egypt—Coptic—by the fourth century. Liturgies and church structures were indigenized. Similar changes occurred in Ethiopia in the fifth century—Scripture translation into the local language of Ge'ez formed a foundation for language use in Ethiopia's early church forms.

In other parts of northern Africa, there was a contrasting approach. Scripture, gospel proclamation, and church practice remained primarily in Greek and later Latin, both foreign languages. The established church was large, with between five hundred and six hundred bishoprics, and known for its orthodoxy. But the Berber laity did not understand the church's primary languages. Their language—Punic—was used for

6. Wycliffe Global Alliance, "2025 Global Scripture Access."

lay instruction within the church, but the meanings behind Scripture, church writings, and practice remained largely incomprehensible to the masses, remaining the domain of church experts.[7]

A look at northern Africa today demonstrates comparative effect. Islam swept through the region in the seventh century. Christianity survived the religious change in Egypt, existing yet today through a population of an estimated ten million followers.[8] It is the same in Ethiopia where Christianity remains vibrant. However, in the parts of North Africa where the church was practiced primarily through foreign languages and forms, the visible church crumpled as common people traded in one religion they did not understand for another, which also used a language not understood, this time Arabic. Christianity still remained for a time. Christian gravestones have been found south of Tripoli dating from 945–1003, written in a local form of Latin. But orthodox church practice without understanding proved a barrier insufficient for Christianity to survive.[9] The vast majority of North Africans in Libya, Morocco, Mauritania, and the Sudan today remain in a religious system that merits practice over understanding. What they worship is not translatable. The lesson deduced? Processes within the translatability paradigm may not assure that Christians as church remain strong, but failure to consider such creates a weak foundation for sustainability. Church instituted through forms not understood does not create a strong foundation for those within, no matter how theologically astute the intent of its leaders.

TRANSLATION AND METHOD

The concept of Christian form and translatability is observable within Christianity and Scripture translation. In the process variation occurs—the result of translation through human boundaries. English versions of Scripture provide an example. Patheos claims over four hundred and fifty Bible translation versions in English alone, with sixty-seven versions available freely on YouVersion, a popular Bible app.[10] Language changes

7. Sundkler and Steed, *Church in Africa*, 228–32.

8. Release International, "Egypt Rebuilds Its Churches."

9. Sundkler and Steed, *Church in Africa*, 28; also Jenkins, *Lost History of Christianity*, 230.

10. Mulhern, "How Many Versions."

and preferences exert themselves, and alternate Scripture versions appear, each with their own reasons for publication.

There are complexities to consider—a wide variety of preferences and decisions. If this were not the case, there could be a single English version to which all adhered. However, the concept of translatability and its processes does not conform to a single preference. Rather, the results of Scripture translation comes in varied linguistic styles. Some hold the words and grammatical forms of Scripture to be inspired and as such to be respected and maintained. Others hold as inspired the meanings of words and grammatical structures of Scripture, and as such they take precedence in the translation process. Others see Scripture as allegorical, with import in the response of the hearer, not the text. All such worldview preferences feed into the translation process and cause variations in translated Scripture text simply because of initial theological suppositions. And then there are differences where cultural boundaries occur, as the translator uses his/her understanding to provide scriptural text for the receptor.

The translation process of a single Bandi[11] language phrase provides the reader a process example. The phrase—*kohunengo le* (with a high tone on the first syllable)—by itself has no meaning for those who do not understand the language. The letters and grammar provide no clues. The meaning is not accessible outside the Bandi context. But the phrase can be translated into English. A literal translator who wishes to preserve form as closely as possible will replicate the original: "[My] stomach-insides-sweet-[state of] it is," the words now in English with Bandi grammar maintained. The receptor determines that some accessibility has been gained but is left to guess much of the phrase's intent. A moderately less literal translation occurs when the grammar structure of the original is dispensed and translated as, "My stomach is sweet." The phrase is now in correct grammatical form for the English receptor, but distortion may still occur trying to deduce how the phrase is to be understood in context. A meaning-accessible translation would be, "I am happy," dispensing with original form so that the underlying meaning is best conveyed through English words and grammatical forms.

There is a continuum in translating—one can seek to maintain form, or one can seek to dispense with form toward meaning, or one can arrive at a solution somewhere in between. Modern Bible translation

11. Southwest Mande language of northern Liberia.

pioneer, William Smalley, uses the term *eavesdropping* to describe the role of the recipients of translated linguistic form.[12] Without inclusion in the translation process, recipient observers of the message overhear as from a distance and supply meanings based upon their own assumptions. The following story illustrates this.

A relatively new Western missionary was learning about the culture in which she was serving in Sierra Leone, West Africa. A young woman from the local population had been struggling to have a child but now was celebrating the arrival of a healthy baby. Friends gathered to rejoice with her. The new missionary knew the trials the woman had gone through. She told the woman, "It just warms my heart to see you with your baby." The reaction was not what was expected. The local woman was confused. In that culture, even though communication could be accomplished in a form of English, the term "warm-heart" indicates anger. The missionary intended to indicate happiness. The local woman accessed the word but not the intended meaning. She rather assumed it as an expression of anger, making the communication very poor.[13] Missiology pioneer Charles Kraft rightly notes, concerning communication, "It is the receptor who has the final say concerning what is communicated."[14]

The obvious conclusion is that translation provides something more or less than the original—exact equivalence is not possible. This means the translation process is not without decision-making cost. The weakest communication occurs where the process is approached primarily as that of the translator, with little consideration of the receptor as the barriers of human limits and boundaries are inserted into the process. William Smalley notes the underlying translation process problem applied to Scripture translation as minimizing the inevitability of distortion in order to maximize the meaning received by the receptor.[15]

Failure to address translation distortions received by the recipient inevitably raises barriers for a translated message through miscommunication and misunderstanding. The purpose for Bible translation in mission is that God's message of salvation comes without barrier to the receiver in order that he or she understands the fullness of the gospel message through the power of the Holy Spirit—a mission task not well

12. Smalley, *Translation as Mission*, 10.

13. The example here is paraphrased from a recounting by a Lutheran Bible Translators' missionary in Sierra Leone.

14. Kraft, *Communication Theory*, 49.

15. Smalley, *Translation as Mission*, 4.

accomplished by the uninformed who may even create distortion unwittingly. Not all languages share the same features; rather, they may differ not only in lexical form (words) but also grammatically and in manners of discourse. Even simple samples exhibit how contrasting features may cause distortion. For example, "I am starving!" in English is an exaggeration, a hyperbole, expressed in a manner not to be taken literally. The underlying meaning is, "I am very much hungry." In another language, hyperbole may not be an existing feature. The result is that a receptor cannot understand "I am starving" as an exaggeration but rather perceives the expressed meaning as a literal "dying from hunger." This may create a distortion of the intent of the directly expressed phrase. Considering the receptor, it may be more suitable to consider a form which contains the desired meaning rather than to maintain a hyperbolic form which misdirects the receptor.

Metaphors and similes are also features of language which contain hidden distortion to be solved in translation, each feature containing a topic, an illustration, and an assumed point of similarity. For example, John the Baptist uses the metaphor "brood of vipers" to refer to Sadducees and Pharisees in Matt 3:7. The metaphor's topic is the Sadducees/Pharisees, and its illustration is "brood of vipers." A receptor assumes the point of similarity as positive or negative. For Western English speakers, the meaning gathered is that of being dangerous, evil, or perhaps devious, all suitable with minimal distortion for indicting the moral character of those John is addressing. For receptors in a different cultural context, a viper may be understood differently—a symbol of fertility and wisdom.[16] A literal rendering of the metaphor used by John raises barriers to John's intent and distorts meaning for those receptors who understand vipers in such manner. Alternately, some languages may not have the same metaphor feature, causing the receptor to picture Sadducees and Pharisees as literal vipers.

In another example, the narrative was told in Liberia of a religious leader who established the Never Die Church. His weak comprehension of direct-speech grammar in the reading of his Bible allowed him to literally perceive the first-person pronouns in John 14:6 to refer to himself when he read, "Jesus said to him, 'I am the way, and the truth, and the life, no one comes to the Father except through me.'" In so doing, and combined with other values within the local context, he reinforced belief

16. Duprey, "Snake Symbolism."

within himself and the cult which followed, where its largely illiterate members believed they would never die as long as they believed in their leader. The cult disbanded when the leader died.[17]

The translator who fails to consider language features and the role of the receptor risks distortion. Translators make choices, and results vary according to preferences applied. Smalley notes that biblical scholars are the most likely to prefer a more literal approach, having already determined meanings through expositional study outside the translated text.[18] But Martin Luther approached translation less rigidly. He defended the more common German receptor in *Defense of the Translation of the Psalms*: "Let my soul be filled as with lard and fat, so that my mouth may make praise with joyful lips. By 'lard and fat' the Hebrews mean joy, just as a healthy and fat animal is healthy and grows fat, and conversely a sad animal loses weight and grows thin. . . . However, since *no German can understand this expression*, we have relinquished the Hebrew words and rendered the passage in clear German like this, 'It would be my heart's joy and gladness, if I were to praise thee with joyful lips.'"[19]

Translation preferences and approach differences within cause difference in result of surface forms. Comparative results can be seen using alternate English versions of Scripture, such as the New American Standard Bible (NASB) and the God's Word (GW) versions. The translated text of the NASB version of Scripture chooses not to attempt to interpret the meaning of the original languages in Scripture, rather attempting to follow the principle of formal equivalence, the words and grammar of the original biblical authors transitioned as closely as possible for English readers. The overtly stated goal of the NASB version is to be the most readable word-for-word translation that is both accurate and clear to English readers.[20] In comparison, the God's Word (GW) version uses the closest natural equivalent approach. It defines itself as easy to read and easy to understand for modern English speakers—grammar simplified, style less formal, and sentences shorter and less complicated.[21] It surrenders literal form in an effort to make meaning accessible for a receptor audience which may not have the same deeper study resources as those who read the more literal NASB version. The provided excerpts provide

17. Personal experience related by one of the authors; see also Gifford, "Liberia."
18. Smalley, *Translation as Mission*, 10–11.
19. Luther, *Defense of the Translations*, 212; emphasis mine.
20. Lockman Foundation, "New American Standard Bible."
21. God's Word Mission Society, "2025 Bible Translation Guide."

example of the two approaches resulting in an alternate surface text expressing the same underlying meaning.

Eph 2:1–10 NASB:
And you were dead in your offenses
and sins, **2** in which you previously
walked according to the course of
this world, according to the prince
of the power of the air, of the spirit
that is now working in the sons of
disobedience. **3** Among them we too
all previously lived in the lusts of our
flesh, indulging the desires of the flesh
and of the mind, and were by nature
children of wrath, just as the rest.
4 But God, being rich in mercy, because of His great love with which He
loved us, **5** even when we were dead
in our wrongdoings, made us alive
together with Christ (by grace you
have been saved), **6** and raised us up
with Him, and seated us with Him in
the heavenly places in Christ Jesus, **7**
so that in the ages to come He might
show the [boundless riches of His
grace in kindness toward us in Christ
Jesus. **8** For by grace you have been
saved through faith; and this is not of
yourselves, it is the gift of God; **9** not
a result of works, so that no one may
boast. **10** For we are His workmanship,
created in Christ Jesus for good works,
which God prepared beforehand so
that we would walk in them.

Eph 2:1–10 GW:
You were once dead because of your
failures and sins. **2** You followed the
ways of this present world and its
spiritual ruler. This ruler continues
to work in people who refuse to obey
God. **3** All of us once lived among
these people, and followed the desires
of our corrupt nature. We did what our
corrupt desires and thoughts wanted
us to do. So, because of our nature, we
deserved God's anger just like everyone else. **4** But God is rich in mercy
because of his great love for us. **5** We
were dead because of our failures, but
he made us alive together with Christ.
(It is God's kindnessthat saved you.)
6 God has brought us back to life together with Christ Jesus and has given
us a position in heaven with him. **7** He
did this through Christ Jesus out of his
generosity to us in order to show his
extremely rich kindness in the world to
come. **8** God saved you through faith
as an act of kindness. You had nothing
to do with it. Being saved is a gift from
God. **9** It's not the result of anything
you've done, so no one can brag about
it. **10** God has made us what we are.
He has created us in Christ Jesus to
live lives filled with good works that he
has prepared for us to do.

No matter what is intended by the one who initiates communication through translation and its inevitable lack of equivalence, the receptor always has the final say in the meaning grasped, sometimes with minor effect and at other times with more. Managing distortions for the receptor is a choice within the translation process resulting in alternate linguistic forms. In the above, the original biblical text is the same. In the more formally presented NASB, the modern reader may not naturally grasp the original meaning of such terms as *sons of disobedience* in verse 2. Rather, a distortion of original meaning must be moderated through additional helps or instruction. In the closest natural equivalence process, the GW version seeks to limit receptor distortion by directly providing an underlying meaning as "people who refuse to obey God." Its casualty is a more dramatic loss of the original form's approximation.

Translatability and the translation process is that of making meaning accessible for the receptor and managing such distortion that may occur as language transitions through time, space, and cultural boundary. This chapter does not seek to provide the reader with a right/wrong position within the translatability paradigm. Rather, it seeks to help the reader to cognitively give thought to translation principles and effects in order to dispense with methods that raise barriers for the recipients of gospel proclamation. The translation process requires more than good intent to negotiate the varieties of language features. No matter what is intended by the one who initiates communication through translation, the receptor always has the final say in what is communicated. Where communication of the message is imprecise, the receptor receives with distortion.

As a closing point, this discussion is not complete without considering the emerging role of artificial intelligence in the Scripture translation process and mission. Artificial intelligence is a tool in the pursuit of efficiency, but it is not a solution to Bible translation in proclaiming the gospel to all nations. Artificial intelligence engines require data. Many of the smaller languages of the world remain unwritten, with little or no recorded data. As such, availability is limited. Artificial intelligence assists in creating new draft translations where existing translations and sufficient data are available. The result depends upon the quality of the existing translation and linguistic data from the target language that is available to the artificial intelligence engine. The closer the two languages, the more accurately a word-for-word process captures the meaning of the original. The more diverse the language features, the more distortion is provided in artificial intelligence drafting. But most important for those serving in God's mission, the concept of Bible translation for mission includes God's people. Martin Luther captures the requirement in *On Translating: An Open Letter*:

> It requires a right, devout, honest, sincere, God-fearing, Christian, trained, informed, and experienced heart. Therefore I hold that no false Christian or factious spirit can be a decent translator.[22]

22. Luther, *On Translating*, 194.

Gospel proclamation and its translatability, whether through linguistic form or other forms which communicate, is more than method applied through such as artificial intelligence or experts who do not know Christ. Rather translation within the translatability paradigm is God's people in mission reducing the barriers that keep others from hearing the message of their salvation too.

TRANSLATABILITY: FORM AND ITS CONTENT IN WIDER CONTEXT

The precepts of translation are applicable beyond linguistic form within the translatability paradigm. All objects, actions, and sounds evoke a communication process. Receptors observe and in effect translate through their own worldviews. In the process, they arrive at conclusions, correct or not. Music, worship styles, and liturgical and structural forms may be transplanted in literal form across cultural boundaries by those from the sending institutions. Or sometimes such forms are modified in an attempt to maintain underlying meanings within the new context. Disagreement occurs in mission process under labels such as indigenous, contemporary, missional, confessional, and/or style/substance. All such positions can be examined through the lens of communication that occurs through form and (its) content since within lies the underlying precept of translatability. Those in cross-cultural mission who fail to consider how form raises or lowers barriers may unwittingly raise barriers to the proclamation process even where the intent is the opposite.

A look at the Reformation period in the sixteenth century provides a historical overview for the notion of translatability in the wider church context. The institutional German church had emerged into one that insisted on correct form in its doctrine by the time of Martin Luther.[23] It had developed a highly ritualized mode of liturgical practice, both among the clerical orders and the laity,[24] as a way of communication in an oral society. But the effect was that ritual had become an end in itself, and underlying gospel content was obscured. Tradition was used for justification. Note the exchange in 1529 Wurttemburg in an investigative document by Hans Wern, the junior bailiff of Urach:

23. Bosch, *Transforming Mission*, 240.

24. Scribner, *Popular Culture*, 22–23.

> The evil spirit should and always [be fought] with the established ordinances ordained for so many years by the holy church, such as blessed salt, water, herbs, the stole, the alb, blessed holy water and the like, which have been used of hundreds of years to expel the evil spirit.[25]

These beliefs were deeply held. A local preacher, Johann Klass, preached against this use of ritual. He stated that belief in magic and the magical use of sorcery was unbiblical and not attested in the gospel.[26] For this he was accused of Lutheranism. He was forced to recant the following Sunday.

> One should seek medicine against sorcery, diabolical spirits and witchcraft, and seek medicine by those doctors permitted by the Christian church, and one should use thereby blessed salt, water, herbs, palms and candles. These things were ordained by the Christian church for the expulsion of diabolical spirits and witchcraft. And he was not saying all this out of his own head but these things had been ordained by the third pope after St. Peter.[27]

Historic liturgy had been developed with good intent to make liturgical content more understandable to the primarily oral society of the day. But over time, original meaning became obscured as laity deduced alternate meanings. Their lack of understanding did not change the truth inside those rituals; rather, laity became practitioners who failed to perceive truth inside. Clergy largely failed to provide correctives and effectively served as partners in practices that had become barriers to the intended content. This led to a time for scriptural reformation, which God used Luther to initiate.

But the debate over form and its content and effect on gospel proclamation is not confined to history. It occurs yet today wherever the processes of translatability play out within missions and the church as God's people. The goal of method for mission is to lower barriers to the proclamation process—providing accessibility to the underlying message for receptors while limiting possible distortions of meaning. The process is similar as those in translation of linguistic form—the arguments range from teaching others how they should observe literally transplanted form, to changing a form to better provide access to meaning. Awareness of

25. Scribner, *Popular Culture*, 262.
26. Scribner, *Popular Culture*, 267.
27. Scribner, *Popular Culture*, 268.

translation processes within the wider concept of translatability informs those who serve in God's mission—the purpose being that we don't proclaim the gospel through barriers that distort the gospel message.

LOWERING BARRIERS—SEEKING BALANCE

There is a continuum within the form and content debate and methods proposed within each position. The surface arguments are similar to the linguistic ones (of Bible translation) where some have entered into the complexities of translation into the many languages used by receptors, while others have proposed to teach the receptors of the world English to enable them to access the many already accomplished translations.[28] Within contemporary debates, some advocate for using church form and music to which receptors have modern affinity. Others propose maintaining historical church form and teaching the proper understanding of the meaning of those forms. Yet the underlying question for mission remains that of translatability—how are surface forms, actions and objects, perceived as they communicate through the act of gospel proclamation to the intended audience.

The gamut of preferences between positions on form and content is entered from opposite suppositions. One position emerges out of the observation that past forms of worship may not meet the needs of new audiences—alternate forms are needed for new receptors. This position assumes new forms as largely empty vessels to be filled with the content desired. Another position advocates to maintain the practice of historically derived forms, Bible versions, liturgy, hymnology, et al. and teaching observers the correct meanings to be contained within those forms. This position equates form and content with two sides of a coin and concludes that one cannot be altered without changing the other.

But both positions are only partially correct. The form-is-empty-waiting-to-be-filled argument is not complete. The observations put forward—historical church forms do not connect—may be true for some, but form is never a completely empty vessel; rather, assumed meanings (even irrelevance) will again be supplied as the worldviews of observers actively seek to determine purpose and meaning (see chapter 7, on worldview). Two young Western missionaries were attending a funeral celebration as a way to learn the culture of the local Zulu community.

28. Cripplegate, "Just Teach Them English."

Food was about to be served. The missionaries noticed two queues (lines) forming, one for men and one for women. They assumed the queues were for washing their hands before the meal. They joined the one for women. The queue shortened until the two missionaries could observe participants dipping their hands into a container of animal intestines. They were horrified but dutifully (and gingerly) dipped their hands into the pot. It was only later that they discovered the purpose was that of purification and respecting ancestors.[29] The line forming before a meal had a different religious purpose than the secular purpose initially supplied by the two young missionaries whose worldviews did not include methods toward placating ancestors.

Changing a form may change the meaning as deduced by observers, but it is not true that maintaining a form maintains meaning from observer to observer or across cultural boundaries. An obvious linguistic form example occurs in Persia where producers had branded their detergent product with the Persian word for *snow*. They then transliterated[30] it using Roman script, perhaps intending to reach a wider audience. The resulting word for that detergent was *BARF*, which most Western English readers understand as the act of vomiting. The attempt to maintain the original by transliterating the Persian form did not maintain the intended meaning, at least in English.[31] No amount of teaching the correct meaning can change the perception of most English receptors—*BARF* will not be perceived as *snow*. In another example, a missionary in Botswana overheard an aged parishioner telling a friend about the merits of baptism—it helped protect the baby against sickness and harm. This understanding was not taught, but rather caught within a context of animist understanding of spiritual powers and ritual. The meaning of a form is not static. The receptor will supply meaning or irrelevance according to his or her own worldview lens until that lens is modified.

The conclusion for mission and mission method is that not all receive forms with the meaning intended by those proclaiming the gospel. No matter the original meaning of actions, hymnologies, and rituals used in mission efforts, context may distort those meanings. As noted in Spears and Kimambo, "Missionaries, their beliefs, their social practices and their languages were all alien, and Africans made of them what they

29. Paraphrase of story told by a former LCMS missionary to South Africa.

30. That is, to write or print a word using the closest corresponding letters of a different alphabet or script.

31. Huesler, "Lost in Translation."

would."[32] Nothing has changed. Just as uninformed laity came to their own conclusions during the time preceding the Reformation, susceptible populations today also observe and apply meaning through their own worldviews and come to their own conclusions. It was reported among the Grebo ethnic group in Liberia that if one vomited after partaking communion it had a meaning—one was not forgiven.[33] Grebo churches of that time were largely Pentecostal. Uninformed members of the Ethiopian Orthodox Church assume the same where sickness follows the Eucharist.[34] Two unrelated church groups, in geography and faith tradition, yet their members arrived at similar conclusions in the absence of accessible scriptural corrective.

Those in mission who dismiss such examples fail to see the barriers that have been erected to understanding the freedom Christians have in Christ. Where meaning is obscured, human reason takes over and assumes other meaning. This human propensity remains operational no matter which argument—two sides of a coin, or empty vessel waiting to be filled—are presented. The reader will note that both positions arrive at the same destination—receptors may need additional information to preserve correct meaning. But preserving form is less important than preserving the meaning understood, a notion to which Luther concurs. He writes,

> But we do not hold that the notes need to be sung the same in all the churches. Let every church follow the music according to their own book and custom. For I myself do not like to hear the notes in a responsory or other song changed from what I was accustomed to in my youth. We are concerned with the changing of the text, not the music.[35]

The concept of translatability seeks balance between form and content, style and substance, contemporary, missional, or confessional. In the maintenance of historical or traditional practice, some receptors determine irrelevance or supply incorrect meaning and purpose. Professor John MacDowell observes that some discourse has a primary commemorative function—forms preservative, abandoning informative intent in the expression of immanent truth—in which meanings must be taught

32. Spear and Kimambo, *East African Expressions*, 127.

33. Rodewald, "Observing Sacred and Profane," 234–35.

34. Rodewald's observation.

35. Luther, *Order of Public Worship*, 31.

through an intensive education process.[36] When such is the case, without corrective instruction, historical and foreign worship forms may stand as barrier to the gospel message proclaimed. David Hesselgrave cautions those in mission out of the Western Christian context, "We err when we (perhaps unconsciously) allow the results of centuries of contextualizing in the Western world to determine the way in which [Western missionaries] present the biblical message to our target culture audiences."[37]

The "empty vessel" approach, in seeking to dispense with the old in favor of the new, similarly needs a caution. For Lutheran Christians with a common understanding of core doctrine, historic forms of gospel proclamation play an important part in how Christians have lived out the gospel. Historicity and its forms need not be lightly dispensed as new peoples and ethnicities determine which forms communicate doctrinal truth with minimal distortion.[38] Rather, for some, historical forms through which the gospel is proclaimed may be readily accepted and understood with minimal distortion of meaning.

Failure to come to a right/wrong conclusion in the form and its content debate is not disastrous within the concept of translatability. Rather, it is a symptom of a fallen world of human worldviews that are not congruent. Forms and language used in gospel proclamation may *not* be understood by some, but the same may be well understood by others who have developed worldviews through additional resources. As example, liturgical dance as a form for gospel proclamation has been used in some churches.[39] To the casual or uninformed visitor distracted by the method, the underlying meanings are distorted. For those that are conversant to forms of dance as gospel proclamation, a more complete understanding may occur.

Where foreign or commemorative form is used as gospel proclamation, it must be accompanied by sufficient knowledge for the worldview of the receptor to receive the underlying meaning of form or ritual without barrier. Where form is instituted and used without concern for the receptor, the worldview of the receptor will dismiss or supply alternate

36. MacDowell, "Folklore as Commemorative Discourse," 403–23.

37. Hesselgrave, *Communicating Christ*, 203.

38. See Rodewald, "Lutheran Church in Africa"; Africa has an identifiable eighty-eight Lutheran church bodies each emerging from varied Lutheran mission efforts. Each exhibits uniqueness in practice as implemented by its founders and instituted practices.

39. Fernandez, "Spreading the Gospel."

meaning, correct or incorrect, the method creating *barrier* rather than implementing understanding. William Smalley's rule of accessibility and distortion is applicable. Form may be maintained or it may be dispensed, but it must contain meaning in a manner that reduces barriers to communication as they occur through the worldviews of intended audiences. A presentation of the gospel message through historical forms may be filled up correctly by recipients familiar with the meanings of those forms. For others, the distractions may point away. Alternate or more readily understood forms may prove less distorted for recipients in the mission context who do not have previous experience of forms within Christianity. At the same time those who see value in historical forms may be so distracted by alternate forms that the new form distorts the intent. Martin Luther captured well the underlying concept of form, its meaning, and translatability within God's people as the Christian church:

> Therefore, it is not in these matters that anyone should either seek or establish as law some indispensable form by which he might ensnare or harass consciences. . . . Further, even if different people make use of different rites, let no one judge or despise the other, but every man be fully persuaded in his own mind [Rom 14:5]. *Let us feel and think the same, even though we may act differently.* And let us approve each other's rites lest schisms and sects should result from this diversity in rites. . . . For external rites, even though we cannot do without them, do not commend us to God.[40]

In gospel proclamation for mission, it is of primary importance that barriers to communication are lowered so that the gospel is provided with a minimum of distortion for the one who hears. Faith is the result of the Holy Spirit working through gospel proclamation. As mission sojourners in God's mission, our part is to lower barriers to the work of the Holy Spirit by proclaiming what can be heard, rather than raising barriers through our mission action.

CONCLUSION

The notion of translatability is foundational to gospel proclamation and missiological precept, not only for Bible translation and linguistic form but also for other forms through which the gospel is proclaimed. The

40. Luther, *Babylonian Captivity*, 31; emphasis mine.

missiological paradigm guides us to examine the forms we use for gospel proclamation. We become aware of translation processes so we do not proclaim versions of the gospel that will not be heard. Christianity is uniquely translatable, equally at home in people from all languages and cultures. Mission into the world is our Trinitarian God calling all to himself using us as his people to carry the good news of the story of our salvation through Jesus. Removing barriers to the work of the Holy Spirit is the missionary task, not only for those so designated within missions but for all who are given the gospel message to witness to others.

10

Partnership in Mission

"If Opportunity Doesn't Knock, Build a Door"[1]

The nineteenth century has often been called the great century of Christian mission. That is mainly because it is a century in which the religious topography of the world was changed. The twenty-first century, however, deserves to be called the greatest century of Christian mission for the following reasons: Firstly, the number of missionaries serving in a country other than their own was never larger than it is now. Missionaries from both the Global North (Western countries) and South (Africa, Asia, and Latin America) have increased their engagement in mission in terms of manpower, capital investment, theological education, and so on.[2] Secondly, there has been a significant increase in schools of mission, increasing mission research, and the rise of non-Western mission forces. This is the reason why Scott W. Sunquist calls it "the unexpected Christian century"![3] Thirdly, churches are forming partnerships for making greater impact in our world today. The Christian churches in the Global North and South have come to realize that for Christian mission to be effective in this new millennia, churches and missions have to develop and build partnerships globally. In the past few decades, several conferences and

1. This chapter began as a lecture at the Concordia Mission Institute Summer Conference, July 9–15, 2023.

2. Galaraga, "Lausanne Report." The terms *Global North* and *Global South* are defined in geopolitical terms according to the United Nations. The Global North includes Europe and Northern America, while the Global South includes Asia, Africa, Latin America, and Oceania.

3. Sunquist, *Unexpected Christian Century*.

mission studies have focused on the issue of partnership in mission and its implication for doing mission effectively.[4] As Robert Wuthnow rightly indicated in *Boundless Faith: Global Outreach of American Churches*, many Western churches have also forged partnerships with the South and are "engaging in faster and more efficient transcultural communication, interacting with a sizable population of refugees and immigrants, and contributing to large-scale international humanitarian and relief organizations."[5]

This chapter attempts to explore the understanding and practice of partnership in mission. In the last five decades, partnership has become a well-established metaphor used to describe mission in the twenty-first century. Emil Brunner once said, "The Church exists by mission, just as fire exists by burning."[6] This means the church cannot be the church without mission because it is missionary by its very nature. The question is, How does the church do mission in this new global age by developing a meaningful mission partnership for effective local and global ministry?

PARTNERSHIP IN MISSION

What is partnership in mission? Partnership in mission is the joining of churches and missions at the local, national, and global levels to engage in mission. Joshua Bowman defines partnership in mission (which he refers to as "cross-cultural missional partnership") as "a kingdom-oriented relationship of culturally diverse groups of believers who share common values and goals, who possess complementary spiritual gifts, skills, and resources, and who mutually engage in the mission of God."[7]

The concept of partnership in mission involves a stronger emphasis on mutuality, sharing, respect, and interdependence among different mission organizations and churches to effectively carry out mission projects. It also involves forming an integrated missional structure and joint

4. See Dharmaraj and Dharmaraj, *Mutuality in Mission*; Cueva, *Mission Partnership*; Braaten, "Toward True Mutuality."

5. Wuthnow, *Boundless Faith*, 1–2. See also Deressa, "What Can the West Learn."

6. Brunner, *Word and the World*, 108.

7. Bowman, *Cross-Cultural Missional Partnership*, 12; missiologist George Peters defines partnership as "a sacred and comprehensive concept of equals bound together in mutual confidence, unified purpose and united effort, accepting equal responsibilities, authority, praise and blame; sharing burdens joys, sorrows, victories and defeats. It means joint planning, joint legislation, joint programming, and involves sending and receiving churches on an equal basis" (Peters, *Biblical Theology of Missions*, 238).

strategizing and planning. Partnership in mission implies partnership with the Triune God and mission partners in the harvest field for the gospel (John 4:34, Rev 14:14). Partnership in mission allows churches and mission organizations to collaborate for the expansion of the kingdom of God.

Partnership in the African context emerged from the African concept of community, which is best described in the Bantu phrase "*umuntu ngamuntu ngabantu*" (I am because we are, and because we are, I am). The Xhosa expression "*ubuntu ungamntu ngabanye abantu*" (each individual's humanity is ideally expressed in relationship with others) also explains clearly why African Christians value partnership, because for Africans it is difficult to define their personal identity except in relation to each other.[8]

The church and theologians have historically always associated the notion of mission with "sending out." Yet mission, as Nigerian scholar Teresa Okure argues, also involves gathering, fellowship, and partnership. Okure rightly argues that mission in the New Testament is essentially a gathering (partnership/fellowship) followed by a going forth. She argues that the Greek name *ekklesia* refers to "the Hebrew *qahal* (synagogue) meaning a gathering or assembly."[9] According to Okure, in the New Testament, the purpose of mission (proclamation of the gospel) was to draw others to join their fellowship.

Lutheran teaching states that the church is a gathering of believers where the gospel is preached without any distortions, and the sacred sacraments are conducted in accordance with the gospel.[10] Therefore, the church is tasked with spreading the message of Jesus Christ's crucifixion and resurrection to people of all nations. This duty applies to both churches and individual Christians, who are called upon to actively participate in materializing the presence of the kingdom of God on earth.

The concept of partnership in mission came into use after World War II (which became also increasingly post-colonial) when Western churches began to consider working in solidarity with younger churches in the Global South. This was the time when a large number of Western missionary personnel were going to the Global South because of the emerging of newly independent churches in countries liberated from colonial powers. It was the objective of missions to plant independent

8. Battle, *Reconciliation*, 39.

9. Okure, "Mission as Gathering In," 14.

10. AC 6.

native churches and move to a new mission area after those native (younger) churches attained total autonomy. This is following the principle of three selves propagated by Henry Venn, general secretary of the Anglican Church Mission Society, and Rufus Anderson, secretary for the American Board of Commissioners for Foreign Missions. According to both Venn and Anderson, the marks of truly independent Indigenous churches are when they are "self-governing," "self-supporting," and "self-propagating."[11] With younger churches growing in autonomy and fulfilling these three selves, the conversation began to shift to defining the relationship between Western and younger churches—and the question was whether to propagate complete independence or find ways for interdependence (partnership in mission).

Partnership in mission was discussed for the first time on the international platform at the International Missionary Council (IMC) meeting held in Whitby, Ontario, in 1947, with its slogan "Partnership in Obedience."[12] The main goal of this conference was to emphasize participation of churches and missions "in God's one mission as equal partners."[13] It was suggested that theologians and leaders of the church should eliminate the use of terminologies such as "dependent" and "autonomous" churches and "younger" and "older" churches, terminologies that were used frequently in describing the relationship between churches in the Global North and South.

Prior to the 1940s, mission was understood as the responsibility of the Western churches, and the Global South was simply at the receiving end of it. Redefining the theology of mission in a new way, the 1947 IMC meeting introduced the concept of mission as "partnership"—emphasizing that participation in mission is the responsibility of the global church and so not limited to the Western churches. This way, schemes such as "sending" and "receiving" churches were eliminated. During this meeting, leaders from both established Western churches and younger churches began to call for a transition away from paternalistic practices to partnership.

At the Willingen conference of 1952, the concept of partnership in mission was reinforced again, redefining the theology of mission from a Trinitarian perspective. At this conference, partnership was defined as "partnership in God's mission (*missio Dei*)," as "entering into partnership

11. See Anderson, *Foreign Missions*, 24; see also Shenk, *Venn*.

12. Bosch, *Transforming Mission*, 379.

13. Marsh, "Partnership in Mission," 371.

with God in history."[14] According to the 1952 statement of IMC, partnership in mission is "an essential condition of effective witness and advance. In the land of younger churches [churches in Africa, Asia, and Latin America] divided witness [witness done without or outside partnership] is a crippling handicap."[15]

In 1972, the Congregational Council for World Mission, which later changed its name to the Council for World Mission (CWM), emphasized the need for local and global partnerships for effective ministry in the world. CWM even used the metaphor of a dining table in Britain to symbolize mutuality and participation in mission. A round table for them denoted equality between all people that are invited to dine around the table. It all implied that all will be sharing from the same meal.[16] For CWM, it was a way of embodying the life of the early Christians in which "no one claimed that any of their possessions was their own, but they shared everything they had. . . . And it was distributed to anyone who had need" (Acts 4:32–35).

Fred Kaan, a prominent hymn writer and former moderator of the Council for World Mission (CWM), employs the metaphor of a round table to depict the church as an inclusive and egalitarian community. In his hymn, he envisions the church as a table without sides or corners—a space where hierarchy dissolves and all participants gather in unity and mutual love. The imagery extends to an "open house," where there are no rigid seating arrangements, symbolizing radical hospitality, shared fellowship, and the abolition of divisions between "them" and "us."[17]

We need partnerships because the Christian church is better equipped for mission when we work together as partners. Partnership provides the means through which each partnering church benefits from the gifts others have to offer. According to Charles Van Engen, "Partnership in mission in the twenty-first century will involve combinations of the following:

- Church with church;
- Mission with mission;
- Sending mission with receiving church;

14. Glasser and McGavran, *Contemporary Theologies*, 92.
15. International Missionary Council, *Missionary Obligation*, 40.
16. Niles, *From East and West*, 33–34.
17. Kaan, "Church Is like a Table."

- Sending church with receiving mission;
- Formerly receiving church, now a mission sender, partnering to serve a new receiving church or mission;
- Multi-cultural teams that draw support from, and are accountable to, persons, churches, or mission agencies all over the globe;
- Local congregations who send their own missionaries, cooperating with older or newer receiving churches or mission agencies;
- Global, multi-lateral cooperative mission endeavors."[18]

BIBLICAL AND THEOLOGICAL UNDERSTANDING OF PARTNERSHIP IN MISSION

Partnership in mission is a biblical concept because it was God who first took the initiative to invite his church to be part of his ongoing creative work in our world. The church is called to partner with the Triune God and is sent to further God's kingdom purpose. Mission as *missio Dei* is God's involvement in the world in and through the church. The idea of partnership in mission is founded on a theocentric biblical concept—God working through the church to break down barriers, creating in Christ "one new humanity" of reconciliation (Eph 2:14–22) and summoning us to cultivate in love "the unity of the Spirit through the bond of peace" (Eph 4:3 NIV).

The very fact that the scope of the Great Commission is global should remind all Christians that we are called to global partnership if we are serious about proclaiming the good news of Jesus Christ to the world. One should also note that the very fact that the Christian faith is not a solitary faith implies the vitality of partnership at every level. In the New Testament, the church is identified as a fellowship of love and worship. The Greek word *ekklesia* means people who are "called out" or "gathered"—a called and gathered community. The concept of church as a building for worship or as an organized institution is entirely strange to the New Testament.

The New Testament understanding of Christian mission in partnership is basically connected to the origin of the Christian church. The *house church* was the center of mission in Acts. It functioned as a place

18. Van Engen, "Toward a Theology," 13.

of worship, fellowship, evangelism, and growth. The house church represented a providential place of partnership in mission where apostles and other Christians came together and proclaimed the gospel across cultural, geographical, social, economic, and sexual boundaries.

The house church was where the Christians gathered for table fellowship (Acts 2:42–46). In those house churches, Luke writes, the early Christians "devoted themselves to the *apostles' teaching* and to *fellowship*, to the *breaking of bread* and the *prayers*" (Acts 2:42; emphasis mine). Besides devoting their lives to studying the apostles' teaching (teachings of Jesus and his life events—death and resurrection), prayer, and breaking of bread (eucharistic life of the Christians), they shared resources and exercised common ownership (see figure 8 below). They looked after each other until all needs were met (4:34), and they all gave according to their ability (11:29). This transformed economic relationship among believers can be described as an expression of their close relationship or unity in heart and soul (4:32). In other words, the inner life of the church (unity in Christ and worship) was reflected in their outer life (a strong sense of community and relationship).

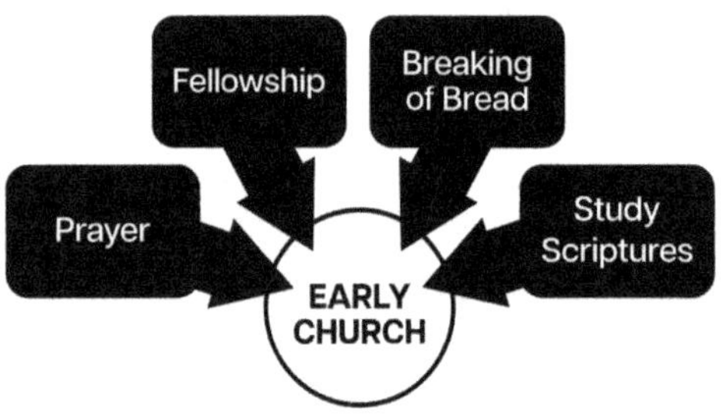

Figure 8:Characteristics of the Early Church

The house church in Acts was a place where God manifested his presence and where the Holy Spirit continued to create new communities of believers. The story of Cornelius, for example, shows that the house church was not only the place where Christians worshiped but was also where gentiles were welcomed and received hospitality—then became part of the renewed community. We also see this in Paul's ministry. In the last section of Acts, it says, "For two whole years Paul stayed there in his *own rented house* and *welcomed all who came to see him*. He proclaimed the kingdom of God and taught about the Lord Jesus Christ—with all *boldness and without hindrance*!" (Acts 28:30–31 NIV; emphasis mine).

What are the forms of partnerships in mission that we can identify in Acts? The first is a *partnership of sharing gifts and resources*. The believers' experience of fellowship and shared communion with Christ is expressed with the biblical concept of *koinonia*. Cathy Ross explains that the word *koinonia* is interchangeable with "partnership" and has been translated as "fellowship," "communion," "participation," or "sharing in Christ."[19] Partnership in *koinonia* is more about "the gift of being" with/by/for partners than sharing material and financial resources.

Partnership in mission in Acts implies that all Christians are called to a shared ministry—which is the proclamation of the gospel. We need each other in mission because we have different skills and gifts, as Acts 2:42–45 and 1 Cor 12 show. Apostles were early missionaries, and they shared ministry with other believers according to their gifts. The Latin word for *missionary* and the Greek word for *apostle* mean "one who is sent." Apostles were elected and trained by Jesus, empowered by the Holy Spirit, and sent as witnesses to the ends of the world. Before his ascension into heaven, Jesus commissioned them to preach, baptize, and make disciples of all nations (Matt 28:19). He commanded them to proclaim the good news by calling people to repentance and forgiveness of sin (Luke 24:47).

Missionaries today are also sent for the same purpose as the apostles, to proclaim the good news of Jesus Christ among people of all nations. Yet the missionary vocation is not a simple extension of the apostolate. The qualification of the apostle was defined as being called, equipped for ministry, and sent by Jesus himself. The apostles of the early church were different because they were present "beginning from John's baptism to the time when Jesus was taken up from [them]. For one of these must become a witness with us of his resurrection" (Acts 1:21–22 NIV). The church, however, was entrusted with the apostolic mission. Just as God sent the apostles to be his witnesses, he bestowed the same ministry upon the church. This ministry is shared among the members of local congregations.

Secondly, we learn to form partnerships in mission by "refusing to understand [ourselves] as a sectarian group" that avoids relating with "others."[20] The early Christians in Acts shared not only resources but were

19. Ross, "Theology of Partnership," 147.

20. Bosch, *Transforming Mission*, 121.

also characterized as sharing "one heart and one soul" (see Acts 2:41–44). This is also what Jesus prayed for his disciples: "Father, just as you are in me and I am in you[,] may they also be in us so that the world may believe that you have sent me" (John 17:20–23 NIV). To be a Christian missionary is to "join up" members of Christ's body on earth and to be his witness. There is no "us" and "them" among members of Christ's body; we are all part and parcel of one family living as witnesses of his eternal kingdom.

Thirdly, as Üllas Tankler emphasized, the Acts provide us with a clear understanding about a *partnership of insight* (vision), which means that "we look at the same situation from different perspectives."[21] The different perspectives, according to Tankler, are very helpful for a successful ministry. He states, "We need each other, as the leaders of the early church in Jerusalem needed Peter and Barnabas to witness to what God had done (Acts 15:12). In modern mission situations, the locals see things up close, and the foreigners may see the larger context. Each perspective is needed for true mutuality."[22]

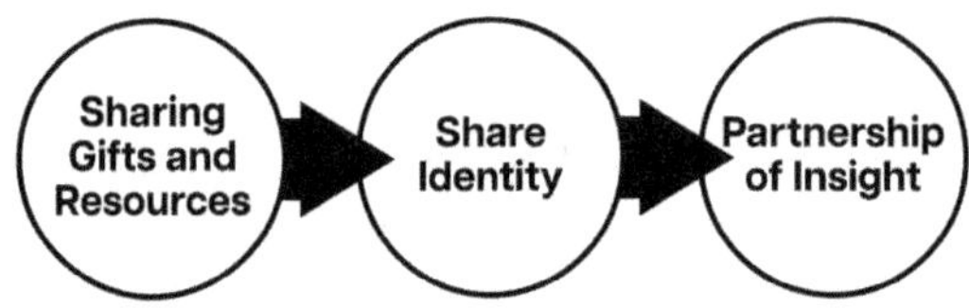

Figure 9: Sharing Partnership in Mission

CHRISTIANITY IN THE TWENTY-FIRST CENTURY: "WE ARE NOT IN KANSAS ANYMORE!"

In the first section of this chapter, I discussed the global conversation on partnership and mission. Partnership in mission has been one of the major issues discussed among church leaders, missionaries, and scholars in the past few decades. It is a relevant issue for the twenty-first-century church because we now live in a different era where the West is no longer the center of Christianity. As missiologist Dana Robert rightly argued, "Today's urgent need for Christian unity [partnership in mission] does not look

21. Tanker, "Theology of Partnership," 81.
22. Tankler, "Theology of Partnership," 81.

like the 1950s and 1960s, when self-satisfied Protestant leaders sometimes pushed for organic union at the expense of diversity of witness. The growth that characterizes World Christianity today means that unity [or partnership] will be taken seriously only where mission is taken seriously."[23]

Many scholars have discussed the shift of Christianity to the Global South. This shift was first reported by David Barrett in 1970 in the *International Review of Mission* and expanded upon in the encyclopedia published in Nairobi by Oxford University Press in 1982.[24] As this report indicates, in the year 1900, 82 percent of Christians lived in the Global North.[25] As you can see on the map below, only 18 percent of all Christians lived in the Global South. In 1970, Europe was home to 40 percent of all Christians. The same year, the ten countries with the largest Christian populations were home to 53.5 percent of all Christians globally. Yet seven of those ten countries were in the Global North (the exceptions were Brazil, Mexico, and the Philippines).[26]

A huge shift began to happen in the early 2000s when the number of Christians in the Global South began to increase at a higher rate. The world's Christians almost quadrupled—from 558 million in 1900 to 1,986 million by the end of the century. And by 2010 only four of the ten countries with the most Christians were in the North. Three years ago, in 2020, fully two-thirds of all Christians were in the Global South, with only one-third in the Global North (33 percent in the North and 67 percent in the South). Yet by 2050, it is expected that 77 percent of all Christians will live in the Global South.[27]

The shift of Christianity to the Global South is now common knowledge. Christianity in the Global South is growing both quantitatively and qualitatively compared to Global North Christianity. As Lamin Sanneh has remarked, "Increasingly, Europe is a new Christian *margin*."[28] However, many church leaders and scholars are still wondering about the implications of this shift in relation to mission theology and practice around the world. What are the implications for the shift of Christianity

23. Robert, "Witness and Unity," 244.

24. Barrett, "AD 2000." For more on Barrett's work in compiling the *World Christian Encyclopedia*, see Zurlo, "Miracle from Nairobi."

25. Johnson and Zurlo, *World Christian Encyclopedia*, 4.

26. Zurlo, "Miracle from Nairobi," 12.

27. Johnson et al., "Christianity 2017."

28. Sanneh, *Whose Religion*, 3.

to the Global South? And how do these implications impact how we do mission in this new age?

One implication of this trend is that the mission movement will be increasingly in the hands of emerging Christian leaders in Asia, Africa, Latin America, and Oceania. As Bryant Myers argued about twenty-five years ago, "Proportionally the Christian church is now non-Western and its theology and mission practice are following suit."[29] As Sebastian Kim and Kirsteen Kim also argued some years ago, many nations with large Protestant populations are rising from the Global South on the global economic and political stage (such as South Korea, Brazil, Nigeria, and China) and are making this prediction a reality. As Sebastian and Kirsteen stated, "As these [African and Asian Protestant churches] become more prosperous and develop their own mission movements, and as the European churches decline relatively in wealth, the ties provided by development activities will no longer be so significant."[30]

How does the mission movement led by leaders of the Global South change the way we understand the Christian movement at present? Historically, resources came from the West and the rest were simply recipients. The change in the shift of Christianity is demanding a change from one-way traffic to two-way traffic. Practical skills, financial resources, human resources, and other resources are to be shared among partners. As Andrew Walls rightly argued, "The design was essentially for one-way traffic. But with the new shape of the world . . . instruments are now needed for two-way traffic; for sharing and receiving."[31]

A second significant implication is the shift in the platforms facilitating global discourse. This transformation occurs in two key dimensions: (1) The demographic composition of participants in theological and missiological discussions will increasingly reflect a greater representation from the Global South than from the Global North. This trend was already evident during the 1966 World Conference on Church and Society in Geneva, which marked "the first large ecumenical conference in which the participants from Western countries were not in a majority."[32] This shift contributed to the Uppsala Assembly's heightened focus on matters of global justice. (2) Future conversations on mission theology will be dominated by issues that arise in the Global South. As Walls states,

29. Myers, *New Context*, 12.

30. Kim and Kim, *Christianity as a World Religion*, 169.

31. Quoted in Rickett, *Making Your Partnership Work*, 36.

32. Newbigin, "Mission to Six Continents," 176.

"The signs suggest that what Christianity of the twenty-first century will be like, in its theology, its worship, its effect on society, its penetration of new areas, whether geographically or culturally, will depend on what happens in Africa, in Latin America, and in some parts of Asia."[33]

The third implication is related to the practice of sending missionaries. Because of the time change, there have been strong voices claiming that the time of mission is over. What they mean by this is that the notion about the "Christian" West sending its missionaries to some "pagan" nations to preach the good news of the gospel (with the agenda to convert them) is over. Yet this is a wrong way to understand mission in our new age. What changed is not the sending of missionaries to the unreached but rather the fact that missionaries in the twentieth century are sent from everywhere to all corners of the world. Mission happens in our neighborhood, at the end of the world, and in all places in between. Therefore, as the West continues to send missionaries to other continents, it also receives those that come from other places to re-evangelize the West.

The impact of the growth of Christianity in the Global South is that the number of missionaries from these continents (Africa, Asia, and Latin America) is on the rise, and countries of the Global North are receiving increasing numbers of missionaries. There were 203,000 missionaries sent from the Global South to North in 2021, up from 31,000 (12 percent of the total) in 1970.[34] Most of these missionaries are from Brazil (40,000), South Korea (35,000), the Philippines (25,000), and China (15,000). The Republic of Korea is positioned as the second largest Protestant missionary-sending country, and by December 2017 it dispatched 27,436 missionaries from denominational mission boards and mission agencies to more than 170 nations.[35] Today, there are over 35,000 Korean missionaries in over 20 countries.

Another surprising fact is that the number of mission societies (organizations) in the Global South is also on the rise. As Larry Keys documented in his research in the early 1990s, there existed 1,094 mission societies in Africa, Asia, and Latin America by 1988 (excluding Catholic and Orthodox). Since then, as Keys argues, there has been a 14 percent increase per year. India alone at present has over 200 mission societies.

33. Walls, *Missionary Movement*, 32.

34. See Zurlo et al., "World Christianity," 17.

35. Korea World Mission Association, "Korea Mission Status."

According to Keys' prediction, the next phase of the global missionary movement will be centered in the Global South.[36]

The United States still continues to send the bulk of long-term missionaries. Northern America and Europe are sending the highest number of cross-cultural missionaries today (53 percent). The number of long-term missionaries from the Global North (Western world) serving in countries other than their own was 227,000 in 2021 (out of 430,000 that were willing to serve), down by 88 percent when compared to the total number of missionaries that served overseas in 1977.[37] This shows that the number of Western missionaries is in decline. This is due to finances but also other factors, such as government limits and the decrease in the number of Western missionaries that are willing to commit to serving among other cultures, to learn the language, and to serve at all costs. As Donal Dorr noted twenty years ago, the great majority of missionaries are also quite old and are not being replaced by younger people.[38]

On the other hand, since the 1980s and 1990s, there has been a dramatic increase in the number of short-term missionaries performing service-oriented projects overseas. According to some studies, between 1 million and 5.5 million people were going abroad annually for short-term missions over a decade ago.[39] Approximately 35,000 American churches, 3,700 North American mission agencies, and 1,000 North American schools engage in short-term mission every year.[40] However, there exists no current data that shows how many short-term missionaries there are in the world. Some church leaders and scholars are also debating whether short-term mission is really "mission" or whether these people are really "missionaries."[41]

36. Keyes, "Toward Third World Missions," 190.

37. See Zurlo et al., "World Christianity," 17.

38. Dorr, *Mission in Today's World*, 9.

39. See Smith and Denton, *Soul Searching*; also Lyman, "Examining Short-Term Mission."

40. Peterson et al., *Maximum Impact*, 252–53.

41. See Priest et al., "Short-Term Mission Movement."

CHALLENGES AND OPPORTUNITIES OF PARTNERSHIP IN MISSION

Little Jackie once famously sang that "The World Should Revolve Around Me."[42] Why partner up with others if this is our resolute belief? In the past two centuries and more, mission work was done by churches from Western countries. In this new age, however, God has given the opportunity for his church to labor in partnership with global mission allies. The work of mission is not the calling of a few but of all Christians. The challenge, however, is how to move from a community of self-interest to a community of common interest—the common interest being the mission of God in the world.

The problem with many churches in the Global South is that they perceive themselves as passive recipients whose duty is to just receive. They have built unhappy dependence on the West which all too often destroys the skills, gifts, and innovations that they could share with others. The problem with the Global North, on the other hand, is that they see themselves as called to share resources and skills with the world without the need to receive anything. They adopted the paradigm that embraced missionary sending and financial support as their primary mandate or calling. While the majority in the Global South wonder what they can share, those in the Global North function with the mindset of the old colonial legacy where the West is always in control of power and money.

Partnership in mission is important for the Global South because they get allies for global mission, allies that can provide them with the means to reach every corner of the world. Partnership is also important for the Global North because the West is no longer able to play a worthy part in the new missionary era unless they can work in partnership with Christian churches in the Global South. This is because the new missionary era requires a profound rethinking of mission strategies and engagement that essentially requires Christians of all six continents to learn from each other and strategize, plan, and engage together as partners in mission. Africans, Asians, Latin Americans, Europeans, and Americans should forge deeper intercultural relationships and collaboration for mission.

What are the benefits of intercultural partnerships among churches and mission organizations globally? Firstly, globalization has changed the way churches, businesses, and governments relate with others. Local

42. Little Jackie, "World Should Revolve."

churches are connected with both their local context, through their outreach ministries, and global context (engaged in global mission). Missiologists have begun to use the term *glocal* to describe this reality—the global and local connections of the church.[43] It is this glocal nature of mission in the twenty-first century that demands partnership in mission. As Craig Van Gelder and Dwight Zscheile emphasized, "Mission [in the twenty-first century] is not the transmission of a particular set of properties, ideas, goods, or concepts to people, but rather entering into relational webs that transform us even as we engage in shaping others."[44]

Secondly, it provides the opportunity for coordinated efforts for world mission to reach the unreached. It also paves the way for the formation of a strategic and holistic ministry alliance that transcends geographical and ethnic boundaries. Facing the many changes confronting the world today demands the motivation of churches to use shared vision, wisdom, cooperation, facilitation, and specialized skills. Resources and expertise shared by Global North can enrich the missionary activities of the growing churches in the Global South and vice versa.

Thirdly, the idea "Although the West is materially rich, the East is spiritually rich" has often been used as a basis of partnership. I am aware that some American and European churches are purposely inviting missionaries from the Global South to come and help revitalize their own communities. I personally have been involved in the discussions initiated by American church leaders on how immigrants can catalyze fresh encounters with gospel and culture. Why do many people, including American leaders, assume that Western Christians have no real spiritual sources to share? D. Preman Niles, a scholar from the Global South, contends that the Western church's lack of real spirituality is due to theological conservatism and traditionalism that refuses to give space to "the different faith expressions which could be the basis for real spirituality."[45]

Fourthly, it provides an opportunity for the Global North, particularly the United States, to learn how to do mission locally and globally. Mission is primarily about communicating the good news of Jesus Christ to all people. It is the same message, and yet the way it is communicated, the language, and the style used must adapt to the context or the situation in which one is communicating. If we don't know how to communicate, the message becomes irrelevant to the hearers or recipients. The United

43. See Van Engen, *Transforming Mission Theology*, 287.

44. Van Gelder and Zscheile, *Missional Church*, 121–22.

45. Niles, *From East and West*, 68.

States is becoming one of the most diverse countries in the world with the increase in the number of migrants from all corners of the world. It is now more culturally and ethnically diverse than it has ever been before. So how is the American church able to communicate the gospel in such a diverse context? Well, it is through partnership in mission that American churches can learn about doing mission among other cultures. For example, they could learn how to effectively engage in mission activities among people of different religions from Asian Christians, whose context has allowed them to be more mature in their understanding of other religions.

Furthermore, American and European Christianity is being impacted by the immigrants from the growing churches of the Global South. The cultural forms of Christianity brought by these immigrants to the United States and Europe are largely non-Western. As scholars observed, two major changes have begun to happen due to these Christian migrants: (1) As Jehu Hanciles rightly contends, "The new immigrant Christian communities are effectively 'de-Europeanizing' American Christianity."[46] (2) The migrant Christians bring with them an international missionary posture and network that invites a new kind of globalized missionary encounter. The passion and witness of immigrant Christians are desperately needed by the West. Therefore, this creates a profound opportunity for American churches to partner with immigrant congregations locally and to use their networks for global missionary encounters.

However, forming a partnership in mission is not an easy task. Even though many church leaders and scholars agree about the significance of partnership for mission, only a few churches and mission organizations have been able to make it practical in the last few decades. According to Üllas Tankler, the reason why missions or churches find it difficult to do mission in partnership is sometimes "*pure arrogance* ('we' think we know best how to do mission), sometimes we fear that other potential partners are not qualified enough or that they lack the right motivation, have a flawed theology, or there are other reasons for our intentional or subconscious reservations to be in mission together."[47] What Tankler refers to as "pure arrogance" is also reflected in what Corbett and Fikkert describe as various forms of paternalism—"resource paternalism" (thinking that "we" have all the right material means), "spiritual paternalism," "knowledge

46. Hanciles, *Beyond Christendom*, 22.

47. Tankler, "Theology of Partnership," 78; emphasis mine.

paternalism," "labor paternalism," and "managerial paternalism"—that we might subconsciously bring into mission partnership.[48]

K. M. Panikkar, in his book titled *Asia and Western Dominance*, argued that the main challenge for Asian and African Christians to work with Western missionaries in the nineteenth century had been the Europeans "sense of superiority which the missionaries perhaps unconsciously inculcated" into their mission practice.[49] According to Panikkar, "During the nineteenth century, the belief in the racial superiority of the Europeans as a permanent factor in human history was widely held in the West [and] the missionaries shared in their belief."[50]

Western missionaries' relationship with churches in Africa, Asia, and Latin America has historically been characterized by paternalism, dependency, inequality, rigidity, and top-down decision-making. For the last few decades, it has been suggested that we need new models of partnership that are genuinely mutual and "bottom-up." Yet, churches have continued to struggle with the question of how to do mission in partnership where a mutual exchange of gifts and resources, respect for each other, and affirmation of both contexts are reflected. They struggled with finding effective ways of communication and collaboration which implies interdependence, reciprocity, and co-participation in God's mission.[51]

A WAY FORWARD: PARTNERSHIP IN MISSION, "IF OPPORTUNITY DOESN'T KNOCK, BUILD A DOOR"

As described above, partnership in mission is the way partner churches and missions engage in joint ventures through developing common goals and strategies. Biblically speaking, partnership in mission is proclaiming the good news of Jesus Christ among all people and nations by joining hands with partner churches. Mission in this new age requires entering into relational webs through which all partners are transformed, challenged, and equipped to serve.

48. Corbett and Fikkert, *When Helping Hurts*, 115.

49. Panikkar, *Asia and Western Dominance*, 455–56.

50. Panikkar, *Asia and Western Dominance*, 455.

51. In 1910 during the Edinburgh Council, V. S. Azariah of India, who later became the first Indian bishop of the Indian church, argued, "The problem of race relationships is one of the most serious problems confronting the church today" (quoted in Stanley, *World Missionary Conference*, 110).

Firstly, churches need to be convinced that partnership in mission is a biblical concept that we all need to adopt in order to effectively reach out to the unreached. In the book of Acts, the house church played a significant role as a place of fellowship and ministry. They were important centers of the apostles' missionary work; they were centers of the life of the newly established communities of believers. It was in those houses that shared Christ's resurrected life that believers contributed to the needs of the saints and practiced hospitality (Rom 12:13). Families in those houses played major roles in building bridges with contemporary society and served as channels for mission.

Secondly, partnership begins with developing trust between two different churches or churches and mission organizations. As William Taylor rightly contends, partners are able to do more together when they have a healthy environment of trust in the relationships.[52] True partnership in mission is founded on mutual trust, even a willingness to risk for the sake of the benefit of our partners in fulfilling the missionary task. Partnership in mission does exist outside trust because it requires "a trusting relationship and fulfill[ing] agreed-upon expectations [among partners] by sharing complementary strengths and resources, to reach their mutual goal."[53]

There is an African proverb that says, "Better to be invited to the kitchen than to the table." It is in the kitchen rather than at the table that true partnership and trust develop. The kitchen provides the space for the guest to collaborate, see the process of participation, and build friendship with the host. In the Ethiopian context, coffee is served with a special ceremony whereby the guest feels honored that the space has been provided to him/her to participate in the process. The idea of partnership in mission demands that all Christian communities be both givers and receivers of mission. Yet it is only where trust exists that true giving and receiving can happen. The question is, How do we develop trust among partners in mission?

What we learn from the early Christians is that they fostered unity and fellowship because they believed it to be the will of Christ for the church and the foundation for God's mission in the world. This fellowship was an authentic fellowship of love, respect, and of bearing each other's burden. Therefore, it is only in the context where the present-day

52. Taylor, *Kingdom Partnership*, 26.

53. Bush and Lutz, *Partnering in Ministry*, 46.

church also follows the same pattern of fellowship that they can develop trust and strong partnerships. The mission of Christ is mission in fellowship and partnership.

Thirdly, it needs to enable local members to think globally, and to see themselves as players in the global mission of Christ. Participation in God's mission is the calling or task given to each Christian that belongs to a local congregation. The question is, How do we help members to be globally sensitive yet theologically and confessionally sound in order to be involved in reaching those without the gospel? There are many churches in the West that have turned inward and have made themselves the goal of the purpose of mission. Yet the church is called to participate in the proclamation of the gospel *to all nations*. The church which is faithful to the Lord's mission in witness and service limits itself to no ethnic or geographical boundaries.

Finally, it is important to let God be in control of mission since it is his mission, the *missio Dei*. One thing I realized living in the US for the last twelve years is the American leaders and missionaries have a strong tendency to have control over day-to-day activities within a closed system. As Anthony Giddens says in talking about the effect of modernity on Westerners, "To be able to control one's life circumstances, colonize the future with some degree of success and live within the parameters of intentionally referential system can, in many circumstances, allow the social and natural framework of things to seem a secure grounding for life activities."[54]

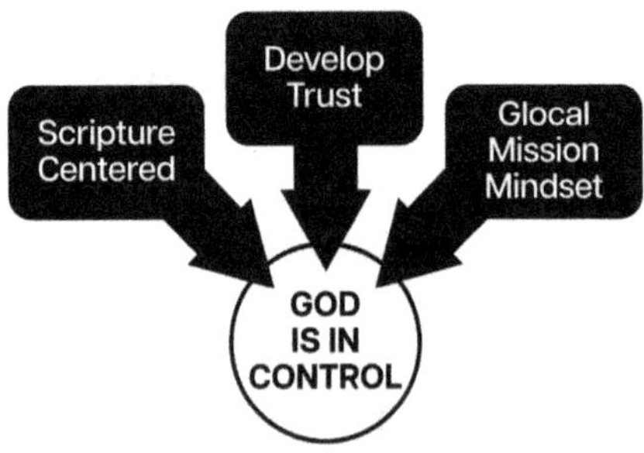

Figure 10: Strategies for Partnership in Mission

54. Giddens, *Modernity and Self-Identity*, 202.

CONCLUSION

Partnership in mission is still one of the major issues discussed among practitioners, church leaders, missionaries, and scholars. It is a relevant issue being discussed because the purpose or mission of the church is taking the whole gospel to the whole world, which in the present age requires partnership in mission. It is a task in which every believer is invited to participate. Partnership in mission facilitates the global church's growth when all parties participate in learning and serving together.

Mission in partnership is also needed because we live in a postmodern world where the cultural paradigm has shifted and become globalized. We live at the time when the world has become connected like never before. This means that the pattern of mission has to change. Communicating the gospel in different cultural settings and over the whole world demands that mission be done in partnership, together with all the saints.

We build mission partnerships by adopting the mindset of "If opportunity doesn't knock, build a door." In our mission to spread the message of hope, love, and faith, we cannot simply wait for opportunities to present themselves. Instead, we must actively seek ways to create opportunities to make a positive impact in the lives of others and share the teachings we hold dear. By taking initiative, being innovative, and boldly stepping forward, we can build doors of opportunity where they may not exist, allowing us to reach out to those in need, touch hearts, and bring about positive change.

During the Edinburgh Council in 1910, Vedanayagam S. Azariah, a representative from India, talked about his and other leaders' experience of unequal relationships among mission workers in his speech titled, "The Problem of Cooperation Between Foreign and Native Workers."[55] His address ended with a plea—"Give us friends!"—and an objection about "a lack of mutual understanding and openness and frank intercourse and friendliness" between Western missionaries and other Christian partners.[56] Today, almost 110 years after this appeal by Azariah was made, I am writing this chapter to appeal to churches of our time to fulfill this plea.

55. Azariah, "Problem of Cooperation."

56. Azariah, "Problem of Cooperation," 315. See also Stanley, *World Missionary Conference*, 124–25.

Bibliography

Al-Asqalani, Ibn Hajar. *Fath al-Bari.* 15 vols. Beirut: Dar al-kutub al-ilmiyya, 1989.

Allen, Wayne. "When the Mission Pays the Pastor." *Mission Frontiers*, 1999. https://www.missionfrontiers.org/issue/article/when-the-mission-pays-the-pastor.

Althaus, Paul. *The Theology of Martin Luther.* Translated by Robert C. Schultz. Philadelphia: Fortress, 1966.

Amanze, J. N. *Botswana Handbook of Churches.* Gaborone: Pula, 1994.

Ambrosino, Brandon. "How and Why Did Religion Evolve?" BBC, Apr. 18, 2019. https://www.bbc.com/future/article/20190418-how-and-why-did-religion-evolve.

Anderson, Gerald H., ed. *Biographical Dictionary of Christian Missions.* New York: Macmillan Reference USA, 1998.

Anderson, Rufus. *Foreign Missions: Their Relations and Claims.* New York: Scribner & Co., 1869.

Andrew, Scottie. "A Guide to Neopronouns, from Ae to Ze." CNN, Aug. 12, 2023. https://www.cnn.com/us/neopronouns-explained-xe-xyr-wellness-cec/index.html.

Arand, Charles P. "A Two-Dimensional Understanding of the Church for the Twenty-First Century." *Concordia Theological Journal* 33 (2007) 146–65.

Aring, Paul G. *Kirche als Ereignis: Ein Belrag zur Neuorientierung der Missionstheologie.* Neukirchen-Vluyn: Neukirchener Verlag, 1971.

Avis, Paul D. L. *The Church in the Theology of the Reformers.* Eugene: Wipf & Stock, 2003.

Azariah, Vedanayagam S. "The Problem of Cooperation Between Foreign and Native Workers." In *World Missionary Conference 1910: The History and Records of the Conference; Together with Addresses Delivered at the Evening Meetings*, 306–15. New York: Revell, 1910.

Barrett, David B. "AD 2000: 350 Million Christians in Africa." *International Review of Mission* 59.233 (1970) 39–54.

Barrett, Lois Y., et al. *Treasure in Clay Jars: Patterns in Missional Faithfulness.* Grand Rapids: Eerdmans, 2004.

Battle, Michael. *Reconciliation: The Ubuntu Theology of Desmond Tutu.* Cleveland, OH: Pilgrim, 1997.

Berger, Helen. "What Is Wicca? An Expert on Modern Witchcraft Explains." Brandeis Now, Sept. 17, 2021. https://www.brandeis.edu/now/2021/september/wicca-berger-conversation.html.

Bernis, Jonathan. "How Many Messianic Prophecies Did Jesus Fulfill in Scripture?" FIRM, Jan. 31 2015. https://firmisrael.org/learn/how-many-messianic-prophecies-did-jesus-fulfill/.

Biermann, Joel. *Wholly Citizens: God's Two Realms and Christian Engagement with the World.* Minneapolis: Fortress, 2017.

Boatwright, Ron. "Lesson 19: Baptism Is Immersion." Interactive Bible. https://www.bible.ca/interactive/salvation-19-baptism-is-immersion.

Bonhoeffer, Dietrich. *The Cost of Discipleship.* New York: Touchstone, 1995.

Born, J. B. "Worlds of the Spirit: Exploring African Spiritual and New Pentecostal Church Relations in Botswana." DTh diss., University of South Africa, 2009.

Bosch, David J. "Evangelism: Theological Currents and Cross-Currents Today." *International Bulletin of Missionary Research* 11 (1987) 98–112.

———. *Transforming Mission: Paradigm Shifts in Theology of Mission.* Maryknoll, NY: Orbis, 1996.

Boudreau, Jen. "Ubuntu: 'I Am What I Am Because of Who We All Are.'" Motivation, Inspiration and Life, June 2, 2012. https://motivationinspirationandlife.wordpress.com/2012/06/02/ubuntu-i-am-what-i-am-because-of-who-we-all-are/.

Bornkamm, Heinrich. *Luther and the Old Testament.* Translated by Eric W. and Ruth C. Gritsch. Philadelphia: Fortress, 1969.

Bowman, Joshua. *Cross-Cultural Missional Partnership: Mediating Relational, Cultural, and Hermeneutical Tensions for Mutual, Faithful Missional Engagement.* Eugene, OR: Pickwick, 2023.

Braaten, Carl. *The Apostolic Imperative.* Minneapolis: Augsburg, 1979.

———. *The Flaming Center: A Theology of the Christian Mission.* Philadelphia: Fortress, 1977.

———. "Toward True Mutuality: Exchanging the Same Commodities or Supplementing Each Other's Needs?" In *Supporting Indigenous Ministries: With Selected Readings,* edited by Daniel Rickett and Dotsey Welliver, 53–64. Wheaton, IL: Billy Graham Center, 1997.

Breen, Mike. "Why the Missional Movement Will Fail (And What We Can Do About It)." Verge. https://my.vergenetwork.org/wp-content/uploads/2015/03/Why-The-Missional-Movement-Will-Fail-Breen.pdf.

Brown, Karen M. "Voodoo." In Lehmann and Myers, *Magic, Witchcraft, and Religion,* 323.

Brunner, Emil. *The Word and the World.* London: Student Christian Movement, 1931.

Bucher, Hubert. *Spirits and Power: An Analysis of Shona Cosmology.* Oxford: Oxford University Press, 1980.

Bush, Luis, and Lorry Lutz. *Partnering in Ministry: The Direction of World Evangelism.* Downers Grove, IL: InterVarsity, 1990.

Carey, William. *An Enquiry into the Obligations of Christians to Use Means for the Conversion of the Heathens.* Leicester: A. Ireland, 1791.

Comaroff, John L, and Jean Comaroff. *Christianity, Colonialism, and Consciousness in South Africa.* Vol. 1 of *Of Revelation and Revolution.* Chicago: University of Chicago Press, 1991.

Corbett, Steve, and Brian Fikkert. *When Helping Hurts: How to Alleviate Poverty Without Hurting the Poor . . . and Yourself.* Chicago: Moody, 2009.

Cripplegate. "Just Teach Them English: The Case for Bible Translation." May 15, 2012. https://thecripplegate.com/just-teach-them-english-the-case-for-bible-translation/.

Cueva, S. *Mission Partnership in Creative Tension.* Carlisle: Langham Monographs, 2015.

Defense Equal Opportunity Management Institute (DEOMI). "Wicca." https://www.deomi.mil/Portals/90/Documents/Toolkit/ReligiousAwareness/FACTS-REL-Wicca-20191106.pdf?ver=2020-01-31-142221-557.

Deressa, Samuel. "Church and Development in Ethiopia: The Contribution of Gudina Tumsa's Holistic Theology." *Lutheran Mission Matters* 25 (2017) 150–64.

———. "Luther on Two Kingdoms Theology and Christian Education." *Lutheran Theological Journal* 55.3 (2021) 151–58.

———. "What Can the West Learn from the Rest? Nurturing the Culture of Global Conversation." *Concordia Theological Journal* 47.4 (2021) 33–44.

Dharmaraj, G. E., and J. S. Dharmaraj. *Mutuality in Mission: A Theological Principle for the 21st Century.* New York: General Board of Global Ministries, 2001.

DiMella, Ashley J. "Flight Passengers' Ritual Touching Airplane Boarding Sparks Mixed Feelings Among Travelers." Fox News, Nov. 27, 2024. https://www.foxnews.com/travel/flight-passengers-ritual-touching-airplane-boarding-sparks-mixed-feelings-among-travelers.

Dorr, Donal. *Mission in Today's World.* Maryknoll, NY: Orbis, 2000.

Duprey, Destiny. "Snake Symbolism and Spiritual Meanings of Seeing Snakes." Your Tango, Nov. 17, 2021. https://www.yourtango.com/2020333991/snake-spiritual-meaning.

Ekengren, Fredrik, and Magdalena Naum. "Sweden in the Delaware Valley: Everyday Life and Material Culture in New Sweden." In *Scandinavian Colonialism and the Rise of Modernity*, edited by Magdalena Naum and Jonas M. Nordin, 169–87. New York: Springer, 2013. https://www.researchgate.net/publication/278661804_Sweden_in_the_Delaware_Valley_Everyday_Life_and_Material_Culture_in_New_Sweden.

Elert, Werner. "Missions." In *The Theology and Philosophy of Life of Lutheranism, Especially in the Sixteenth and Seventeenth Centuries*, 385–402. Vol. 1 of *The Structure of Lutheranism*, translated by Walter A. Hansen. St. Louis: Concordia, 1962.

Engelsviken, Tormod, et al., eds. *The Church Going Glocal: Mission and Globalisation.* Regnum Edinburgh Centenary 6. Oxford: Regnum International, 2011.

Facts and Details. "Muslim Beliefs About Angels, Satan, Idols, and Saints." https://africame.factsanddetails.com/article/entry-875.html.

Fairchild, Mary. "Southern Baptist Beliefs." Learn Religions, last updated June 25, 2019. https://www.learnreligions.com/southern-baptist-beliefs-700524.

Fashole-Luke, E. W. "The Quest for an African Christianity." *Ecumenical Review* 27 (1975) 261–72.

Fernandez, Jean Marie. "Spreading the Gospel Through Dance." Global Sisters Report, Mar. 30, 2021. https://www.globalsistersreport.org/spirituality/spreading-gospel-through-dance.

Fitch, David E., and Geoff Holsclaw. *Prodigal Christianity: Ten Signposts into the Missional Frontier*. San Francisco: Jossey-Bass, 2013.

Friederich, Otto. "New Age Harmonies." In Lehmann and Myers, *Magic, Witchcraft, and Religion*, 412–19.

Frost, Michael, and Alan Hirsch. *The Shaping of Things to Come: Innovation and Mission for the 21st Century*. Peabody, MA: Hendrickson, 2003.

Galaraga, Caleb Maglaya. "Lausanne Report: Most Missionaries Are Reaching the Reached." *Christianity Today*, Sept. 25, 2024. https://www.christianitytoday.com/2024/09/lausanne-missions-state-great-commission-christianity-polycentrism/.

Gensichen, Hans-Werner. "Bartholomäus Ziegenbalg." In Anderson, *Biographical Dictionary*, 761.

———. "Plütschau, Heinrich." In Anderson, *Biographical Dictionary*, 540–41.

Giddens, Anthony. *Modernity and Self-Identity*. Stanford, CA: Stanford University Press, 1991.

Giebel, Rolf W., trans. *The Varocanabhisambodhi Sutra*. Berkeley, CA: Numata Center for Buddhist Translation and Research, 2005.

Gifford, Paul. "Liberia: Never-Die Christians." *Journal of Modern African Studies* 30 (1992) 349–58. https://doi.org/10.1017/S0022278X00010764.

Glasser, Arthur E., and Donald McGavran, eds. *Contemporary Theologies of Mission*. Grand Rapids: Baker, 1983.

Gmelch, George. "Baseball Magic." In Lehmann and Myers, *Magic, Witchcraft, and Religion*, 295–301.

God's Word Mission Society. "2025 Bible Translation Guide." https://godsword.org/pages/bible-translation-guide.

Grenstedt, Staffan. "Ambaricho and Shonkolla." PhD diss., University of Uppsala, 2000. http://www.diva-portal.org/smash/get/diva2:169585/FULLTEXT01.pdf.

Gritsch, Eric, and Robert Jenson. *Lutheranism: The Theological Movement and Its Confessional Writings*. Philadelphia: Fortress, 1976.

Guder, Darrell L., ed. *Missional Church*. Grand Rapids: Eerdmans, 1998.

Guznik, David. "2 Kings 3—War Against Moab." Enduring Word. https://enduringword.com/bible-commentary/2-kings-3/.

Haider, Mowlana Syed Aftab. "Dogs in Islamic Culture and Our Etiquette Towards Future Events." AFOSA, Apr. 7, 2022. https://afosa.org/dogs-in-islamic-culture-our-etiquette-towards-future-events/.

Hanciles, Jehu. *Beyond Christendom: Globalization, African Migration, and the Transformation of the West*. Maryknoll, NY: Orbis, 2008.

Harris, Marvin. "Why We Became Religious and the Evolution of the Spirit World." In *Magic, Witchcraft and Religion: An Anthropological Study of the Supernatural*, 4th ed., edited by Arthur C. Lehmann and James E. Myers, 6–9. Mayfield, CA: Mayfield, 1997.

Henry, Matthew. "Commentary on 2 Kings 3 by Matthew Henry." Blue Letter Bible, last updated Mar. 1, 1996. https://www.blueletterbible.org/Comm/mhc/2Ki/2Ki_003.cfm.

Hesselgrave, David. *Communicating Christ Cross-Culturally*. Grand Rapids: Zondervan, 1991.

Hickman, Claude. "14 Reasons for Missions." Traveling Team. https://www.thetravelingteam.org/articles/14-reasons-for-missions.

Hiebert, Paul G. "The Flaw of the Excluded Middle." *Missiology* 10 (1982) 35–47.

Hiebert, Paul G., et al. *Understanding Folk Religions: A Christian Response to Popular Beliefs and Practices*. Grand Rapids: Baker, 1999.

Hill, Harriet. "Witchcraft and the Gospel: Insights from Africa." *Missiology* 24.3 (1996) 323–44.

Hoekendijk, Johannes Christiaan. *The Church Inside Out: Adventures in Faith*. Philadelphia: Westminster, 1966.

———. *Kirche und Volk in der deutschen Missionswissenschaft*. München: Kaiser, 1967.

Hogg, W. R. *Ecumenical Foundations: A History of the International Missionary Council and Its Nineteenth-Century Background*. Eugene: Wipf & Stock, 2002.

Holl, Karl. "Luther und die Mission." In *Die Westen*, vol. 3 of *Gesammelte Aufsätze zur Kirchengeschichte*, 234–43. Tübingen: Mohr Siebeck, 1928.

House of Joppa. "Relics of Saints: What You Need to Know." https://www.houseofjoppa.com/blogs/news/relics-of-saints-what-you-need-to-know.

Huesler, Stephanie. "Lost in Translation: Barf." Mar. 28, 2016. https://stephaniehuesler.com/2016/03/28/lost-in-translation-barf/.

Hunsberger, George R. "Called and Sent to Represent the Reign of God." In Guder, *Missional Church*, 94–107.

Hutchison, William R. "A Moral Equivalent for Imperialism: Americans and the Promotion of 'Christian Civilization.'" In *Missionary Ideologies in the Imperialist Era: 1880–1920*, edited by William R. Hutchison and Torben Christensen, 167–78. Aarhus: Christensens Bogtrykkeri, 1982.

IMB. *Foundations*. Richmond, VA: IMB, 2022. https://www.imb.org/wp-content/uploads/2022/06/Foundations-2022-FINAL-FILE-spreads-0623-opt.pdf.

International Missionary Council. *The Missionary Obligation of the Church: Willingen, Germany, July 5–17, 1952*. London: Edinburgh House, 1952.

Jacobson, David. Review of *Churches That Make a Difference*. *Journal of Missional Practice* 10.2 (2005) 45–47.

James, R. Alton. "Post-Reformation Missions Pioneer." In *Discovering the Mission of God: Best Missional Practices for the 21st Century*, edited by Mike Barnett and Robin Martin, 250–56. Downers Grove, IL: IVP Academic, 2012.

Jarvis, Heath. "Defending the Word-Faith Movement." Heath Jarvis Ministries, Oct. 1, 2004. www.heathjarvis.com/october1st2004.htm.

Jenkins, Philip. *The Lost History of Christianity*. New York: HarperCollins, 2008.

Jeyaraj, Daniel. *Der Beitrag der Dänisch-Halleschen Mission zum Werden einer indisch-ein-heimischen Kirche, 1706–1730*. Erlangen: Ev.-Luth. Mission, 1996.

———. "Mission Reports from South India and Their Impact on the Western Mind: The Tranquebar Mission of the Eighteenth Century." In Robert, *Converting Colonialism*, 21–42.

Johnson, Todd M., and Gina A. Zurlo. *World Christian Encyclopedia*. 3rd ed. Edinburgh: Edinburgh University Press, 2019.

Johnson, Todd M., et al. "Christianity 2017: Five Hundred Years of Protestant Christianity." *International Bulletin of Mission Research* 41 (2016) 41–52.

Kaan, Fred. "The Church Is like a Table." In *Rejoice and Sing: Hymnal of the United Reformed Church in the United Kingdom*, by the United Reformed Church, #480. Oxford: Oxford University Press, 1991.

Kabbani, Muhammad Hisham. *Remembrance of Allah and Praising the Prophet.* Vol. 2 of *Encyclopedia of Islamic Doctrine.* 2nd ed. Mountain View, CA: As-Sunna Foundation of America, 1989.

Kane, J. Herbert. *A Concise History of the Christian World Mission.* Grand Rapids: Baker, 1982.

Kato, Byang H. "The Gospel, Cultural Context, and Religious Syncretism." In *Let the Earth Hear His Voice*, edited by J. D. Douglas, 1216–23. Minneapolis: World Wide, 1975.

Kim, Chul Hwan. "Central Issues in Proclaiming the Gospel to Korean Shamanists." PhD diss., Concordia Theological Seminary, 1999.

Kim, Sebastian, and Kirsteen Kim. *Christianity as a World Religion.* London: Continuum, 2008.

Kimball, Dan. *The Emerging Church: Vintage Christianity for New Generations.* Grand Rapids: Zondervan, 2003.

Kirk, Andrew. *What Is Mission? Theological Explorations.* Minneapolis: Fortress, 2000.

Koinange, Jeff. "In Gambia, AIDS Cure or False Hope?" CNN, Mar. 17, 2007. https://www.cnn.com/2007/WORLD/africa/03/15/koinange.africa/index.html.

Kolb, Robert. "Luther on the Two Kinds of Righteousness: Reflections on His Two-Dimensional Definition of Humanity at the Heart of His Theology." *Lutheran Quarterly* 13 (1999) 449–66.

———. "Two Realms." In *Dictionary of Luther and the Lutheran Traditions*, edited by Timothy J. Wengert, 756–57. Grand Rapids: Baker Academic, 2008.

Kolb, Robert, and Charles Arand. *The Genius of Luther's Theology: A Wittenberg Way of Thinking for the Contemporary Church.* Grand Rapids: Baker Academic, 2008.

Kolb, Robert, and Timothy Wengert, eds. *The Book of Concord: The Confessions of the Evangelical Lutheran Church.* Minneapolis: Fortress, 2000.

Korea World Mission Association (KWMA). "Korea Mission Status Report 2023." Research and Development Office, 2024. https://kwmaorg.direct.quickconnect.to:5500/sharing/0c43rU73A.

Kraft, Charles H. *Communication Theory for Christian Witness.* Nashville: Abingdon, 1983.

Krige, Eileen. *The Social System of the Zulus.* Pietermaritzburg: Shuter & Shooter, 1950.

Latourette, Kenneth Scott. *The Christian World Mission in Our Day.* New York: Harper & Bros., 1954.

———. *The Great Century: Europe and the United States of America, A.D. 1800–A.D. 1914.* Vol. 4 of *A History of the Expansion of Christianity.* New York: Harper & Bros., 1941.

———. *Missions Tomorrow.* New York: Harper, 1936.

Lingenfelter, Sherwood G., and Marvin K. Mayers. *Ministering Cross-Culturally.* Grand Rapids: Baker, 1986.

Little Jackie. "The World Should Revolve Around Me." Track 2 on *The Stoop*, S-Curve, 2008.

Lehmann, Arthur C., and James E. Myers, eds. *Magic, Witchcraft, and Religion: An Anthropological Study of the Supernatural.* 2nd ed. Mountain View, CA: Mayfield, 1989.

Lehmann, E. Arno. *It Began at Tranquebar: The Story of the Tranquebar Mission and the Beginnings of Protestant Christianity in India: Published to Celebrate the 250th Anniversary of the Landing of the First Protestant Missionaries at Tranquebar in 1706.* Translated by M. J. Lutz. Madras, India: Christian Literature Society, 1956.

Lobdell, William. "Pastor's Empire Built of Acts of Faith, and Cash." Los Angeles Times, Sept. 19, 2004. https://www.latimes.com/archives/la-xpm-2004-sep-19-me-tbn19-story.html.

Lockman Foundation. "New American Standard Bible (NASB)." https://www.lockman.org/new-american-standard-bible-nasb/.

Löhe, Wilhelm. *Die drei Bücher von der Kirche*. Vol. 1 of *Wilhelm Löhe Gesammelte Werke*, edited by Klaus Genzert. Neuendettelsau: Kessinger, 1954.

Lohse, Bernhard. *Martin Luther's Theology: Its Historical and Systematic Development*. Translated and edited by Roy A. Harrisville. Minneapolis: Fortress, 1999.

Lumpp, David. "Luther's 'Two Kinds of Righteousness': A Brief Historical Introduction." *Concordia Journal* 23 (1993) 27–38.

Luther, Martin. *Auslegung über etliche Kapitel des andern Buchs Mosi*. In *Reihenpredigten über 2. Mose 1524/27*. Vol. 16 of WA.

———. *The Blessed Sacrament of the Holy and True Body and Blood of Christ, and the Brotherhoods*. In *Word and Sacrament 1*, edited by Philip S. Watson and Helmut Lehmann, 45–73. Vol. 35 of LW.

———. *The Bondage of the Will*. In *Career of the Reformer 3*, edited by Philip S. Watson and Helmut Lehmann, 3–307. Vol. 33 of LW.

———. *Commentary on Psalm 8*. In *Selected Psalms 1*, edited by Jaroslav Pelikan, 95–135. Vol. 12 of LW.

———. *Commentary on Psalm 45*. In *Selected Psalms 1*, edited by Jaroslav Pelikan, 195–300. Vol. 12 of LW.

———. *Commentary on Psalm 51*. In *Selected Psalms 1*, edited by Jaroslav Pelikan, 303–410. Vol. 12 of LW.

———. *Commentary on Psalm 82*. In *Selected Psalms 2*, edited by Jaroslav Pelikan, 39–72. Vol. 13 of LW.

———. *Commentary on Psalm 117*. In *Selected Psalms 3*, edited by Jaroslav Pelikan, 1–39. Vol. 14 of LW.

———. *Commentary on Zechariah*. In *Lectures on the Minor Prophets 3*, edited by Jaroslav Pelikan. Vol. 20 of LW.

———. *Concerning the Ministry*. In *Church and Ministry 2*, edited by Jaroslav Pelikan, 3–44. Vol. 40 of LW.

———. *Concerning the Order of Public Worship*. In *Liturgy and Hymns*, edited by Jaroslav Pelikan et al., 7–40. Vol. 53 of LW.

———. *Defense of the Translation of the Psalms*. In *Word and Sacrament 1*, edited by Jaroslav Pelikan et al., 203–32. Vol. 35 of LW.

———. *Die ersten 25 Psalmen auf der Koburg ausgelegt, 1530*. In *2. Psalmenvorlesung 1519/21*. Vol. 5 of WA.

———. *D. Martin Luthers Werke: Kritische Gesamtausgabe*. 136 vols. Weimar: Herman Böhlau, 1883–2009.

———. *The Freedom of a Christian*. In *Career of the Reformer 1*, edited by Jaroslav Pelikan, 327–77. Vol. 31 of LW.

———. *Heidelberg Disputation*. In *Career of the Reformer 1*, edited by Jaroslav Pelikan, 35–70. Vol. 31 of LW.

———. *In Genesin Declamationes, 1527*. In *Reihenpredigten über 1. Mose (1523/24)*. Vol. 24 of WA.

———. *Lectures on Genesis, Chapters 31–37*. Edited by Jaroslav Pelikan and Hilton C. Oswald. Vol. 6 of LW.

———. *Lectures on Genesis, Chapters 45–50*. Edited by Jaroslav Pelikan and Walter A. Hansen. Vol. 8 of LW.

———. *Lectures on Isaiah*. Edited by Hilton C. Oswald and Jaroslav Pelikan. Vol. 17 of LW.

———. *Luther's Works, American Edition*. Edited by Jaroslav Pelikan and Helmut Lehmann. 55 vols. St. Louis: Concordia; Philadelphia: Fortress, 1955–1986.

———. *On the Babylonian Captivity of the Church*. In *Word and Sacrament 2*, edited by Jaroslav Pelikan, 3–126. Vol. 36 of LW.

———. *On Translating: An Open Letter*. In *Word and Sacrament 1*, edited by E. Theodore Bachmann and Helmut Lehmann, 175–208. Vol. 35 of LW.

———. *Ordinance of a Common Chest, Preface*. In *Christian in Society 2*, edited by Jaroslav Pelikan, 159–94. Vol. 45 of LW.

———. *Predigt am Sonntag nach Ostern über die Taufe*. In *Predigten 1538*. Vol. 46 of WA.

———. *The Sacrament of the Body and Blood of Christ—Against the Fanatics*. In *Word and Sacrament 2*, edited by Jaroslav Pelikan, 329–60. Vol. 36 of LW.

———. *Sermons on the First Epistle of Saint Peter*. In *The Catholic Epistles*, edited by Jaroslav Pelikan, 3–145. Vol. 30 of LW.

———. *Sermon: The Gospel for the Main Christian Service*. In *Sermons 2*, edited by Jaroslav Pelikan, 41–88. Vol. 52 of LW.

———. *Short and Long Sermons on Usury*. In *Christian in Society 2*, edited by Jaroslav Pelikan, 231–310. Vol. 45 of LW.

———. *That a Christian Assembly or Congregation Has the Right and Power to Judge All Teaching and to Call, Appoint, and Dismiss Teachers*. In *Church and Ministry 1*, edited by Jaroslav Pelikan, 301–14. Vol. 39 of LW.

———. *To the Christian Nobility of the German Nation Concerning the Reform of the Christian State*. In *Christian in Society 1*, edited by Philip S. Watson and Helmut Lehmann, 115–217. Vol. 44 of LW.

———. *A Treatise on the New Testament, That Is, the Holy Mass*. In *Word and Sacrament 1*, edited by Philip S. Watson and Helmut Lehmann, 75–111. Vol. 35 of LW.

Lutheran World Federation. "Resolution on Being Church in Context and Its Role in Mission." Twelfth Assembly of the Lutheran World Federation, Windhoek, Namibia, 2017. https://2017.lwfassembly.org/en/resolution-being-church-context-and-its-role-mission.

———. *Together in God's Mission: A LWF Contribution to the Understanding of Mission*. LWF Documentation 26. Geneva: Lutheran World Federation, 1988.

Lyman, Margaret. "Examining Short-Term Mission from a Globalization Perspective: Factors in the Emergence of Today's Mission Boom and Validity Issues for a Global Church." PhD diss., Fuller Theological Seminary, 2004.

Maddix, Mark A., and Jan Akkerman. *Missional Discipleship: Partners in God's Redemptive Mission*. Kansas City, MO: Nazarene, 2014.

Majestic Quran. "Can the Quran Be Translated?" Sept. 16, 2020. https://www.majesticquran.co.uk/can-the-quran-be-translated/.

Margalit, Baruch. "Why King Mesha of Moab Sacrificed His Oldest Son." Biblical Archaeology Society Library, 1986. https://library.biblicalarchaeology.org/article/why-king-mesha-of-moab-sacrificed-his-oldest-son/.

Marsh, Colin. "Partnership in Mission: To Send or Share?" *International Review of Mission* 91.366 (2003) 370–81.

Marthaler, Berard L. *The Creed.* Mystic, CT: Twenty-Third, 1987.

McGavran, Donald A. *Understanding Church Growth.* Grand Rapids: Eerdmans, 1970.

Moltmann, Jürgen. *The Church in the Power of the Spirit: A Contribution to Messianic Ecclesiology.* London: SCM, 1977.

Montgomery, John Warwick. "Luther and the Missionary Challenge." In *In Defense of Martin Luther*, 159–72. Milwaukee, WI: Northwestern, 1970.

Mulhern, Kathleen. "How Many Versions of the Bible Are There?" Patheos, last updated Oct. 25, 2023. https://www.patheos.com/answers/how-many-versions-of-the-bible.

Murdoch, Iris. *The Sovereignty of Good.* New York: Routledge, 1970.

Myers, Bryant. *The New Context of World Mission.* Monrovia, CA: Mission Advanced Research and Communication Center, 1996.

Neill, Stephen. *Creative Tension.* London: Morries & Gibb, 1959.

———. *A History of Christian Missions.* Harmondsworth: Penguin, 1973.

Newbigin, Lesslie. *Foolishness to the Greeks: The Gospel and Western Culture.* Grand Rapids: Eerdmans, 1986.

———. *The Gospel in a Pluralist Society.* Grand Rapids: Eerdmans, 1989.

———. *The Household of God: Lectures on the Nature of the Church.* The Kerr Lectures. New York: Friendship, 1954.

———. "Mission to Six Continents." In *1948–1968,* edited by Harold C. Fey, 171–97. Vol. 2 of *The Ecumenical Advance: A History of the Ecumenical Movement.* London: SPCK, 1970.

———. *The Other Side of 1984: Questions for the Churches.* The Risk Book Series. Geneva: World Council of Churches, 1983.

New Song Church. "Why Did the King Sacrifice His Baby?" Mar. 8, 2025. https://newsongpeople.com/btonline/why-did-the-king-sacrifice-his-baby.

Nida, Eugene A. *Message and Mission.* New York: Harper & Bros., 1960.

Norrish, Howard. "The Great Century." In *Discovering the Mission of God: Best Missional Practices for the 21st Century*, edited by Mike Barnett and Robin Martin, 288–90. Downers Grove, IL: IVP Academic, 2012.

Öberg, Ingemar. *Luther and World Mission: A Historical and Systematic Study.* Translated by Dean Apel. St. Louis: Concordia, 2007.

O'Connor, Elizabeth. *The New Community.* 1st ed. New York: Harper & Row, 1976.

Okure, Teresa. "Mission as Gathering In: A Biblical and African Perspective." Paper presented at a gathering of missionaries in Maynooth, Ireland, 1994.

Ott, Craig. *The Mission of the Church: Five Views in Conversation.* Grand Rapids: Baker Academic, 2016.

Ovid. *Metamorphoses.* Translated by Samuel Garth et al. http://classics.mit.edu/Ovid/metam.8.eighth.html.

Panikkar, K. M. *Asia and Western Dominance.* London: Allen & Unwin, 1953.

Peck, M. Scott. *People of the Lie: The Hope for Healing Human Evil.* New York: Simon & Schuster, 1983.

Peterson, Cheryl. "The Church." *Lutheran Quarterly* 30 (2016) 43–59. https://muse.jhu.edu/article/612160.

Peterson, Roger, et al. *Maximum Impact Short-Term Mission: The God-Commanded, Repetitive Deployment of Swift, Temporary, Non-Professional Missionaries.* Minneapolis: STEMPress, 2003.

Pieper, Francis. *Christian Dogmatics.* Vol. 1. St. Louis: Concordia, 1962.

Pless, John T., and Larry M. Vogel, eds. *Luther's Large Catechism with Annotations and Contemporary Applications.* St. Louis: Concordia, 2023.

Priest, Robert J., et al. "Researching the Short-Term Mission Movement." *Missiology* 34 (2006) 431–50.

Rekstis, Emily. "Healing Crystals 101: Everything You Need to Know." Healthline, last updated Nov. 14, 2023. https://www.healthline.com/health/mental-health/guide-to-healing-crystals##science.

Release International. "Egypt Rebuilds Its Churches." July 10, 2023. https://releaseinternational.org/egypt-rebuilds-its-churches/.

Rice, Chris, et al. "Reconciliation as the Mission of God." LOP 51 (2004). https://lausanne.org/occasional-paper/lop-51-reconciliation-as-the-mission-of-god#roots-and-realities-vignettes.

Rickett, Daniel. *Making Your Partnership Work.* Spokane, WA: Partners International, 2002.

Robert, Dana L. *Christian Mission: How Christianity Became a World Religion.* Chichester: Wiley-Blackwell, 2009.

———, ed. *Converting Colonialism: Visions and Realities in Mission History, 1706–1914.* Studies in the History of Christian Missions. Grand Rapids: Eerdmans, 2008.

———. "Witness and Unity in 21st-Century World Christianity." *Transformation* 30 (2013) 243–56.

Robinson, Neil. "The Bible Is Fantasy." Rejecting Jesus, Aug. 11, 2023. https://rejectingjesus.com/2023/11/08/the-bible-is-fantasy/.

Rodewald, Michael K. "Barriers to the Gospel: Approaching Contextualization from a Confessional Lutheran Perspective." *Missio Apostolica* 22 (2014) 43–60.

———. "The Lutheran Church in Africa: Thirty Years of Growth." *Journal of Lutheran Mission* 4 (2015) 95–104.

———. "Mwali in Historical and Regional Context: Part Two." *Botswana Notes and Records* 42 (2010) 22–30.

———. "Observing Sacred and Profane in Animist Worldview." PhD diss., Concordia Theological Seminary, 2007.

———. "An Outside Look at the Missio Dei in 2 Kings 5." *Lutheran Mission Matters* 26 (2018) 262–72.

———. "Understanding Mwali as Traditional Supreme Deity of the Bakalanga of Botswana and Western Zimbabwe: Part One." *Botswana Notes and Records* 42 (2010) 11–21.

Ross, Cathy. "The Theology of Partnership." *International Bulletin of Missionary Research* 34.3 (2010) 145–48.

Roxburgh, Alan J. "Missional Leadership: Equipping God's People for Mission." In Guder, *Missional Church*, 128–44.

———. *Missional Map-Making: Skills for Leading in Times of Transition.* 1st ed. Leadership Network. San Francisco: Jossey-Bass, 2010.

Sainz, Adrian. "Mississippi River Flood of 2011 Caused $2.8B in Economic Damage: Army Corps." *Insurance Journal*, Feb. 27, 2013. https://www.insurancejournal.com/news/national/2013/02/27/282875.htm.

Sanneh, Lamin. "Christian Missions and the Western Guilt Complex." *Christian Century*, Apr. 8, 1987, 331–34. https://www.religion-online.org/article/christian-missions-and-the-western-guilt-complex/.

———. "Gospel and Culture: The Ramifying Effects of Scriptural Translation." In *Bible Translation and the Spread of the Church in the Last 200 Years*, edited by Philip Stine, 133–52. Leiden: Brill, 1990.

———. *Translating the Message: The Missionary Impact on Culture*. Maryknoll, NY: Orbis, 1989.

———. *Whose Religion Is Christianity? The Gospel Beyond the West*. Grand Rapids: Eerdmans, 2003.

———. "World Christianity and the New Historiography: History and Global Interconnection." In *Enlarging the Story: Perspectives on Writing World Christian History*, edited by Wilbert Shenk, 94–114. Maryknoll, NY: Orbis, 2002.

Scherer, James. *Gospel, Church, and Kingdom: Comparative Studies in World Mission Theology*. Minneapolis: Augsburg, 1987.

Schlesinger, Arthur, Jr. "The Missionary Enterprise and Theories of Imperialism." In *The Missionary Enterprise in China and America*, edited by John F. Fairbank, 336–73. Cambridge: Harvard University Press, 1974.

Schulz, Klaus Detlev. "The Missional Significance of the Doctrine of Justification in the Lutheran Confession." ThD diss., Concordia Seminary, 1994.

———. *Mission from the Cross: The Lutheran Theology of Mission*. St. Louis: Concordia, 2009.

———. "Nineteenth-Century Lutheran Missions." *Logia* 29.4 (2020) 51–70.

Scribner, R. W. *Popular Culture and Popular Movements in Reformation Germany*. London: Hambledon, 1987.

Shenk, Wilbert. *Henry Venn—Missionary Statesman*. Maryknoll, NY: Orbis, 1983.

Sider, Ronald J., et al. *Churches That Make a Difference: Reaching Your Community with Good News and Good Works*. Grand Rapids: Baker, 2002.

Simpson, Gary M. "Being Neighbor in the Coming Pandemic Crisis: Thinking with Luther in the 21st Century." *Caring Connections* 5 (2008). http://lutheranservices.org/wp-content/uploads/2022/06/CaringConnections_2008_vol05_1.pdf.

Singh, Brijrah. *The First Protestant Missionary to India: Bartholomaeus Ziegenbalg (1683–1710)*. New Delhi: Oxford University Press, 1999.

Smalley, William. *Translation as Mission*. Macon, GA: Mercer University Press, 1992.

Smith, Christian, and Melina Lundquist Denton. *Soul Searching: The Religious and Spiritual Lives of American Teenagers*. Oxford: Oxford University Press, 2009.

Snyder, Howard A. *The Problem of Wine Skins: Church Structure in a Technological Age*. Downers Grove, IL: InterVarsity, 1975.

Song, C. S. *Tell Us Our Names: Story Theology from an Asian Perspective*. Maryknoll, NY: Orbis, 1984.

Spear, Thomas, and Isaria N. Kimambo, eds. *East African Expressions of Christianity*. Athens, OH: Ohio University Press, 1999.

Spickard, Paul R., and Kevin M. Cragg. *A Global History of Christians: How Everyday Believers Experienced Their World*. Grand Rapids: Baker Academic, 1994.

Stanley, Brian. *The World Missionary Conference, Edinburgh 1910*. Grand Rapids: Eerdmans, 2009.

Stetzer, Ed. *Planting Missional Churches: Your Guide to Starting Churches That Multiply*. Nashville: B&H Academic, 2016.

Steyne, Philip. *Gods of Power: A Study of the Beliefs and Practices of Animists*. Houston, TX: Touch, 1990.

Stolle, Volker, ed. *The Church Comes from All Nations*. Translated by Klaus Detlev Schulz. St. Louis: Concordia, 2003.

———. "How Lutherans Have Done Mission: A Historical Survey." *Lutheran Mission Matters* 24 (2016) 128–31.

Stoner, Peter W. *Science Speaks: An Evaluation of Certain Christian Evidences*. Chicago: Moody, 1958.

Stott, John. *Christian Mission in the Modern World*. Downers Grove, IL: Intervarsity, 1975.

Study.com. "How Many Nouns Are in the English Language?" https://homework.study.com/explanation/how-many-nouns-are-in-the-english-language.html.

StudyLight. "2 Kings 3:27." https://www.studylight.org/commentary/2-kings/3-27.html.

Sundermeier, Theo. "Gensichen, Hans-Werner." In Anderson, *Biographical Dictionary*, 238.

Sundkler, Bengt, and Christopher Steed. *A History of the Church in Africa*. Cambridge: Cambridge University Press, 2000.

Sunquist, Scott W. *Understanding Christian Mission: Participation in Suffering and Glory*. Grand Rapids: Baker Academic, 2013.

———. *The Unexpected Christian Century: The Reversal and Transformation of Global Christianity, 1900–2000*. Grand Rapids: Baker Academic, 2015.

Tankler, Üllas. "The Theology of Partnership in Mission: Reflections on Interdependence." *European Journal of Theology* 31 (2022) 73–91.

Taylor, William. *Kingdom Partnership for Synergy in Mission*. Pasadena, CA: William Carey Library, 1994.

Tenney, Merrill C, and Richard N. Longenecker. *John and Acts*. Vol. 9 of *The Expositor's Bible Commentary*. Edited by Frank E. Gaebelein. Grand Rapids: Zondervan, 1981.

Theological Education Fund. *Ministry in Context: The Third Mandate Programme of the Theological Education Fund, 1970–77*. Bromley, UK: Theological Education Fund, 1972.

Thomas, Douglas E. *African Traditional Religion in the Modern World*. Jefferson, NC: McFarland & Co., 2005.

Thorne, Susan. *Congregational Missions and the Making of an Imperial Culture in Nineteenth-Century England*. Sanford, CA: Stanford University Press, 1999.

Trueblood, Elton. *The Incendiary Fellowship*. 1st ed. New York: Harper, 1967.

Tucker, Ruth. *From Jerusalem to Iran Java: A Biographical History of Christian Missions*. Grand Rapids: Zondervan, 2004.

Unwene, Nelson. "Some Annang Christians Revert to Spiritism." PhD diss., Concordia Theological Seminary, 1999.

Van Engen, Charles. "Toward a Theology of Mission Partnership." *Missiology* 29 (2001) 11–44.

———. *Transforming Mission Theology*. Pasadena, CA: William Carey Library, 2017.

Van Gelder, Craig. *The Essence of the Church*. Grand Rapids: Baker, 2000.

Van Gelder, Craig, and Dwight Zscheile. *The Missional Church in Perspective: Mapping Trends and Shaping Conversation*. Grand Rapids: Baker Academic, 2011.

Vicedom, Georg. *The Mission of God: An Introduction to a Theology of Mission*. Translated by Gilbert A. Thiele and Dennis Hilgendorf. St. Louis: Concordia, 1965.

Walls, A. F. "Building to Last: Harold Turner and the Study of Religion." In *Exploring New Religious Movements*, edited by A. F. Walls and Wilbert R. Shenk, 1–18. Elkhart, IN: Mission Focus, 1990.

Walls, Andrew. *The Missionary Movement in Christian History: Studies in the Transmission of Faith*. Maryknoll, NY: Orbis, 1996.

Walsh, Chris, and William McKenzie. "Pluralism Is a Big Deal." George W. Bush Presidential Center, Mar. 16, 2023. https://www.bushcenter.org/publications/pluralism-is-a-big-deal.

Wan, Enoch Yee-nock. *Diaspora Missiology: Theory, Methodology, and Practice*. Portland, OR: Institute of Diaspora Studies, Western Seminary, 2011.

Warneck, Gustav. *Outline of a History of Protestant Missions from the Reformation to the Present Time: A Contribution to Modern Church History*. Translated by George Robson. New York: Revell, 1902.

Webber, Daniel, ed. *William Carey and the Missionary Vision*. Edinburgh: Banner of Truth Trust, 2005.

Whiteman, Darrell L. "Contextualization: The Theory, the Gap, the Challenge." *International Bulletin of Missionary Research* 21 (1997) 2–7.

Willard, Dallas. *The Great Omission: Reclaiming Jesus' Essential Teachings on Discipleship*. New York: HarperCollins, 2014.

Williams, Peter. "The Church Missionary Society and the Indigenous Church in the Second Half of the Nineteenth Century: The Defense and Destruction of the Venn Ideals." In Robert, *Converting Colonialism*, 86–93.

Winter, Ralph. "The Kingdom Strikes Back: Ten Epochs of Redemptive History." In *Perspectives on the World Christian Movement: A Reader*, edited by Ralph Winter and Stephen C. Hawthorne, 4th ed., 210–24. Pasadena, CA: William Carey Library, 2009.

———. "Three Mission Eras and the Loss and Recovery of Kingdom Mission, 1800–2000." In *Perspectives on the World Christian Movement: A Reader*, edited by Ralph Winter and Steven C. Hawthorne, 4th ed., 263–78. Pasadena, CA: William Carey Library, 2009.

———. *The 25 Unbelievable Years, 1945–1969*. Pasadena, CA: William Carey Library, 1970.

World Meteorological Organization. "UN Warns Half the World Not Prepared for Disasters." Oct. 13, 2022. https://wmo.int/media/news/un-warns-half-world-not-prepared-disasters.

Wright, N. T. *Simply Christian*. San Francisco: Harper SanFrancisco, 2006.

Wuthnow, Robert. *Boundless Faith: The Global Outreach of American Churches*. Los Angeles: University of California Press, 2010.

Wycliffe Global Alliance. "2025 Global Scripture Access." https://www.wycliffe.net/resources/statistics/.

Ziegenbalg, Bartholomaüs. *Genealogy of the South Indian Deities: An English Translation of Bartholomäus Ziegenbalg's Original German Manuscript with a Textual Analysis and Glossary*. Edited and translated by Daniel Jeyaraj. London: Routledge Curzon, 2005.

Zizioulas, Jean, and Paul McPartlan. *Communion and Otherness: Further Studies in Personhood and the Church*. New York: T&T Clark, 2006.

Zurlo, Gina A. "A Miracle from Nairobi: David B. Barrett and the Quantification of World Christianity, 1957–1982." PhD diss., Boston University, 2017.

Zurlo, Gina, et al. "World Christianity and Mission 2021: Questions About the Future." *International Bulletin for Mission Research* 45 (2021) 15–25.

Index

Note: Page numbers in **bold** refer to tables, and references following "n" refer to the notes.

www.ingramcontent.com/pod-product-compliance
Lightning Source LLC
LaVergne TN
LVHW050619100826
845148LV00011B/1650
* 9 7 9 8 3 8 5 2 6 2 1 6 8 *